D1444697

THE PRINCES
OF WALES

By Wynford Vaughan-Thomas

Portrait of Gower. *Robert Hale*
Anzio. *Longman*
Wynford Vaughan-Thomas' Wales. *Michael Joseph*
The Countryside Companion. *Webb & Bower*
Shell Guide to Wales (part author)

THE PRINCES
OF WALES

Wynford Vaughan-Thomas

Kaye & Ward · Kingswood

Design by Victor Shreeve

Copyright © 1982 by Wynford Vaughan-Thomas

Index compiled by Indexing Specialists

Published by
Kaye & Ward Ltd
The Windmill Press
Kingswood, Tadworth, Surrey

Filmset in Monophoto Garamond by
Northumberland Press Ltd, Gateshead

Printed in Great Britain by
Fletcher and Son Ltd, Norwich

ISBN 0 7182 5890 8

CONTENTS

Introduction

'A country of memorable honour.'
EDMUND SPENSER

On the sunlit morning of 29 July 1981 Charles, Prince of Wales, rode with his radiant bride in the State Coach from their wedding at St Paul's Cathedral to give Londoners – and indeed the whole of Britain – the happiest, most colourful and popular royal occasion for a very long time. Nearly 500,000 people poured down The Mall to cheer Charles and Diana as they stood together in mutual happiness on the balcony of Buckingham Palace. The vast crowd roared with delight as the Prince, after a quick glance for the Queen's approval, kissed his bride; perhaps the first time royalty had deliberately kissed in public since Charles I embraced Nell Gwynn. They made the very picture of the Prince and Princess of fairy tale. And well they might be. Prince Charles is the twenty-first holder of a title that has gathered around it through over seven hundred long and eventful years an irresistible air of glamour and romance.

We have no need to look further back than Prince Charles's immediate predecessor, the Duke of Windsor, to sense that special quality of romance, drama and even tragedy inseparable from the office of Prince of Wales. The New York débutantes fought for the honour of touching his hand, while the popular cabaret artists sang: 'I've danced with a man who danced with a girl who danced with the Prince of Wales.' This same young man became in later life 'the King who gave up a Throne for Love'. And the Duke's own predecessor, who eventually became Edward VII, certainly created a dashing image of social elegance during his long career as Prince.

So the long line of princes stretches back through the years, even to the thirteenth century, in a fascinating procession of extraordinarily varied characters. Warriors, statesmen, frustrated artists and spectacular sinners all find their place in the roll-call of the Princes of Wales. Their fates were extraordinarily varied as well. Some, like the eldest sons of Henry VII and James I, died before entering their inheritance.

Others, like the Prince Regent and Edward VII, waited an intolerably long time in the wings before stepping onto the centre of the stage. Princes of Wales have been brutally slaughtered on the battlefield, secretly murdered or ruthlessly removed from their inheritance. Many of them were married against their will. All, from birth, were bound to be pawns in the great game of politics.

The younger historians these days tend to shy away from assigning undue importance to individuals and personalities. They need not necessarily be imbued with Marxist theories to feel that there are general tendencies, maybe dictated by changes in methods of production, which lead inevitably to changes in society as a whole. Perhaps they are right, but I am old-fashioned enough to think that individual character still has a vital part to play in shaping the pattern of events, even if it operates within the framework established by outside forces. I comfort myself by remembering that Marx himself wrote, 'History does nothing, possesses no enormous wealth, fights no battles. It is rather man, the real, living man, who does everything, possesses, fights.' In my heart of hearts I cannot believe that our past is entirely moulded by tendencies, committees, resolutions, manifestos and correct assessments of party lines. Behind all this are human beings, impatient and fallible, moved by the same emotions and carried away or downcast by triumph or disappointment exactly like ourselves. I am fascinated by history because, through its study, I imagine that I can cross the vast gulf of the years and meet again those men and women, those princes and princesses of the past. At second hand I can share their joys and sorrows and perhaps, through sympathizing with them, reach a better understanding of the problems of our own restless age.

I plead guilty to another historical heresy. From time to time I cannot resist indulging in what serious historians disparagingly call the 'Cleopatra's Nose Theory of History'. It is pointless, they insist, to speculate on what would have happened if Cleopatra had been a long-nosed frump, incapable of ensnaring the impressionable Mark Antony. But as we now start to trace the story of our Princes of Wales, we cannot resist speculating on the 'Might-Have-Beens'. Why shouldn't we breathe a sigh of relief that the eldest son of George II, the unpleasant Frederick, died while his father was still alive? Or that the unstable Prince 'Eddy', the heir of Edward VII, was replaced by his utterly dependable and dutiful younger brother, George V?

Through all this runs the persistent theme of the relationship between father and son; doubly difficult when the father is king of England and his son his destined successor. Even in the early years of the title, we find the Black Prince fretting as he saw his father, Edward III, once so glorious, lose his grip on affairs and sink towards dotage.

And if the popular story, used with such effect by Shakespeare, is to be trusted, Prince Hal himself – the future hero-king Henry V – was somewhat over-eager to assume the mantle of his father, Henry IV.

It is because I am sure that most people still think the individual to be important and believe that personalities still influence events that I have brought together these short accounts of the lives of the Princes and Princesses of Wales. I feel that I can trace, in the growing prince, some of the qualities that emerged, for better or worse, in the character of the king. I stop my account as soon as the prince becomes the king.

There have now been twenty-one Princes of Wales since the title was first granted to his eldest son by the king of England at the beginning of the thirteenth century. Not every English monarch has been a Prince of Wales in his youth. The title is not automatically assumed by the heir to the throne as soon as he is born. It came to the English crown by right of conquest after Edward I had crushed Llywelyn ap Gruffydd, the only native-born prince to bear undisputedly the title of Prince of Wales. The unlucky Welshman is usually and unfairly disregarded when tracing the line of the Princes of Wales. This is now reckoned to start with Edward of Caernarfon, the son of Edward I, who came to the throne as Edward II. The honour lies in the gift of the monarch and he can decide when – and indeed if – he grants it. Edward I did not create his heir Prince of Wales until 1301, some considerable time after he had conquered Wales. Queen Victoria, on the other hand, made her son Prince of Wales a month after his birth. Our present Queen announced the elevation of our present prince to the honour in a message sent to the Commonwealth Games at Cardiff in 1958 and read by Prince Philip. The new Prince of Wales was then nine years and eight months old.

As the honour is in the absolute gift of the monarch, he can in theory give it to any one of his sons. In practice he always gives it to the eldest, for the principle of primogeniture lies at the very root of the English monarchy, and, indeed, may account in part for its success. Other monarchies have been elective, as was the Polish, or the inheritance was divided among the heirs, as in the old Celtic kingdoms. But with the advent of the Normans, primogeniture became the rule in England. It was the eldest son who automatically ascended the throne. The rule had one great merit. It eliminated the crowning evil of a disputed succession. It also had one drawback. The eldest son was not always the fittest son to succeed. The long line of our kings has some duds on the list. Henry VI was hardly a king who stirred the imagination of his people. We will also come across some providential 'near misses' in our survey; Princes of Wales who luckily never succeeded. But to be fair, the successful princes far outweigh the misfits. Primogeniture hasn't done too badly for Britain.

In these days of Women's Lib, we note with interest that no woman has ever been created Prince of Wales – or should we say Princess? – in her own right. Again in theory, there is no reason why the king should not give the title to a daughter, if she is his only heir. In France, the so-called Salic law prevented the accession of females to the throne. Luckily this rule never applied in Britain. If it had, we would have lost the glories of the Elizabethan era. We would have missed the splendours of Queen Anne's reign. There would have been no Victoria and our present Queen would not have been crowned. 'Bloody Mary' was the only one of our female rulers since the Middle Ages who was not an outstanding success. But in the early days the title of Prince of Wales could also carry with it important administrative duties. As he grew to manhood, its holder might be expected to be sent to govern the principality. In the case of Henry V as Prince of Wales he even had to fight for his inheritance. The medieval mind did not take kindly to the idea of women leading armies. One Joan of Arc was enough, and she was eventually burnt as a heretic.

Court flattery occasionally caused the king's eldest daughters to be called Princesses of Wales in Tudor and Stuart times but to this day, the only way a woman can become Princess of Wales is to follow the example of Lady Diana Spencer and marry her prince.

Not all Princes of Wales have married Princesses. Some died before they could marry and some only married after they had become king. Henry VIII married his deceased brother's wife and George V married the bride who had been pledged to his elder brother. So while there have been twenty-one Princes of Wales there have been only eight Princesses.

The Prince of Wales has, of course, other titles that have accrued to the office over the centuries, and they make a splendid roll-call of titles, all reflecting the history of the monarchy and the union of the Scottish and English crowns under James I as well as the far earlier conquest of Wales in the thirteenth century. Prince Charles is thus His Royal Highness Prince Charles Philip Arthur George, Prince of Wales and Earl of Chester, Duke of Cornwall in the Peerage of England, Duke of Rothesay, Earl of Carrick and Baron of Renfrew in the Peerage of Scotland, Lord of the Isles and Great Steward of Scotland.

The arms of the Prince of Wales still contain reminders of our French wars in the Middle Ages. A well-loved story relates that the famous three ostrich feathers on the Prince's crest together with the motto *Ich dien*, were won by the Black Prince on the field of Crécy. The blind king of Bohemia insisted on being led into the thick of the fight. When it was over his body and those of the two knights who had led him were found dead on the field. The Prince picked up the ostrich feathers that decorated the king's helmet, and also appropriated his motto, *Ich dien*.

Unfortunately contemporary accounts of the battle do not mention the incident, and the motto may have come into the princely arms through his mother's connection with her family house of Hainault in Flanders.

The time has long gone when the Prince's titles implied power over the areas described or administrative duties of any kind. The one exception is the Duchy of Cornwall. The land owned by the Prince in the Duchy still has the practical purpose of supplying a great part of the Prince's revenue, although half is now handed over to the Government.

This was not true of the office in the Middle Ages and well on into the seventeenth century. The Princes of Wales governed Wales, put down rebellion in Wales and, later on, started their apprenticeship in the art of ruling by presiding over the Council of the Marches in Ludlow, then the centre of the government of Wales. But the Hanoverians broke the connection with the land from which the Prince took his title. Few of them ever bothered to visit their Principality. George IV condescended to make one short excursion there when he was prince. He happened to be staying in Shropshire and was persuaded to ride over the border near Welshpool. He received the homage of the gentlemen of Montgomeryshire and within an hour was safely back over the border and on his way to the arms of Mrs Fitzherbert.

Our present Prince Charles has triumphantly reversed the attitude of some of his forebears of polite indifference. No Prince of Wales in recent times has tried so hard and so successfully to identify himself with his Principality. He has even achieved the unparalleled feat – at least for an English Prince of Wales – of making a speech in public in Welsh. As he spoke, the minds of many of his Welsh listeners in the audience, went back seven hundred years to the birth of the first non-Welsh Prince of Wales in Caernarfon Castle. So it is there, on 25 April, St Mark's Day, in 1284, that we must begin the long, romantic and eventful chronicle of the Princes of Wales.

I

The Prize of Conquest

'Ruin seize thee, ruthless king,
Confusion on thy banners wait.'
THOMAS GRAY

It is a curious fact that the eldest son of the king of England takes his title from a country that is still fiercely conscious that it is not English. In the Middle Ages the monarch had numerous apanages that he might have bestowed on his heir. Our own Charles might now be known as Prince of Cornwall or of Lancaster. But seven hundred years ago Edward I of England laid his heavy hand on the neighbouring principality of Wales. The title of Prince of Wales came with the conquest and Edward naturally reserved it for his son. After all, Prince is a more resplendent title than a mere Duke, but there is more to the title than prestige. The honour of Prince of Wales had a special significance in the context of thirteenth-century politics. Taking it away from the Welsh and vesting it in an English prince marked an important step in the realization of a cherished dream that had beset every English ruler all through our national history – the ultimate unity of the whole of the islands of Britain under the English crown. Edward regarded the title as a jewel in his own crown and handed it on to his son with pride.

But how did it originate in the first place? Was there a long line of Welsh princes whose ancient heritage had been violently dispossessed by Edward? His newly acquired principality already had a complex story, romantic and tragic in turn. The very survival of Wales, next door to its overpowering neighbour, England, is one of the surprises of history. Again and again the little country seemed to be erased from the map. The Romans overran it and held it in a vice-like grip of forts and military roads. The Anglo-Saxons drove the Welsh from the fertile lowlands, and Offa of Mercia marked the boundary in the great earthen dyke that still bears his name. The rapacious Normans carved Marcher lordships out of the fertile valleys of South and Mid-Wales, but some-how, against all the odds, there remained a corner of Wales that still nourished its independence. By the end of the twelfth and the beginning of the thirteenth century Welshmen even dared to hope that most of Wales might become a self-governing political reality.

A powerful line of able princes had established themselves in Gwynedd in North Wales. They had a strong base in the mountain wilds of Snowdonia with the fertile island of Anglesey beyond. Here they could defy any invader and then spread themselves out over the rest of Wales. When the kings of England were in difficulties, as were King John and Henry III, the princes of Gwynedd could turn these difficulties to their advantage. By 1220 the most astute of them, Llywelyn ap Iorwerth, had built up a strong principality, with its own castles and its own administrative structure, a small but well-organized state, functioning on the same lines as the similar, if bigger, states of England and France. When he died in 1240 a Cistercian annalist could write of him:

> Thus died that great Achilles the Second, the lord Llywelyn ... whose deeds I am unworthy to recount. For with lance and shield did he tame his foes; he kept peace for the men of religion; to the needy he gave food and raiment. With a warlike chain he extended his boundaries; he showed justice to all ... and by meet bonds of fear or love bound all men to him.

Curiously enough, Llywelyn ap Iorwerth, who is rightly known to Welsh history as Llywelyn the Great, never gave himself the title of Prince of Wales. He was a man with a clear sense of political reality. He was careful to pay formal homage to the king of England and was content to call himself Prince of Aberfraw (his favourite residence) and Lord of Snowdon. He preferred real power to surface panache. His son, David, was the first of the Welsh princes who actively sought the supreme princely title.

Among his many political innovations in Welsh politics, Llywelyn had sought to introduce the rule of primogeniture in regulating the succession. The old Welsh custom of dividing the inheritance among the heirs had always been a serious source of weakness in the state. Not long before he died, Llywelyn ap Iorwerth summoned all his barons and made them swear allegiance to David. Old customs, however, die hard. David found his heritage strongly disputed by his half-brother, Gruffydd. In the troubled times that followed, David undoubtedly felt that his position would be immeasurably strengthened if he was formally acknowledged by the outside world as Prince of Wales. Titles were vitally important in the Middle Ages for they directly reflected the realities of power. David had no hope of being recognized under the title by the King of England. He turned instead to that other source of authority in Europe, the Pope. Matthew Paris, the greatest of the English medieval chroniclers, makes the somewhat sarcastic comment, under the year 1244:

> David, intending to free his neck from the yoke of fealty to the lord king, took flight to the wings of papal protection, pretending that he held a part of Wales from the pope directly.

In a few documents David actually used the proud title – he was the first man in our history to do so – but the Pope soon withdrew his support. As far as the Papacy was concerned, the English monarchy had more 'muscle'. David returned to the less controversial form of 'Prince of North Wales'. It was left to his successor, Llywelyn ap Gruffydd, to be fully acknowledged as Prince of Wales by the King, the Pope, the Lords Marcher and his own barons. Llywelyn was a worthy descendant of his grandfather, Llywelyn the Great. He, too, profited by the troubles of Henry III and the revolt of Simon de Montfort to advance the expansion of Gwynedd and its development on true feudal lines. The peak of his success was marked by the Treaty of Montgomery in 1267. Not only did most of Wales now bow before him as overlord but the King of England agreed to his assuming the title of Prince of Wales. Llywelyn ap Gruffydd is thus the first true native-born Prince of Wales.

He was also the last. Henry III died in 1272. He was succeeded by a king of a very different character. Edward I was a notable soldier and a first-class organizer with a clear-cut legal mind. No doubt to such a man the very existence of an independent Wales was administratively untidy. Llywelyn should have carefully watched his step, but this was exactly what he did not do. Perhaps he had been elated by his success at Montgomery, or perhaps he was nursing a grievance that his bride, Eleanor, the daughter of Simon de Montfort, had been detained by Edward in England. What ever the reason, he repeatedly delayed paying his homage to the new King. This was a fatal mistake when dealing with the meticulous Edward. War was inevitable and it was a war that Llywelyn could not win. The big battalions were on Edward's side.

In two brilliant campaigns Edward used the fleet of the Cinque Ports to cut Llywelyn off from the source of his supplies in Anglesey.

In 1277 Llywelyn was humiliated. In 1282 he was utterly defeated. In December of that year he slipped out of the grip of Edward's armies that were closing in on Snowdonia. He hoped to raise support in South Wales but he was surprised on a lonely hillside near Cilmery, near Builth in the Wye Valley. An English knight ran him through. His head was cut off and sent to Edward in Anglesey. The King sent it on to London as evidence of his triumph. Llywelyn's headless body was laid to rest in the now ruined abbey of Cwm Hir among the deeply wooded hills of Mid-Wales far from his native Gwynedd. But a great stone, quarried from the rocks of Snowdonia, stands as his memorial at the spot where he met his death. The court poet marked the end of the last native Prince of Wales with the bitter cry,

O God! that the sea might engulf the land!
Why are we left to long-drawn weariness?

The victor lost no time in bringing a new order to his conquest. The Statute of Rhuddlan recast the structure of Llywelyn's principality on English lines, and Edward made certain of his grip on North Wales by building an iron ring of castles around the redoubt of Snowdon and separating it from Anglesey. They now form a magnificent tourist attraction, for this was the greatest scheme of castle building ever undertaken in medieval Europe. Welshmen of the time, however, could hardly be expected to admire their new prison walls. The most impressive of these new castles is Caernarfon. On it, Edward's architect, Master James of St. George, in charge of the 'King's Works in Wales', lavished all his skill. Caernarfon was to be the administrative centre of the new principality. Master James set out to make it a place of imperial splendour. Did he go for inspiration to the great walls of Byzantium, which still impress the spectator with the strength of their rectangular towers?

In April 1284, these walls of Caernarfon were still under construction when Edward brought his wife, Eleanor of Castile, to join him in Wales. Temporary apartments had been erected in the upper ward and here on 25 April Queen Eleanor gave birth to a son, who, according to the custom of the day, was known as Edward of Caernarfon.

Here we come to one of those delightful stories that were scattered through our long history and entranced us in our childhood. We learnt about King Bruce of Scotland and his spider and King Alfred burning the cakes at the same time as we heard the story of King

Edward presenting his infant son to the Welsh people. Legend maintains that the victorious king summoned the defeated and dejected Welsh barons to meet him at Caernarfon, where he promised them a new prince who was born in Wales and could not speak a word of the hated English tongue. Whereupon he produced the infant Edward of Caernarfon, who was indisputably born in Wales and certainly could not speak a word of English – or any other language for that matter!

A pretty story but, alas, without real foundation. It seems to have appeared in Tudor times. It first appears in Dr David Powel's *Historie of Cambria* three hundred years after the Edwardian conquest of Wales. Edward of Caernarfon was formally created Prince of Wales in 1301 when he was seventeen. In any case, he was not the heir to the throne in 1284: his elder brother, Alfonso, was still alive. He it was who had acted on the King's behalf when he had presented the spoils of the Welsh campaign to the Church at Westminster Abbey. But in August 1284, the young Prince suddenly died. Edward of Caernarfon thus became first in the line of succession. Wales missed having an Alfonso as its first prince by a few short months!

The future career of the infant born at Caernarfon was eventful enough without the celebrated story, and contained all the elements that characterized the history of all succeeding Princes of Wales, including the inevitable conflict between father and son. Edward I was forty-four when his son was born. He was an impressive and intimidating figure, with an European reputation as a soldier and statesman. He was also handsome and physically strong with the furious and ungovernable temper of the Plantagenets. Such a man was hardly likely to have much time or affection to spare for the small boy who had so unexpectedly become his heir. Two years after he had put the affairs of Wales in order, the King went overseas for a prolonged stay in his French domains in Aquitaine.

The Prince's mother, Eleanor of Castile, was a remarkable woman whose deep devotion to her husband has gone down in history. But she went abroad with her husband and she died on her return three years later. Little Edward was thus deprived not only of a father's interest but of a mother's love. He had to take affection wherever and in whatever form he could find it. This might be one explanation for many of his subsequent troubles. He was summoned from time to time to attend the King at public functions, but his early life was mainly spent in the country. His formal education was entrusted to Sir Guy Frere.

Sir Guy was a scholar and a courtier of the old school, who had served the Prince's grandfather. He had been a crusader in the Holy Land and had acted as Steward to the Prince's grandmother, Eleanor of Provence. The Prince became much attached to this kindly and upright veteran who was to be his governor for eight of his early and formative years. Under Sir Guy's guidance Edward grew up to be a healthy, lively and intelligent youth who soon acquired a reputation as a superb horseman. All his life he was devoted to the chase and one of the earliest English treatises on hunting was written by his chief huntsman. At the age of seventeen a chronicler described him as 'a well-proportioned and handsome person' who managed his steed wonderfully well and who took every occasion to demonstrate his skill.

He was undoubtedly literate for we know that he possessed books in Latin and in the Norman French habitually spoken in court. His letters have an individual style and betray a well-developed sense of humour. They give us a slightly different portrait from the usual stereotyped picture of a medieval prince. He was also deeply devoted to music. He had his pipers, singers and drummers constantly around him, and even sent to Wales for a 'crwth', an early form of violin, to be played to him at Windsor. He also delighted in plays and dramatic performances of all sorts, even, as his enemies complained, buffoonery. This may simply mean that he exercised his wit at the expense of the dull-witted.

As he grew to manhood he was granted the manor of Langley in Hertfordshire, later to be known as King's Langley. This became a favourite residence. Here he could breed horses and greyhounds, and even keep a few exotic beasts like camels and lions. He also became skilled in country crafts, from gardening to hedging and ditching. All this may seem highly commendable to modern observers. Here we have a young prince getting an understanding of the real life of ordinary people. Unfortunately it seemed anything but commendable to his contemporaries. They were living in a feudal society, where rank was of vital importance and the rights and duties of all classes were rigidly defined. They were distressed to see their future king stepping out of his own class, and thus betraying the central assumptions that held feudal society together.

Soon they found another defect in him. Edward showed no enthusiasm for that most important medieval institution as far as the governing classes were concerned – the tournament. This extraordinary ritual involved armoured knights charging each other along a barrier in front of an excited audience of high-born ladies. It had begun as a training for warfare and was an extremely rough affair. By the time Edward of Caernarfon was growing up the tournament had developed from a semi-murderous mêlée into an elaborate ritual, with strict rules and tempting prizes. Some knights even made a business of attending tournaments, touring Europe with the medieval equivalent of the modern professional tennis 'circus'. Edward I had been a famous 'tournayer'. In his youth he had journeyed to France, and although he was badly beaten in 1260 and lost armour and horses, this did not quench his enthusiasm. When he became king he used the tournament to the full as a political weapon. He gave a particularly splendid one at Nevin to celebrate his conquest of Wales. His barons naturally expected his son to continue the tradition and were deeply disappointed to find that Edward of Caernarfon was lukewarm in his attitude to their favourite entertainment. The contemporary anonymous chronicler who wrote the *Vita Edwardi Secundi* noted with regret that 'if the prince had given to arms the labour he expended on rustic pursuits, he would have raised England aloft; his name would have resounded through the land.' Instead doubts circulated through the land about the physical courage of the heir to the throne. Unjustly so, for in later campaigns in Scotland Edward proved that, whatever were his other shortcomings, he had the usual Plantagenet bravery in battle. Later on, still darker suspicions were to cloud the barons' judgement of their prince and future king.

Meantime the Prince of Wales had to serve his apprenticeship in the business of government. His father's expansionist policy had overcome the Welsh. He now turned on the Scots. A disputed royal succession gave him the chance to interfere in Scottish affairs, which were to haunt him for the rest of his life. First Wallace and then Bruce kept alive the flame of Scottish resistance, draining away King Edward's strength, patience and cash. He was to leave this dangerous heritage to his son, who was to pay for his father's misjudgement about Scottish resistance years later on the fateful field of Bannockburn. The King's first campaigns in Scotland went reasonably well, and the Prince of Wales also acquitted himself well at the siege of Caerlaverock Castle in Dumfriesshire.

The King must have been reasonably satisfied at this time with the way the Prince was developing. In 1299 his marriage came under discussion. King Edward's beloved wife Eleanor had died and the King felt he had to remarry for political reasons. He sought an alliance with France and at Montreuil he pledged his troth to Margaret, sister of Philip IV of France, and contracted young Edward, aged fifteen, to

Philip's daughter Isabella, aged eight. The King celebrated his wedding to Margaret at Canterbury with great splendour, and the Prince of Wales had a stepmother to whom he became greatly attached. His own marriage had perforce to wait until his bride reached a suitable age. She waited off stage, in the wings as it were. When she finally took the stage it was to play a sinister and tragic part.

In 1301, the King's satisfaction with the progress of his son was marked by his creation as Prince of Wales. This honour, new in the monarchy of England, was confirmed at the session of Parliament held at Lincoln. It was combined with the Earldom of Chester. With it went the Welsh lands of the Principality, a rich and princely inheritance indeed! We have no record of the actual investiture ceremony, but there must have been one since subsequent grants of the title refer to insignias being presented 'according to custom'. We may legitimately assume that an investiture ceremony was performed in the chapter house at Lincoln when the King presented the Prince with a coronet for his head, a ring for his finger and a silver rod for his hand. So our own Prince Charles was invested at Caernarfon in 1969.

The new Prince of Wales left on a tour of his Welsh estates and made progress through North Wales, receiving the homage of his new vassals. He visited Flint, Ruthin, Rhuddlan and Conway. He did not return to his Principality until his last tragic days when he fled before his enemies for refuge in South Wales. Surprisingly enough, considering that they had risen in violent revolt only a few years before, the Welsh received their new Prince of Wales with respect if not with enthusiasm. They sent him petitions when he returned to England. He had Welsh musicians at his court and Welsh archers fought for him on his Scottish campaigns.

For the next three years the Prince of Wales carried out his public duties. He was at his father's side in parliaments and on diplomatic missions. He took his full share of the hardships of campaigning in Scotland. Again he proved himself, if not a brilliant soldier, at least a brave and respectable one. He may still have shown no interest in tournaments, and remained overfond of rustic pursuits, but the King must now have hoped that his son had the stuff of successful royalty in him.

Then out of a clear sky came a bombshell. On 14 January 1305, the King banished his son from court. He then cut off all financial support from the Royal Exchequer. The Prince of Wales was in disgrace, and the cause was a mystery. On the face of it the excuse given by the King for taking this severe line was an alleged trespass for poaching on the estates of the royal treasurer. Not a particularly serious affair for a high-spirited young man, and one which might have merited a reprimand and a suitable apology. Was there some deeper reason that provoked the King's wrath?

Here we come to the central problem in the strange and tragic career of Edward of Caernarfon – his relations with and curious attachment for the handsome, witty and brave young Gascon, Piers Gaveston. The name of Gaveston was to echo like a sinister undertone through the whole story of Edward of Caernarfon, both as prince and king. What was the secret bond that held together a man in the highest position in the land and a comparatively base-born foreigner? Edward's enemies had only one explanation. The Prince was a homosexual and the bond that bound Edward and Gaveston was a shameful one, prohibited by the Church and vigorously condemned by most of his subjects. Other English monarchs have been suspected of this tendency, including William Rufus and Richard the Lionheart, but Edward of Caernarfon had to face the severe criticism of his own contemporaries. The higher baronage were suspicious from Gaveston's first appearance in the royal household.

Piers's father had served Edward I in his early days, and young Piers had come to the King's notice for his good conduct during the Flanders campaign of 1298. It was the King himself who appointed Gaveston as companion to his son. The two young men soon became inseparable, for Gaveston also enjoyed theatricals and had a mordant wit that delighted the Prince and infuriated the baronage. Gaveston was with Edward at the time of the affair of the poaching on the treasurer's estates. The King might have heard the gossip and this may account for his explosion of Plantagenet temper.

Victorian historians were prepared to leave Edward's true relationship to Gaveston in a cloud of doubt. The good Bishop Stubbs wrote that 'it was reserved for later generations to discover an element of vice in what his contemporaries viewed with pitying indignation as a simple but faithful infatuation.' This is hardly the impression we get, however, when we read the contemporary accounts. They speak of Gaveston 'loving the king's son inordinately', and in return 'Edward's son so much loved him that he called him his brother'. One chronicler states bluntly, 'And when the king's son saw him he fell so much in love that he entered on an enduring compact with him.'

Christopher Marlowe, the great Tudor dramatist had no doubt about the matter. He thought that the chroniclers were right, when he came to write his powerful drama *Edward II*. Foreign observers at the time were positive that Edward was a homosexual. The chronicler of Meaux Abbey in France plainly states, 'The prince was much given to sodomy.' This surely settles the matter. And the Prince of Wales's peculiar taste lay at the centre of all the disagreements between prince and king.

This first row eventually died down. Father and son were reconciled at the Feast of St Edward the Confessor, but as long as Gaveston was still in the Prince's company further outbursts of Plantagenet temper were inevitable. A particularly violent clash occurred between the King and his heir in February 1307. In the previous year the King had felt that perhaps the relationship of Gaveston with his son was fading. He had marked this, for him, happy turn of events by creating the Prince Duke of Aquitaine and then knighting him, and three hundred other young aspirants to knighthood, in a splendid ceremony at Westminster. But the following year the Prince had again provoked the terrifying wrath of his father. Edward's latest campaign against the Scots had not gone well and at Lanercost Priory in Cumbria the Prince chose this inopportune moment to ask that the small territory of Ponthieu in Northern France should be given to Gaveston. The King burst out in furious rage, 'You base-born whoreson, do you want to give away land now, you who never gained any?' He seized the Prince by his hair and pulled out tufts of it. Gaveston was to go into exile and the King forced the Prince to swear that he would not communicate with him in any way. Prince Edward had to agree. He accompanied Gaveston to the coast and loaded him with farewell gifts on the way. No doubt they did not think of Gaveston's stay in Gascony as lasting more than a few months, for the King was now clearly ill and exhausted. Yet still his indomitable will kept him going.

The stage was set for that memorable last scene in the life of Edward I. The King ordered his army to march out from Carlisle. Surely this last time he would finish with that persistent and pestiferous rebel, Robert the Bruce. The King had to be lifted onto his horse. Slowly the army crept forward, but soon it was evident that the old warrior's strength was fading. But still he insisted on moving forward, held up on his horse by his attendants. At last, at Burgh-by-Sands he could go no further. The 'Hammer of the Scots' died within sight of the Border, but on the English side. His son came up from the south, where he had been seeing Gaveston depart for Gascony, and standing by his father's bier, he realized that he was now king.

One of the first acts of the new King was to recall Gaveston. He also carried out the contract arranged by his father and married Isabella of France. Later scandal claimed that Edward gave his wife's marriage jewels to his favourite. The new reign began with evil omens and it ended in tragedy, and the basis of that tragedy had already been laid during Edward's career as Prince of Wales. Here was a king out of sympathy with his baronage. His nobles could not help contrasting him with his mighty father. Edward II was seen to be a king who would govern through favourites, one who did not attend scrupulously to business, and who had inherited a legacy of debt which only a strict and economical administration could control. Edward was neither economical nor business-like. There remained a further and dangerous heritage – the war with Scotland. Edward was no coward but he was not a general of the same class as his father. Would the Hammer of the Scots ever have committed himself to that dangerous, premature charge that brought the crowning disaster of Bannockburn?

Rule by favourites usually ends in the favourite's death. Murder can sometimes be the only way to change a government. Gaveston inevitably came to a sticky end at the hands of Lancaster, Hereford, Arundel and others; Thomas of Lancaster, Edward's chief opponent among the barons was a distinctly unpleasant fellow and we can understand the King's distaste for such counsellors. The King's final attempt to govern through favourites precipitated the last act of the tragedy. Young Despenser was not a homosexual and he was not inefficient – neither for that matter was Gaveston who had made a good job of governing Ireland. The real cause of discontent was their ousting of the powerful magnates who felt that they had a traditional right to share in the government of the realm. Queen Isabella had gone to France on the pretext of a diplomatic mission. For obvious reasons she had been alienated from her husband, and this gave her enmity a particular venom. Even more than Margaret of Anjou, she was a 'she-wolf of France'. She allied herself with Roger Mortimer, a powerful baron from the Welsh Marches, where he had clashed with the Despenser family. He was a man in the sense that Edward was not. Mortimer landed with Isabella on the Suffolk coast. Edward's support fell away from him. He and young Despenser were compelled to flee, with Mortimer and Isabella relentlessly hunting them westward. They hoped to get to Ireland but finally were trapped in South Wales. The harassed King had brought some of his treasure and records with him. They had been sent on to Neath Abbey and Swansea Castle, but the King was overtaken by his enemies before he could follow. Tradition maintains that he was betrayed by a Welshman in whom he had trusted, and they still point to the dingle known as Pant y Brad, the little valley of treachery, near Tonyrefail, where the foul deed was done. Edward was dragged back to his shameful death in Berkeley Castle. He lies buried in Gloucester Cathedral, where the serene face on his funeral effigy adds irony to his story. Strange relics of his last flight still keep turning up in South Wales. When Neath Abbey was being restored a great cache of Edwardian coins was discovered buried beside one of the pillars in the nave. The strangest relic of all came to light at the end of the nineteenth century when a doctor in Swansea was called to attend a farmer's wife in Gower. At the end of the visit the farmer declared that he had no money at hand to pay but added, 'Will this do?' He put his hand in the thatch and pulled out a box. It contained an old parchment which was submitted to the experts for examination. It turned out to be the marriage contract between Edward as Prince of Wales and Isabella of France. The parchment is still on display in the museum of the Royal Institution in Swansea, a sad relic, so evocative of royal suffering six hundred years ago. It must surely always remain in Wales, for according to the Wakefield chronicler, the Welsh had always shown kindness to the first English Prince of Wales who had been born at Caernarfon.

When Scotland would rebel against him and all England would rid herself of him, the Welsh in a wonderful manner cherished and esteemed him and, as far as they were able, stood by him, grieving over his adversities both in life and in death, composing mournful songs about him in the language of their country, the memory of which lingers to the present time and which neither the dread of punishment nor the passage of time have destroyed.

2

Princes of Chivalry

'He was a verray parfit gentil knight.'
GEOFFREY CHAUCER

The career of the first Prince of Wales ended in stark tragedy. We remember the horror of his last moments as Marlowe saw them, with the wretched king crying out to his approaching murderers,

I feel a hell of grief. Where is my crown?
Gone, gone!

The image of the second Prince of Wales is in sharp contrast.

Edward of Woodstock never wore the crown that brought such misery to Edward of Caernarfon, but he gained endless glory on the field of battle and his contemporaries regarded him as a pattern of chivalry, the very model of the perfect knight. The legends gathered around him. Froissart, that eloquent glorifier of the fighting aristocrats of the Middle Ages, has given us a whole series of memorable pictures of the Prince in action – winning his spurs at Crécy and picking up the ostrich feather plumes of the dead King of Bohemia to be his future crest, and waiting humbly on the captured King John of France after his resounding victory at Poitiers. How true some of these stories are is another matter, but at least they show us the atmosphere of chivalric romance that surrounded the Prince throughout his career.

We call him the Black Prince, although the men of his time never knew him under such a name. Like so many other cherished names and stories in our national history, we owe the title to the writers and antiquarians of Tudor times who thought that Edward of Woodstock always wore black armour, or perhaps because of the supposed ruthlessness with which he treated the French. No matter. Edward of Woodstock has been known as the Black Prince for the last four hundred years. It would now be pedantic to call him by any other name.

He was born when his father, Edward III, was about to overthrow the guardianship of his mother, Isabella, and her infamous paramour,

Mortimer. Edward III's wife was Philippa of Hainault, who had long been marked out as the bride of the young king. We have a description of her at the age of nine from Bishop Stapleton, who, according to the custom of the age, had been sent to the Low Countries by Edward II to make a detailed examination of the future Queen of England. Bishop Stapleton was precise.

> The lady whom we saw has not uncomely hair, between blue-black and brown. Her head is clean-shaped, her forehead high and broad and standing somewhat forward. Her face narrow between the eyes, and the lower part of her face is still more narrow and slender than the forehead ... Her teeth, which have fallen and grown again, are white enough, but the rest are not so white ... Her neck, shoulders and all her body and lower limbs are reasonably well shaped; all her limbs are well set and unmaimed; and nothing is amiss so far as a man may see.

The good bishop's account reads more like the sales-bill of a thoroughbred mare at Tattersalls than a description of a royal bride. The reputation of her house for fertility was also vitally important. It was not until the nineteenth century that royal princes were allowed a free choice in brides. In the Middle Ages beauty was desirable, but fertility was better. Ripeness was all!

Philippa turned out to be the perfect partner for young Edward III. She tempered his occasional brusque outburst of Plantagenet temper, and made a graceful centre-piece for the brilliant court he created around her. The handsome, virile young king and his charming queen were a welcome relief after the miseries of a dark decade that had seen the murder of a king and the rule of a profligate queen and her lover. By a deft *coup d'état* Edward had begun his personal rule. Mortimer was executed and his mother packed off to comfortable retirement in a convent. Edward and his young queen inaugurated a new age which was to be marked by military glory and a remarkable flowering of the arts. This was the high noon of the age of chivalry, when the descendants of the tough and rough knights of the early medieval times had learnt to live by an elaborate code of conduct, which involved honour for a brave enemy beaten in battle and courtesy towards women. High-born ladies and knighted aristocrats, of course! Chivalry wore thin and the further you went down the ranks of society. For Froissart, the Black Prince was the flower of chivalry.

Edward of Woodstock grew to manhood when his father was preparing his country for an intoxicating period of military glory. The Prince spent most of his early years at Woodstock in Oxfordshire, where the splendid eighteenth-century palace of Blenheim now stands and where Winston Churchill was born. His mother, Queen Philippa, carefully supervised his education. Her almoner, Walter Burley, was appointed his tutor. Burley was a scholar of repute, but the Black Prince did not grow up bookish, nor was he devoted to lowly rustic pursuits, like his grandfather. The story that he was once a scholar at Queen's College, Oxford, seems to be an eighteenth century invention. The Prince early delighted in the pursuit of arms. By 1338 his accounts show that he possessed a quantity of armour with such picturesque names as bascinets, poleyns, a pisane, a ventail, vambraces and rerebraces. The list already brings with it an air of romantic chivalry. He also possessed a small personal tent, modelled on those used in the military campaigns of the time. Edward III looked on the development of the growing boy with approval and the Black Prince never joined the ranks of those Princes of Wales who were at loggerheads with their fathers. We have a pleasant picture of him playing dice with his father as they floated down the Thames on a state barge on their way to a pilgrimage at Canterbury. The Prince delighted in jewellery and fine clothes and was an avid lover of the tournament. From an early age he was well fitted for his future role as the showpiece in his father's glittering court. Earlier he had been made Earl of Chester and then Duke of Cornwall, the fist time that the title of Duke was attached to a royal apanage in England.

In 1343, Edward III made his son Prince of Wales. He himself had never held the title. The troubled closing years of Edward II's reign were hardly the time for the giving of honours. Now, at a Parliament held in Westminster Hall, the Black Prince was invested 'according to custom' with a coronet, a ring and a silver rod. He also received the rights to all the royal lands in Wales. The Black Prince, however, never visited his Principality and took no interest in its national life. He valued it chiefly as a recruiting ground for his soldiers. He would soon need all the Welsh recruits he could get, for the time was coming when his father would break with France, and that seemingly endless contest between the two nations would begin, which we call the Hundred Years War although it consisted of short periods of violent action punctuated by periods of uneasy truce. The war was to twist the whole course of English history into a new pattern and to end in ultimate disaster. The comparatively short life of the Black Prince – he died at the age of forty-six – spanned the period of success and glory.

The causes of the war with France were many and complex but, at the heart of the matter, lay the awkward fact that the King of England owned a vast part of south-western France – Aquitaine. This had come into English hands when Henry II had married Eleanor of Aquitaine and, by feudal custom, the English king had to do homage for his French lands to the king of France. This was a constant source of irritation to the French crown. It seemed dangerous to the king of France to have a powerful vassal who was also king of an independent country. It threatened the unity of the French state. It was doubly dangerous when the succession to the French throne was in dispute and the English king was a possible claimant. This is exactly what happened when his mother Isabella's brother, Charles, died early in the reign of Edward III. The French preferred Philip de Valois and, for the moment, Edward III had to agree, but when, after interfering in the Anglo/Scottish dispute, Philip ordered the seizure of Gascony, Edward decided on war. He revived his own claim to the French throne. He was all the more confident of ultimate victory because he had devised new tactics of battle in his Scottish campaigns. He had combined massed archers, mostly Welsh, with his armoured knights in a deadly and effective manoeuvre. His knights now awaited the enemy onslaught on foot. As his opponents rode forward Edward unleashed his archers at them from the flanks. The longbow, developed in South Wales and the Marches, was the machine-gun of the Middle Ages. The crossbow was more powerful, but the longbow was faster. The attacking knights had their horses killed under them and crashed to the ground in their heavy armour under the arrow-storm.

It must be admitted that the Welsh were regarded in Europe as the Gurkhas of the day. The French felt that they were a very wild lot indeed. A Flemish chronicler visited them in their camp and was surprised by what he found.

> There you saw the peculiar habits of the Welsh. In the very depth of winter they were running about bare-legged ... Their weapons were bows, arrows and swords. They also had javelins ... They wore linen clothing. They were great drinkers. They endangered the Flemings very much. Their pay was too small and so it came about that they took what did not belong to them.

However unruly the Welsh may have been off the battlefield, there was no doubt about their effectiveness on it. They were a major factor in the victory of Crécy in 1346, the battle that first established the fighting reputation of the Black Prince. The result startled Europe. The French knights were universally regarded as the foremost warriors of their age. They and their horses went down like ninepins before the Welsh arrows. Worse still, the wild men from the hills thought nothing of running up to the fallen knights, helpless in their armour, and cutting their throats. Froissart was shocked. Warfare should have the chivalry of a tournament on a larger scale, and besides, what a loss of ransom money! As Froissart says, Edward III was 'after displeased' for he had hoped that they would be taken prisoner.

The young prince, however, had covered himself with a glory that never left him. He was only sixteen at the time, but men went early to battle in those days. We cannot be certain that Edward III replied 'Let the boy win his spurs', when the Prince, or his advisers, appealed to him for help in the height of the battle, but the blind King of Bohemia was certainly led to his death in the fight and his plume of three ostrich feathers went to the Prince as his spoil of victory.

The Crécy campaign carried Edward III and his son forward on a vast tide of popularity. England had suddenly become a factor to be reckoned with in European politics. In this mood of confidence, Edward created the Order of the Garter. It was proclaimed in a great feast held at Windsor on St George's Day, 1348. Again we have to turn to Tudor historians for the legendary origin of the name. It is Polydore Vergil who tells the story of how the Queen or one of Edward's mistresses dropped her garter at a great ball held to celebrate the foundation of this new order of chivalry. The courtiers tittered but the King silenced the unseemly mirth of his knights by picking up the garter with the words, *'Honi soit qui mal y pense'* – Shame to him who thinks evil of it. True or not, the tale reflects the atmosphere of high chivalry in which the Order was created. The Prince of Wales was naturally the leading member under the King. Among the original Knights of the Garter were commanders who had won fame in the French campaigns and many who were to form a devoted band of experienced warriors around the Prince.

For the career of Edward of Woodstock was to be firmly based on the business of war, and all through the long campaigns in France, the Prince never lost sight of the commercial aspect of it. Victories could be made to pay, and the revenue from ransoms was vital in the maintenance of the state and splendour with which he surrounded himself. It was to this splendour and to his lavish rewards to his companions in arms that he owed much of his prestige. The war in

27

France was resumed after the comparative lull that had followed Crécy and the sea fight against the Castilians off Winchelsea in 1350 – the only occasion when a Prince of Wales has fought at sea!

The centre of interest was now transferred from Northern France to the English possessions in the south-west. There was no question that the inhabitants of the country around Bordeaux preferred English rule to that of the French king. London was further away than Paris and interfered less. The Black Prince was entrusted with the defence of Aquitaine as an experienced warrior in his own right. His strategy was to lead long, damaging raids deep into French territory, thus destroying the enemy resources and weakening his will to resist. These forays have been compared to the bombing raids on Germany in World War Two. In this case the raiders also returned with fat and acceptable loot. On one of these raids, known as 'chevauchées', King John of France intercepted the Black Prince's army near Poitiers with a vastly superior force. The result was an English victory even more extraordinary than Crécy.

The French tried to vary their tactics and moved forward slowly on foot. But the Prince, by an alert use of his archers and a cavalry charge at the right moment, smashed the French line. It was a victory of a small, well-led and well-disciplined, battle-tested army over a larger but less disciplined force. In the mêlée, the King of France himself was captured. The Prince made a triumphal return to London with his prisoners. A splendid series of tournaments was held at Smithfield to celebrate his success. King John, thinking of the heavy ransoms yet to be paid, remarked wryly that he had never before seen a tournament financed not with silver and gold but with tallies.

The eventual price of Poitiers was not only ransoms but a treaty signed at Brétigny immensely favourable to the English. In the uneasy peace that followed two important events occurred in the life of the Black Prince. First he got married, not for diplomatic reasons but apparently for love – and a certain amount of money. The bride was Joan, Countess of Kent in her own right. She already had a complicated matrimonial history, for she had been secretly married to Sir Thomas Holland. This had not prevented her from being married, in his absence abroad, to the Earl of Salisbury. Sir Thomas returned to England and was naturally furious. Eventually the union with the Earl of Salisbury was dissolved and Sir Thomas conveniently died, leaving Joan a desirable widow. It took some complicated negotiations with the Papacy before the way was cleared for the Black Prince to claim his bride, universally acknowledged to be one of the greatest beauties of her day. She amply deserved her nickname of the Fair Maid of Kent. She was a beautiful ornament in the lavish court he now established in Aquitaine. For the King had now vested the whole of this splendid apanage in the Black Prince. This was the climax of the Prince's career. He even added to his already high military reputation by a victory at Najara during a campaign in Spain in 1367. As the chroniclers claimed, he had ennobled the title of Prince of Wales until it resounded throughout the Christian world.

Indeed, he was the man who first brought the very name of Wales to the notice of Europe. Welshmen were always prominent in his armies; men like Sir Hywel ap Gruffydd, known as Sir Hywel of the Axe. He had wielded his battleaxe with conspicuous gallantry at Poitiers and was even credited with the actual capture of the King of France. The Prince had been so impressed that he is said to have ordered this fearsome weapon to be placed in the hall, where a ration of beef was served daily before it. Sir Hywel was appointed constable of Criccieth and died in 1381.

But an equally celebrated Welshman fought on the other side in the service of France. Yvain de Galles the French called him, but the Welsh back in Wales celebrated him as Owain Lawgoch, Owen of the Red Hand. Owen was the last representative of the princely house of Gwynedd, being the grandson of Llywelyn the Last's youngest brother, Rhodri. He also acquired a formidable reputation as a fighter, and was specially denoted by the English with the epithet of 'enemy and traitor to the Lord Prince'. He claimed that he, not the Black Prince, was the rightful Prince of Wales. He even persuaded the French to back him in an invasion of his native land, but this got no further than Guernsey in 1372. It would be interesting to speculate what would have happened if a Welsh Prince of Wales had set up his standard in the Principality while the English Prince of Wales was heavily engaged in his French wars. Owen Lawgoch might have anticipated the later rebellion of Owain Glyn Dŵr and perhaps with more permanent results. Owen's career ended in a strange and tragic accident when he was besieging the small town of Mortange-sur-Mer in Poitou. He was a handsome man, much admired by the French ladies and was proud of his fine head of hair. He was in the habit of combing it before the town every morning, while discussing the tactics of the day with his commanders. He sent his squire, John Lambe, back for a special comb but when Lambe returned, it was with a dagger with which he stabbed Owen to death. Thus, at the hands of a mercenary traitor, perished the last scion of the noble line of the Princes of Gwynedd.

The Black Prince's own career was already clouding over towards its end. The French could never willingly accept the Treaty of Brétigny. War flared up again and the French relentlessly gnawed away at the boundaries of Aquitaine. The Prince was in continual need of money to maintain his extravagantly expensive court at Bordeaux, but the French war had long ceased to be a good business proposition. Besides, he was an ailing man. His eldest son had died and his heir was now the four-year-old Richard, born at Bordeaux. It is strange how often in our past history the eldest son of royalty dies and the second son becomes the heir. Joan and little Richard accompanied the Prince back to England.

It was a very different country from the land he had left eight years before to become Duke of Aquitaine. Edward III had lost his wife, Philippa, and his zest and interest in kingship. He was falling increasingly under the influence of his rapacious mistress, Alice Perrers. The reins of government were slipping out of his hands. Parliament was restive and the Black Prince had to tackle a continual series of political crises. His health made him unequal to the task. He died on 8 June 1376, and was buried in an elaborate tomb at Canterbury Cathedral, where a replica of his helmet still hangs above his noble effigy. Thomas Brinton, Bishop of Rochester, preached an eloquent sermon after the Prince's death, in which he praised the one quality that his contemporaries most admired in the Black Prince.

> His wisdom appeared in his manner of acting and habit of speaking prudently, because he did not merely talk like the lords of today but was a doer of deeds, so that he never began a great work without bringing it to a praiseworthy end.

A doer of deeds! That is what the men of the Middle Ages required their kings and princes to be. Above all, a doer of deeds in battle, a leader who would make decisions. Edward III and the Black Prince, with their love of the tournament and of lavish display, shared the tastes of their baronage. It was the secret of their success. The monarchs who failed in the Middle Ages – Edward II, Richard II, and Henry VI – might have been more learned, more cultured and even more saintly, but they were not 'doers of deeds'. They all came to a sticky end.

The heir to the Black Prince's glory was a boy of nine when his father died. Prince Richard had been born in Bordeaux and had received a good education from his father's old comrade-in-arms Sir Simon Burley. He was a lively, intelligent lad and fond of the arts. Perhaps too fond for his less cultured barons. They looked askance at his taste for fashion, his interest in the art of cookery – he was praised in one of our earliest cookery books as 'the best and ryallest vyander of all christen Kynges'. He has even been credited with the invention of the handkerchief. At any rate, his clerk recorded the purchase of 'little pieces made for giving to the lord King for carrying in his hand to wipe and clean his nose'. Mr Anthony Steel has called this the 'chef d'oeuvre of a dilettante of genius'. Perhaps that very phrase gives the clue to the failure of Richard II. He was a dilettante in government, not a doer like his father.

No one questioned his courage. He rode fearlessly up to the rebellious mob led by Wat Tyler in the Peasants' Revolt and imposed his will on the rioters: he was a lad of fourteen at the time. Although he was deeply interested in the life of his grandfather, Edward II, he was no homosexual. He was devoted to his first wife, Anne of Bohemia, and tender to his second, the twelve-year-old Isabella of Valois, whom he had married for political reasons. Under Richard, England reached high peaks in architecture, painting and poetry, but through it all, Richard remained curiously detached from his great nobles, who felt that they had an ancient acknowledged right to participate in the business of government. Richard had high ideas about the sanctity of monarchy. He was a James I two hundred years before his time, theorizing on the Divine Right of Kings. Above all he was not a warrior, a fighting king. His nobles could say, with Langland's *Piers the Plowman*;

There the cat is a kitten, the court is full ailing.

A kitten-reign is bound to have stresses and strains. When the Lords Appellant humbled Richard he bided his time with feline malice and took his revenge. If he is seen at his best as the builder of the great hammer-beam roof of Westminster Hall, he shows his worst side in his dealing with John of Gaunt's son, Henry Bolingbroke, Earl of Derby, Duke of Hereford and heir to the vast Lancaster estates. The two men were not made to understand one another, but when Richard finally exiled Henry and confiscated the whole of the Lancaster lands, there could only be one outcome. Henry would return to reclaim his inheritance and he would have most of the baronage behind him. Henry did indeed return to England in 1399 at an awkward time for Richard. The King was in Ireland and had to hurry back to his kingdom only to find that his support had fallen away from him. From the tower of Flint Castle, which still stands overlooking the wide levels of the estuary of the Dee, he had the mortification of seeing the host of Bolingbroke advancing in overwhelming strength. He was taken to Henry at Chester to meet his conqueror. It was the end. Richard was deposed and disappeared, but not before Adam of Usk had met him in the Tower and had recorded his moving cry of despair.

> My God, a wonderful land is this and a fickle, which has exiled, slain and destroyed so many kings, nobles and great men which is ever touched and tainteth with shame and variance and envy.

The land had indeed been 'tainted' with an unprecedented deed of political violence. Edward II had been deposed and murdered but had been succeeded by his son. The direct line of Plantagenet descent had not been broken. Now the rightful king had been flung ruthlessly from his throne and had been replaced by the scion of a younger member of the vast brood begotten by Edward III. Edward had had five surviving sons as well as many daughters. Why should the descendant of the third son, John of Gaunt, claim any precedence over those of the second son? The way was open to other claimants, and the potent and prolific Edward III had supplied them in plenty. The dark deed of 1399 would only be expiated eighty-six years later at the battle of Bosworth Field. These long years of strife, envy and violence we call the Wars of the Roses would be broken by only one period of national glory – the reign of Henry V.

The future hero-king was a boy of twelve when his father, Bolingbroke, usurped the throne. He was a Prince of Wales who never expected to become one. He was also the only one who had to fight for his inheritance. He was born in the castle of Monmouth in the south-east Marches of Wales. He received the education proper for a nobleman's son for no one imagined in the Lord Henry's youth that he would one day become king of the whole realm. The accounts of Henry's youth are sparse but we know that he had a serious illness when he was eight years old. He did not see much of his father, for Henry Bolingbroke was a famous jouster and a crusader with the Teutonic Knights in East Prussia. He travelled in Bohemia, Hungary and Cyprus and actually went on a pilgrimage to Jerusalem. Meantime, the young Lord Henry was at home, attached, as was the custom for the further education of youths of distinction, to the royal court. He grew up in an environment in which the arts and social graces were valued. All his life he was devoted to music, and without being a

Above *Caernarfon Castle.*
Left *The legendary presentation of the infant
Prince to the people of Wales by Edward I.*

Below *The Black Prince's homage to his father,
Edward III.*

Effigy of Edward III on his tomb in Westminster Abbey.

Richard II and his patron saints. From the Wilton diptych.

Prince Hal being knighted by Richard II.

Valle Crucis Abbey in Owen Glendower country.

Henry V after victory at Agincourt. Laurence Olivier as the King in the Rank film of Shakespeare's play.

Above *Henry VI.*

Above centre *The battlefield before Tewkesbury Abbey, where Henry VI's son, Edward, Prince of Wales, was killed in 1471.*

Left *Richard III.*
Right *The Princes in the Tower await their murderers.*

Edward IV, the first Yorkist king, and father of Edward V.

Henry VII, victor at Bosworth Field and founder of the Tudor dynasty.

Arthur, Prince of Wales, who died before his father, Henry VII.

scholar he was well educated, in the terms of medieval aristocratic society.

We can get an idea of the kind of curriculum the Lord Henry might have had to follow from the rhyming chronicle of John Hardynge, who later followed King Henry to Agincourt. At four, the young lad should begin to learn his letters. At six he should study languages and 'learn to sit at meat seemly'. By the time he was twelve he would have learnt to 'revelle, daunce, and synge and speke of gentlenesse'. In short he would have become the perfect fifteenth century young gentleman.

Richard II was fond of the young boy and continued to show him favour even after he had fallen out with his father. Henry, in turn, never ceased to remember the kindness shown to him by the unlucky king. When he himself became king, he took care to bring back Richard's body from obscure burial at King's Langley to a splendid tomb in Westminster Abbey. Henry accompanied Richard on his expedition to Ireland in 1398 and was knighted by him. He got his first introduction to the realities of war in pursuit of rebels around the bogs of Ireland. When Bolingbroke landed in England, Richard reluctantly imprisoned the lad in the castle of Trim from which he was rescued by a trusted sea-captain sent by his father, who brought him safely to the usurper's side.

In a few dizzy months, the young Lord Henry's world changed with dramatic speed. In the spring of 1399 he had been at Richard's side, high in his favour. By October of the same year his father had become Henry IV. On 12 October he knighted his son again, together with his younger brother. The next day, the Lord Henry carried the sword Curtana, the symbol of mercy, at his father's coronation. On 23 October he became Duke of Aquitaine. On 8 November he was made Prince of Wales, Earl of Chester and Duke of Cornwall in a ceremony of particular splendour carried out before the Commons of Parliament. Two days later he received the Duchy of Lancaster with all its vast estates. No Prince of Wales has ever received such rapid and powerful promotion. His breathless rush through the list of honours was surely due to the usurper's wish to legitimize his own position as soon as possible. All traces of Richard II's regime had to be swept away. Unfortunately the obliteration of the late king's memory was not so easily accomplished. Certainly not in the new Prince of Wales's own Principality.

The French minstrel-knight Creton had been with Richard II and the Lord Henry in Ireland. Now he wrote about the new Prince of Wales,

Then arose Duke Henry. His eldest son, who humbly knelt before him, he made Prince of Wales and gave him the land, but I think he must conquer it before he will have it. For, in my opinion, the Welsh will on no account, allow him to be their lord, for the sorrow, evil and disgrace which the English, together with his father, had brought on King Richard.

Creton was right. Within a year after the Lord Henry had knelt before his father in that impressive Investiture ceremony, another claimant to the title of Prince of Wales was in the field. That violent, social explosion we call the revolt of Owen Glendower – more correctly, in Welsh, Owain Glyn Dŵr – had begun its fiery and furious course.

It caught Henry IV utterly unprepared. Glendower must have seemed the last person to lead a rebellion. He was a well-to-do, cultivated, landed gentleman of forty-five, who had been educated at the Inns of Court and had served with distinction in Richard II's expedition to Scotland. He was even prepared to accede to Henry IV's accession. Unfortunately Glendower was already involved in a long-standing quarrel with his neighbour, Lord Grey of Ruthin, over the ownership of land in the Dee valley. Glendower was summoned by Henry IV to take part in his expedition to Scotland. This summons had to pass through the hands of Lord Grey who saw to it that Owen never got it. Owen was declared in default of his duty to his feudal overlord. The Welshman had no other course open to him but rebellion. Henry did not realize how serious the outbreak would be. He led a perfunctory expedition through North Wales accompanied by young Henry. Glendower simply retreated into the hills and prepared for a more widespread revolt.

By 1402, Glendower had begun to rally the whole of Wales to his cause. What had begun with a dispute over land was rapidly turning into a national crusade. There were even deeper forces working than irritation over English rule. The destruction wrought by the Black Death in 1348–50 had shaken the Welsh social structure as strongly as it had the English, and Glendower's rising took on some of the aspects of the earlier English Peasants' Revolt. Henry IV found that he had a large-scale war on his hands. Owen went from strength to strength. Even the rebellion of Harry Percy, 'Hotspur', and his subsequent defeat at Shrewsbury, did not stop the progress of the rebellion in Wales. The years between 1404 and 1406 were the high-water mark of the Glendower rising. The royal castles of Harlech and Aberystwyth fell into Owen's hands and gave him a firm base of operations.

Distinguished Welshmen, leading clerics and experienced administrators, came over to his side. His plans took on an impressive amplitude. He held a Parliament at Machynlleth and planned two universities in North and South Wales. He formed an alliance with France and boldly took the title of Prince of Wales, bearing the old arms of Llywelyn the Last. In 1405, with the help of his French allies, Glendower penetrated into England as far as Worcester.

Owen's independent Wales made a marvellous show for a few years and has haunted the Welsh imagination ever since as a symbol of Welsh nationality. Modern Wales, some historians have maintained, begins with Glendower. It could not last. As soon as Henry IV had crushed the rebellion in England he had the resources to break the rising in Wales. The crushing of the rebellion was entrusted to Henry of Monmouth who gained his mastery of the art of war in his long and difficult campaigns against the Welsh. In his very first campaign he burnt Owen's pleasant country seat and birthplace at Syncharth near the Welsh border. He matured as a general by learning to do much with little. He learnt the art of siegecraft in the capture of Owen's two strongholds at Harlech and Aberystwyth. He also learnt to be ruthless. There were atrocities on both sides, with the destruction of monasteries and the burning of country houses and the wrecking of towns in a scorched-earth policy that left its mark on Welsh life for the rest of the century. But in the end the sheer strength of England was bound to prevail. Owen's cause began to fade. The rebellion flickered on for years but the heart had been torn out of it. In the end the old hero disappeared into the mists. When he came to the throne Henry V offered his old rival a pardon but no reply came from the Welsh hills. No one knows where Glendower died but his memory has never faded from the Welsh mind. He left a legend that still has power over Welshmen of today.

After 1408 the Prince felt that he had completed his real task in Wales, and that others could attend to the beating out of the embers of the rebellion. He came back to London and the centre of power to find his father a sick and saddened man, worn by the cares of state, and with the effort of establishing his power on a restive country. The Prince might well have become impatient with his father's faltering conduct of affairs, and there is evidence of periods of strong disagreement between them. The pattern of friction between monarch and heir was re-establishing itself. These stories may have been the basis for the legend of the roistering Prince Hal so brilliantly exploited by Shakespeare.

The genius of Shakespeare has given us a picture of the Prince which is hard to banish from our minds. We will not lessen or tarnish that picture by looking more closely at the hard facts. When we do so we find to our sorrow that Sir John Falstaff must disappear. There was indeed a Sir John Fastolf who lived during this period, but he was a highly respected East Anglian soldier and Privy Councillor who would have turned in his grave if he thought that he had been the model for the fat and bibulous knight. There actually was a Bardolph and a soldier was certainly hanged on the march to Agincourt for stealing a sheep. But the soldier was unnamed in the chronicles and the Bardolph of history was Sir William Bardolph, again a loyal knight of the utmost respectability. Must Sir John, Bardolph, Nym and Doll Tearsheet and the rest of the rip-roaring, roistering and immortal crew of the Boar's Head Tavern disappear into the mists of pseudo-history? Alas, they must. But a slight trace of fact may remain. It seems that the Prince may still have sown his oats a little wildly when back on winter's leave from his Welsh campaigns. An Italian reporting about 1437 records the tradition that the Prince of Wales 'exercised nightly the feats of Venus as well as those of Mars and other pastimes of youth, as long as his father lived.'

When his father died the nation saw a different prince. The King appeared as a serious minded soldier, who, in his determination to stand well with the Church, could tolerate the burning of Lollard heretics, who was single-minded in leading the nation into what he was convinced was a just war with France. A leader and inspirer of men who would give the country a new respect for itself. Shakespeare may have dramatized that change in the public character of the Prince as King when he wrote that deeply moving scene of the rejection of Falstaff, at the end of the play of Henry IV.

I know thee not, old man: fall to thy prayers;
How ill white hairs become a fool and a jester!

Prince Hal had disappeared. The hero-king had taken his place, who moves on to Agincourt and military glory. Somehow we prefer Prince Hal, the young lad who grew up in the court of Richard II and still loved and honoured the fallen king, the brave young soldier learning his trade by sharing the discomforts of his men in the rain of the Welsh mountains, and then having a temporary 'night out on the town' when on leave in London, to the pious and enormously successful king.

The King had learnt the art of war as Prince of Wales in the Welsh

44

mountains, and Welshmen were again enlisting in his armies. Like the Highlanders who enlisted in the Highland regiments after the '45 Rebellion, fighting Welshmen had nowhere else to go.

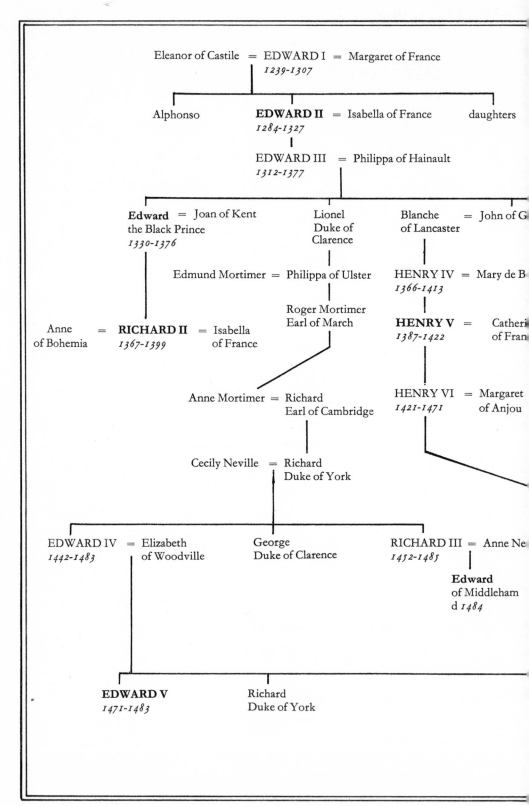

Eleanor of Castile = EDWARD I = Margaret of France
1239-1307

Alphonso   EDWARD II = Isabella of France   daughters
1284-1327

EDWARD III = Philippa of Hainault
1312-1377

Edward = Joan of Kent   Lionel   Blanche = John of G
the Black Prince   Duke of   of Lancaster
1330-1376   Clarence

Edmund Mortimer = Philippa of Ulster   HENRY IV = Mary de B
                                        1366-1413

Roger Mortimer
Earl of March

Anne = RICHARD II = Isabella   HENRY V = Catheri
of Bohemia   1367-1399   of France   1387-1422   of Fran

Anne Mortimer = Richard   HENRY VI = Margaret
                Earl of Cambridge   1421-1471   of Anjou

Cecily Neville = Richard
                 Duke of York

EDWARD IV = Elizabeth   George   RICHARD III = Anne Ne
1442-1483   of Woodville   Duke of Clarence   1452-1485

                                               Edward
                                               of Middleham
                                               d 1484

EDWARD V   Richard
1471-1483   Duke of York

Houses of Plantagenet, Lancaster and York

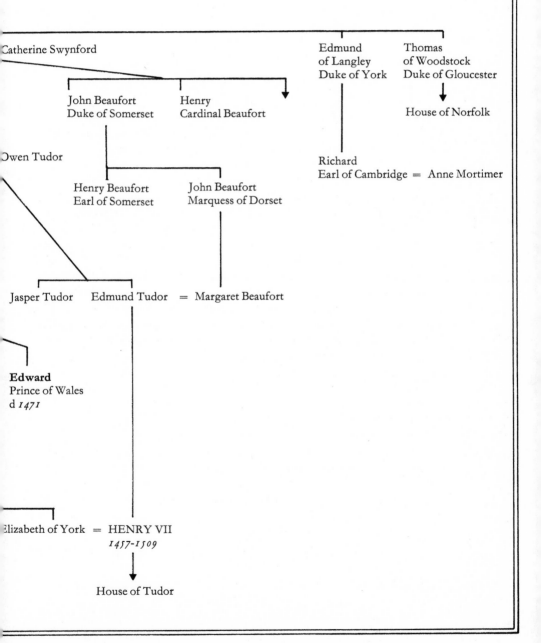

Catherine Swynford

John Beaufort
Duke of Somerset

Henry
Cardinal Beaufort

Edmund
of Langley
Duke of York

Thomas
of Woodstock
Duke of Gloucester

House of Norfolk

Owen Tudor

Henry Beaufort
Earl of Somerset

John Beaufort
Marquess of Dorset

Richard
Earl of Cambridge = Anne Mortimer

Jasper Tudor   Edmund Tudor   = Margaret Beaufort

Edward
Prince of Wales
d *1471*

Elizabeth of York = HENRY VII
1457-1509

House of Tudor

3

Blood on the Tapestry

'. . . the intestine shock
And furious close of civil butchery.'
WILLIAM SHAKESPEARE

Agincourt was a legendary personal triumph. It put Henry V on a
pinnacle of national prestige from which he has never been deposed.
Again the Welsh archers played their vital part in crushing the lum-
bering advance of the heavily armoured French knights, and their
prowess is still celebrated in the little hilltop town of Llantrisant, in
the Vale of Glamorgan, where the Black Hundred Society meets to
toast their ancestors who sent a hundred archers to join Henry in that
famous victory. Like so many battles that seemed overwhelming at the
time, it took many years of further fighting before the full fruits of
victory could be gathered. At last Henry signed the Treaty of Troyes
with the French and it must have seemed to him that he had hit the
jackpot! France was to be his for the taking. The unhappy, half-mad
French king agreed to give Henry his daughter in marriage, to make
the English king Regent of France with the reversion of the kingdom
on his death. The Dauphin, Charles, would naturally have nothing to
do with such a wholesale giving away of his inheritance, and he still
had two-thirds of France behind him. He would do his best to upset
that triumphant Treaty of Troyes.

For the moment the skies must have seemed sunny and clear to the
English conqueror. He married young Catherine of France and brought
her back in triumph to be crowned as his queen in Westminster Abbey.
In 1421 his triumph must have seemed complete when Catherine gave
birth to a son at Windsor, the future Henry VI. The King had done
his best to secure a safe delivery for his wife by sending her a precious
relic captured in France. This was none other than the foreskin of the
infant Christ, removed at his circumcision and guaranteed to be of
special help to women in labour.

Henry never saw his son. He had to resume his campaigns in France.
At the long and bitter siege of Meaux he fell ill of a fever, probably

dysentery. He died at Vincennes in August 1422. He was approaching his thirty-fifth birthday and his infant son was just nine months old. Henry VI was thus never made Prince of Wales. There was to be a gap of thirty-one years before the next prince succeeded to the title.

Long minorities were usually a signal for disaster in a medieval state and the minority of Henry VI was no exception. In his early days he was naturally in the hands of his counsellors who were faced with a rising tide of difficulties. The war in France was a dangerous heritage. Henry V might have eventually carried it to complete success, but Henry VI's advisers were faced with Joan of Arc. They took the little boy across the channel and crowned him King of France in Paris, the only English king who could thus claim to have actually sat on the French throne. It did him no good. He grew up against a background of ever increasing disaster to the English arms in France. He also grew up excessively pious, well-versed in Latin and French, devoted to the arts, kind-hearted and utterly unfitted to be a medieval king. Again we meet with a monarch who lacked the will to govern, a fatal defect in the English monarchy of the Middle Ages where the whole machinery of government depended upon the driving power of the king. Posterity may remember Henry with gratitude as the founder of Eton and the builder of that masterpiece of late Gothic architecture, King's College Chapel, Cambridge. His contemporaries were less appreciative. They looked at him with dismay as the government of the country fell apart in his witless hands. Worse still, there were times when his wits actually left him and he sat dumb and unspeaking, oblivious of all around him. His ministers and his courtiers were reduced to despair. What could they do with such a king?

Later, Tudor propaganda sought to depict Henry as a man of 'holy simplicity', almost made a saint by his sufferings. The Tudors needed to whitewash Henry as vigorously as they needed to blacken Richard III, for they were the inheritors of the Lancastrian claim to the throne. But much of the anecdotage about Henry comes from the so-called *Life of the King*, allegedly written by his confessor, John Blackman. Serious doubts have recently been thrown on this work. At any rate, if Henry was a saint he was the most incompetent one in the calendar.

It was his sheer incompetence that mattered when the times cried out for a strong king. The collapse of English rule in France had left the baronial class without those useful supplies of French loot and there were plenty of old soldiers about who could be recruited into private armies. There were also deeper causes for that unrest that grew in Britain as the fifteenth century progressed. The old feudal system was breaking up. New developments were changing the pattern of trade. The old medieval certainties were being challenged. And in the centre of this changing world was an incompetent king. But if Henry did not feel fit to govern there were others who did. Ambitious men looked at the monarchy and felt that it was ripe for capture. Such a man was Richard, Duke of York. He felt that he had as good a right to the throne as any descendant of the House of Lancaster. After all, the Lancastrian Bolingbroke had usurped the throne from its rightful owner, Richard II. From that usurpation all the subsequent troubles followed. It gave the Wars of the Roses their peculiar bitterness and savagery. The name Wars of the Roses was only applied in Tudor times to the struggle for supreme power between the houses of York and Lancaster, but as in the case of the Black Prince, it would now be pedantic to change it. The Tudors certainly left their mark in the history books in more ways than one!

Savage these wars undoubtedly were, at least in the higher echelons of English society, and fortunes changed with bewildering regularity. In the heart of the Lancastrians stood Henry VI's queen, Margaret of Anjou. He had been married to her for political reasons, in pursuit of a political settlement in France, but she soon established a powerful influence over her weak-willed husband. She was only fifteen when she first came to England after a stormy voyage that seemed prophetic of the political storms that awaited her. A chronicler of the time reported that she lay sick at Southampton, 'by the labour and indisposition of the sea by which a pox had broken out on her'. She soon recovered in time for her marriage and coronation, but eight years were to pass before she presented her husband with a son and heir, a future Prince of Wales.

Much happened in those eight years, including the final collapse of English rule in France, the rebellion of Jack Cade and, arising directly from these events, the Yorkist determination to claim the throne. Lancastrian fortunes were at a low ebb when, in the spring of 1453, Margaret discovered that at last she was pregnant. She had not been popular in England but all that would change if she presented the King with an heir to the throne. York's pretensions to the crown would now have to be put aside. But as the year progressed, Margaret faced disaster. The King was stricken with a mysterious mental illness amounting to complete prostration. He sat limp and speechless. He could not move his limbs. He became wholly dependent upon his attendants who washed, clothed and fed him while he remained in a perpetual silence. Margaret's baby was born on 13 October, St Edward the Confessor's

Day. Six days later she brought him to the King at Windsor. We have a contemporary account of the pitiful scene that followed. First the Duke of Buckingham presented the child, 'and the king made no answer'. Then the Queen, herself, tried to arouse Henry's interest in his own son.

> The Queen came and took the Prince in her arms and presented him in like form as the Duke had done, desiring that he should bless it. But all their labour was in vain, for they departed thence without any answer of countenance, saving that once he looked on the Prince and cast down his eyes again, without any more.

A strange beginning to a young life that was to end in tragedy. The Prince at once became the centre of Queen Margaret's life, her inspiration in all the trials that followed. She fought like a tigress for her son's right to succeed to the throne. The King eventually came to his senses again in 1455 and was excited to discover that he was the father of a son. He gave thanks for a miracle – as well he might!

The King's recovery meant that York had to retire for the moment. There could be no question of his retaining the Regency he had exercised during Henry's illness. He had behaved with some restraint as Regent. He had even allowed little Edward to be invested as Prince of Wales and the title was sanctioned by Parliament, the only occasion when this occurred. To make doubly sure that no doubt should be cast on her son's right to be Prince of Wales, the Queen made Henry summon Parliament to Westminster in 1455, when he confirmed his son in his new honour. Alas, the title so carefully ratified proved to be a dangerous heritage for young Edward and, eventually, a passport to death.

No Prince of Wales ever spent a more disturbed youth. As the Wars of the Roses now began in earnest and fortune changed sides with bewildering rapidity, the Queen had perforce to take the boy with her on her campaigns. He early became acquainted with the rough side of life. No wonder then that in one of the few glimpses we have of him at this time, it was reported that the Prince would talk of nothing else but the cutting off of heads and the making of war. By 1460, the pathetic king was a puppet in Yorkist power. He was actually weak enough to recognize Richard of York as his heir, thus disinheriting his own son. York was to have the rents of the Principality and of the Duchy of Cornwall, and young Edward of Westminster would only retain the title of Prince of Wales as long as his father was alive.

Margaret managed to hustle her son out of the Yorkist clutches,

They spent some months in the safety of Harlech Castle and then crossed the border into Scotland. From this position of comparative safety she rallied the great families of Northern England to her cause. She had an army again. She marched south with her forces, bringing her son with her and the soldiers sporting his crest of the three ostrich feathers. In the second battle of St Albans they defeated the Yorkists who were led by the redoubtable Earl of Warwick. After the fight the victors found King Henry VI with his guards seated under a tree. They almost regarded him as one of the spoils of war. He did, however, knight his young son on the evening after the battle. Young Edward, in his turn, knighted thirty of his followers, including one gallant old soldier, Andrew Trollope, who had been injured in his foot. Said Trollope, 'My Lord, I have not deserved it for I slew but fifteen men, for I stood still in one place and they came unto me. But they still abode with me!' Yorkist partisans paint an unpleasant picture of the Prince being made by his mother to preside over the tribunal that condemned so many of the defeated to immediate beheading after the battle. I prefer to think of the young boy saluting bravery in the person of Andrew Trollope.

Unfortunately for them the Lancastrians delayed after St Albans and Warwick slipped back to London, where he was joined by the young Earl of March. He was the son of Richard, Duke of York, and as York had been killed earlier on at Wakefield, he was the heir to the Yorkist claim to the throne. Edward, Earl of March, proved to be the trump card in the Yorkist pack. He turned out to be a brilliant soldier. While Warwick was fighting at St Albans, he had inflicted a crushing defeat on the Lancastrians on the Welsh border at Mortimer's Cross. The victor raced at high speed to join Warwick. There was no time to lose. The Yorkists now boldly proclaimed Edward of March as Edward IV of England and declared Henry VI, Queen Margaret and the Prince of Wales all deposed. The new king immediately put his title to the test by ordeal in battle. He caught up with the Lancastrians at Towton near York. The battle was fought with great brutality in a blinding snowstorm. Towton was a shattering defeat for the Lancastrians. Margaret fled with her son and husband, and Edward IV was firmly in power. As Henry Bolingbroke had deposed Richard II, so Edward, Earl of March, had deposed Henry VI.

Margaret had no alternative but to take her son into exile on the Continent. Her husband fell into Edward's hands and was packed off to the Tower. The Queen began her exile in the pleasant valley of the Meuse, and this absence from England had one advantage: she could now seriously begin the long-neglected education of her son. Accompanying her into exile was the very man to undertake the task of training the heir to a throne. Sir John Fortescue was a distinguished lawyer who had remained faithful to the Lancastrian cause. He was the author of a celebrated treatise analysing the theory of monarchy in England and the nature of its laws. Its title, *On the Governance of England*, came in useful later when a recent Prime Minister also gave us his thoughts on the constitution. Edward of Westminster would certainly be well prepared for his position when he came to the throne, but would the throne ever come to him? Edward IV seemed firmly established on the throne and there was no hope of any Lancastrian rising in England. Towton had broken the heart of the Lancastrian cause. But then came a strange reversal of fortune. Edward IV was proving himself a vigorous ruler. He held the country firmly in his grip and few people cast longing eyes in the direction of that shadowy figure in the Tower or on the Prince over the Water. Edward IV, however, proceeded to make a false step in his highly successful career. He married a young widow, Elizabeth Woodville.

There was nothing surprising in the King's marrying. In fact, it was high time he did. The young monarch was acquiring a reputation as an accomplished amorist among the pretty wives of the city aldermen of London. But the Lady Elizabeth Woodville was a surprising choice. She was the widow of a Lancastrian knight who had been killed at St Albans. Her family could not compare in standing with the long-established Nevilles, Greys, Bohuns and the rest of them. Edward further irritated his aristocratic supporters by promoting members of the Woodville clan to important positions in the state. The Woodvilles were clever and able, but a little too eager to get on. Friction was bound to occur, especially with Edward's greatest supporter, Richard Neville, Earl of Warwick. The tension built up over the years and ended in Warwick breaking completely with Edward and going into disgruntled exile in France. A last surprising chance was offered to Queen Margaret.

Warwick was at the court of the French king, that remarkable but slippery monarch, Louis XI. Louis felt that he could use Warwick in his devious and complex struggles with Burgundy. He persuaded Margaret to meet her old enemy. With great reluctance, Margaret agreed. Sir John Fortescue was firm in his opinion that an alliance with Warwick, however distasteful, was the only hope of a Lancastrian restoration. Margaret had to face one more condition hurtful to her pride. The alliance had to be sealed by the betrothal of Anne, Warwick's daughter, to the Prince of Wales. There was nothing for it but to agree. The strange and unnatural alliance between Yorkist magnate and Lancastrian queen had now to be put to the test.

Warwick landed in Devon and raised the southern counties. Edward was caught on the hop. He had to slip overseas and get help from the old enemy of France, Burgundy. Meanwhile, Warwick had released Henry VI from the Tower. Once again the shadow monarch was proclaimed King of England and once again the Lancastrian's luck deserted them. Margaret delayed her return to England. Instead, Edward returned with his usual speed and lost no time in marching south from the Humber. He met Warwick in battle at Barnet and in the fight Warwick was killed. When Margaret and her Prince of Wales eventually landed at Weymouth it was to receive the disastrous news that their chief supporter was dead. Should they return immediately to France? This would have been the wisest course, but the Lancastrian cause was strong in the West and still stronger on the Welsh border. The fatal decision was taken to march to Wales.

Gloucester closed its gates to the Lancastrians and they had to march upstream to the next crossing at Tewkesbury. They took up position before the ancient Abbey. Edward IV was now an experienced and successful commander, and he had his brother, Richard of Gloucester, in command of his west wing. His attack was overwhelming. The Lancastrian front was broken and the survivors fled towards the safety of the Abbey. In the flight, his enemies caught up with the Prince of Wales. Accounts differ as to how he was killed, but it was certainly not Richard of Gloucester who did the deed, as Richard's enemies maintained. But whoever did it, the unfortunate Edward of Westminster was killed, the only Prince of Wales to be killed in battle. Poor Queen Margaret had watched the whole dreadful tragedy. She and Anne Neville were hurried away to Malvern where they fell into the Yorkist hands. She was eventually ransomed and allowed to return to France, a heart-broken woman who had nothing further to live for. Her husband disappeared in the Tower; Edward could not afford to leave him alive.

The body of the slain prince was placed in his tomb in Tewkesbury Abbey. It bears an inscription in Latin which must be the most touching of all epitaphs on a Prince of Wales. 'Here lies Edward, Prince of Wales, cruelly slain while still a youth, May 4, 1471. Alas, for the fury of men.'

In these violent and murderous proceedings, one Prince of Wales had been slaughtered on the battlefield at almost the same time as his successor was being born. When Warwick had suddenly landed in

England and caught Edward IV on the hop, Queen Elizabeth Wood-ville had fled for sanctuary to Westminster Abbey. There she gave birth to her first son, who was therefore known as Edward of the Sanctuary. He came into a world which was now being firmly remodelled by his father. This may have well been the reason why Edward was made Prince of Wales as soon as possible, namely at the age of seven and a half months.

Edward IV turned out to be a forceful, capable king. He may have been a dedicated amorist who could not control his passions, but there can be no question that he knew how to control England. He had a Machiavellian ruthlessness and efficiency and gave the country a fore-taste of that absolutism, tempered by parliamentary consent and popular acclaim, that was the keynote of the Tudor system of government. There were signs too of the approaching change in the intellectual climate of the medieval world that we call the Renaissance. It was during Edward IV's reign that Caxton established his press at West-minster.

We can detect this coming change in the education of the Prince of Wales. In addition to the traditional warlike exercises and training in courtly manners, the Prince was encouraged to take an interest in the classics and the arts. His father, like so many other royal fathers, drew up a strict curriculum for his son's studies. The prince was to get up 'at a convenient hour according to his age' and was to spend his morning 'in such righteous learning as his age shall suffer him to receive'. While he ate his midday meal, he was to listen to a reading from a virtuous book. In the afternoon he was to indulge in courtly exercises and there was to be a period of play after supper. The little prince was to be put to bed by eight o'clock, when the curtains were to be drawn. He was naturally expected to attend the masses and the other numerous celebrations of the medieval church, but the emphasis on real learning strikes a new note in the education of a Prince of Wales. Edward IV also insisted that no one of bad character should be permitted to come near the Prince and no foul language should be used in his presence. Was the amorous king easing his own conscience in his instructions for his son's education? He did however, encourage the Prince's attendants to force themselves to make him 'merry and joyous towards his bed'.

The young Prince did not spend much time at court. We hear of him being taken on an official pilgrimage to Canterbury by his father, but he mainly resided at Ludlow Castle on the Welsh border. This was the headquarters of the Council for the Welsh Marches, which

Edward had created to bring order in the turbulent affairs of Wales. The Prince was officially head of the Council but the actual administrative work was done by Bishop John Alcock of Worcester. The Prince's governor was Anthony, Earl Rivers, a member of the Woodville clan that had come to power after the King's surprising marriage. Earl Rivers was a man of culture and there is no question that the Prince benefited by his guardianship. The few glimpses we have of Edward growing up show us a bright, precocious boy, gifted with more learning than was usual for princes of his time, and with considerable personal charm. He had the Yorkist handsome face and strong physique. Altogether an attractive picture which makes all the more tragic the fate that awaited Edward of the Sanctuary.

At this point a sinister figure comes onto the stage, a dark character who was always waiting in the wings in the age-old drama of the Princes of Wales – the Wicked Uncle. When a monarch died leaving his heir a minor, his younger brother could naturally expect to be given the regency until his nephew came of age. The position of regent could offer temptation to an unscrupulous and ambitious man. People remembered that King John had done away with his nephew, Arthur of Britanny. Suspicions of wicked uncles even emerged as late as the nineteenth century in the early years of Queen Victoria. Richard of Gloucester is, however, the pre-eminent Wicked Uncle in our history. A dark cloud hangs over his memory. From our earliest days we have been taught the story of the Princes in the Tower. We see the two innocent boys clasped in fear in each other's arms as they hear the stealthy step of their murderer creeping up the stairs of the Bloody Tower. As their death approaches, their Wicked Uncle prepares to take the crown. He is a sinister hunchback, racked by ambition.

Deformed, unfinished, sent before my time
Into this breathing world, scarce half made up.

So Shakespeare paints Richard for us, a stereotyped Machiavellian villain

subtle, false and treacherous.

Of recent years a strong movement has developed to rehabilitate Richard III. The whitewashing of the Wicked Uncle has gone to great lengths in some quarters. It has even been suggested that the children were still alive in the Tower when Henry VII defeated Richard at Bosworth Field in 1485, and that it was therefore the successful Welshman who got rid of them. I confess that when I hear this I echo the celebrated remark of the Duke of Wellington when a certain gentleman addressed him as 'Mr Jones, I believe'. 'If you believe that', growled the Duke, 'you'll believe anything!'

What then should we believe about Richard and, above all, about the murder of the Princes in the Tower? A. L. Rouse, in his forthright way, has dismissed the more fervent 'Richard-olators' as 'amateurs who proliferate in this field as about Shakespeare: people who are not qualified to hold an opinion, much less express one'. After that, one almost hesitates to say a good word for Richard. But before the usurpation, he had been a loyal supporter of his brother Edward IV, and had won a reputation as a soldier. He had firmly defended the northern frontier against Scotland, and had won the loyalty of his tenants in Yorkshire and along the Border. After she had lost her Prince of Wales in the slaughter at Tewkesbury, Richard had married Anne Neville and the marriage had turned out to be a reasonably happy one, although we can hardly follow the whitewashers when they emphasize their hero's deep devotion to domestic life. He had several bastards, one of whom, Richard Plantagenet, very sensibly went into hiding after Bosworth. His repulsive appearance however appears to have been an exaggeration of his enemies. We need not believe the story that he was born with teeth and a loathsome caul of dark hair. Richard may have been dark, but he was no misshapen 'crookback'.

He was nevertheless a man of his age. The Wars of the Roses had created a certain ruthless atmosphere. Ambitious men were almost expected to remove their rivals by force. Richard may have been tempted from his loyalty by his brother's sudden death. Edward IV had always seemed to be in robust health. Neither he nor his counsellors envisaged his early departure from the scene. There was no thought of a minor coming to the throne, and no elaborate arrangements had been made to cope with the situation that arose when Edward died after a short illness of a few days. He was not yet forty-one.

Edward, Prince of Wales, was at Ludlow when the news reached him that he had unexpectedly become king. Richard was in the North of England. Lord Rivers set out for London with his charge. Richard came racing down from the North. The two parties met near Stony Stratford. Richard acted with speed. He succeeded in removing Earl Rivers and lost no time in chopping his head off. He now had the King in his possession. He brought him to London under heavy guard, 'since', as a contemporary, Dominic Mancini, an Italian in London observed, 'the Welsh could not bear to think that owing to their stupidity, their prince had been carried off.' Queen Elizabeth was alarmed and feared what was to come. Again she took sanctuary in Westminster Abbey with her second son, Richard, Duke of York. Richard now set the machinery of usurpation in motion. He persuaded the Queen to send the Duke of York, now ten years old, out of Sanctuary on the pretext that he was needed at his brother's coronation. Needless to say that coronation never took place. Richard was firmly in the seat of power. The inconvenient sons of Edward IV gradually disappeared from the scene into the obscurity of the Tower of London. By a series of cunning manoeuvres, Parliament and the nobility were persuaded to agree that Richard was the right man to come to the throne. There were the usual accusations of the bastardy of Edward V and his brother, and the carefully stage-managed invitation by the Duke of Buckingham to the Protector to accept the throne. On 6 July 1483, the usurper was crowned king with considerable pomp in Westminster Abbey. We can well imagine the feelings of the widowed queen, hiding in the safety of the Church nearby.

The young princes had now been lost from sight in the Tower for some time, and soon the rumours started to circulate in London, sinister rumours that the sons of Edward IV had actually been done to death by orders of his own brother. The testimony of that observant Italian, Mancini, gives a fascinating account of the events of Richard's reign. The manuscript was unearthed from a forgotten corner in the municipal library at Lille in 1934. Mancini has been described as the 'unexpected witness', and his short history goes far to confirm the popular story. He tells us that the young King already had an intuition of the fate that awaited him. His physician, Dr Argentine, reported that young Edward, 'like a victim prepared for sacrifice, sought remission of his sins by daily confession and penance, because he believed that death was facing him.' Or, as another chronicler put it, 'And so the new king was removed from his legal servants and received with kisses and embraces like an innocent lamb falling into the hands of wolves.' Mancini noted that many prominent men 'burst into tears when his name was mentioned and already there was a suspicion that he had been done away with.'

How the King and his brother were actually done away with remains uncertain. Apparently Richard entrusted the dirty work to Sir James Tyrrell, who received the keys of the Tower for one night by Richard's special order. Tyrrell's two thugs were Miles Forrest, 'a fellow flushed in murder before time', and John Dighton, 'a big, broad, square, strong knave'. They are said to have smothered the boys in their feather-bed and, after calling Tyrrell to look at the bodies, buried the corpses at the foot of the stairs. The story received a grim confirmation two hundred years later.

In 1674, while repairs were being carried out to the White Tower, the bones of two boys were discovered in exactly the place described by Sir Thomas More in his *History of Richard III*. By order of King Charles II, they were placed in an urn which is now on top of a monument in Westminster Abbey. Young Edward V was the fourth medieval king of England to be put cruelly out of the way by his successor. The others were Edward II, Richard II and Henry VI. The English had an unenviable reputation in Europe as monarch murderers.

Try as he would, Richard could never eliminate the disgust his deed had produced. He did his best to win popularity by lavish display, and like all usurpers hurried to ensure the continuity of his dynasty by making his son, Edward of Middleham, Prince of Wales. This Edward is a wraith-like figure in our procession of Princes. He was born at Middleham Castle in Yorkshire in 1473 and remained the only child of the marriage of Richard with Anne Neville. He seems to have spent most of his short life at Middleham and was clearly not a healthy or robust child. The traditional physical well-being of the Yorkist dynasty seems to have passed him by. His father, however, staged a splendid Investiture ceremony for him in York. He had created him Prince of Wales by royal patent and was obviously in a hurry to observe all the ceremonies that would establish him firmly on the throne. He and Queen Anne made a slow and splendid state progress to the North after his coronation. Here he was among his friends and supporters, away from the doubts and suspicions of London. York gave him a splendid reception, and young Edward was suitably escorted in state from Middleham in Wensleydale to join his parents. He may have been a sickly child but his father was proud of him. In the letters patent he had referred to his son and 'the singular wit and endowments of nature wherewith, his young age considered, he is remarkably furnished'. We are reminded of another Prince of Wales, only a year before, who was equally well-endowed.

Edward of Middleham was invested in due form in York Minster, wearing his golden coronet and carrying his rod and sword. The fanfares of trumpets went echoing through the splendid arches as the three royal personages, all crowned, walked down the long nave to show themselves to the populace outside who 'extolled King Richard to the skies'. This ceremony at York was probably the only public appearance of the new Prince of Wales, and the country had no time to assess his quality for, in April 1484, he suddenly died. Richard's grief was intense.

He must have pinned great hopes on this boy. Only a month before he had summoned all the lords temporal and spiritual to the palace and made them swear an oath of loyalty to the Prince, in case anything should happen to the King. This has a slightly suspicious ring about it. Richard knew only too well what could happen to Princes of Wales who came to the throne as minors. Another personal sorrow fell upon Richard. His wife, the long-suffering Anne, also died. Richard must now have begun to feel that the fruits of usurpation were turning sour. Why had he done the desperate deed if he had no son to succeed him? All his hopes for the future seemed buried in that tomb at Sheriff Hutton church in Yorkshire which contains the mortal remains of young Edward of Middleham. The tomb is not elaborate and the effigy on it is worn. Richard had planned to found a splendid chantry at Sheriff Hutton, but as with so many of his other plans, that fatal day at Bosworth Field put an end to them all.

The usurper's troubles were now gathering around him. Try as he would he could not eliminate from his subjects' minds the fate of the Princes in the Tower. Even his strongest supporter, the Duke of Buckingham, staged a rebellion against him. Richard had tried his best; he had been lavish and efficient, but now he was suspicious. Buckingham's rebellion had gone off at half-cock and its leader had gone to the block, but the interesting thing is that this notable Yorkist supporter had staged his rebellion against Richard in the name of the Lancastrian claimant, Henry Tudor. Henry Tudor based his claim on his descent from Margaret Beaufort and he had become the hope of the Lancastrians after the killing of Edward, Prince of Wales, at the battle of Tewkesbury. Even so, he would have remained in obscure exile in Brittany if Edward IV had been peacefully succeeded by Edward V. It was, again, the business of Richard's usurpation – that break in the line of rightful succession – that gave Henry Tudor his support and his hope for the throne.

In 1485 he put that hope to the test. On 1 August, he landed near Dale on Milford Haven and marched up through Wales. The Welsh rallied enthusiastically to a Tudor. His army grew as he entered England. All the discontentment with Richard's rule now came into the open. Some of the greatest of the discontented magnates could not yet show their support. Henry marched on in the hope that they would change sides at the critical moment. At Bosworth Field that hope was triumphantly fulfilled. Bosworth was won by the deceit of the Stanleys who hovered on the outskirts when the battle was joined and then came in on Henry's side. Bosworth Field was won not by tactics but by treachery. Richard died fighting bravely to the end. Nothing became his life more than his leaving of it. Richard's crown had been found on the battlefield. It was brought to Henry and Lord Stanley placed it on his head at the spot they still call Crown Hill, while his exultant soldiers shouted 'King Henry. King Henry. God save King Henry'. The naked body of the dead Richard was flung ignominiously across the back of a horse and so brought to the Grey Friars church in Leicester. A new age had begun.

4

Tudor Triumph

'Now civil wars are stopp'd, peace lives again.'
WILLIAM SHAKESPEARE

On the first day of February in 1461, a middle-aged Welshman, who had been captured at the Yorkist victory at Mortimer's Cross, was brought for execution to the market place at Hereford. His name was Owen Tudor, and until the last moment when the axe fell he was sure that his life would be spared. The scene is vividly described in the chronicle of William Gregory. Owen trusted that he would escape 'until he saw the axe and block, and that, wherein that he was in his doublet, he trusted to pardon and grace till the collar of his red doublet was ripped off. Then he said, "That head shall lie on the stock that was wont to lie on Queen Catherine's lap," and put his heart and mind wholly unto God and full meekly took his death.' His head was set on the highest point of the market cross. A mad woman came and combed the hair, washed the blood off the head that once lay in a queen's lap and set candles about it. The extraordinary, amorous career of Owen Tudor had come to an end.

This once obscure North Wales gentleman had indeed married a queen, none other than Queen Catherine, the widow of the hero-king, Henry V. Young Owen had been taken as a page into Henry's entourage. His ancestors came from the family of Ednyfed Fychan, who had been important officials of the Princes of Gwynedd before the Edwardian conquest. They had then served the English crown, but many of the family had joined the rising of Owen Glendower. Some were executed after the rising or lost their estates. Marudedd (Meredith), the youngest brother, managed to get his son into the safety of the King's court. The records of his service at court are scanty. He may have gone on the Agincourt campaign, but not as a fighting man. He won his greatest victory without fighting at all!

King Henry V had died unexpectedly in 1422, leaving his young French wife with an infant son, the future Henry VI. A widow in a strange land, she must have felt desperately lonely. She turned to an attractive Welshman of her same age, who may also have felt a stranger in a strange land, but who was also gifted with irresistible charm. Never has sexual attraction had such a profound influence on the history of Britain, for Owen and Catherine – the ex-Queen and the comparatively humble Welshman – got married in secret. It sounds like something out of a romance in a woman's magazine! But married they were, and had four children – three sons and a daughter. They seem to have lived happily together with no comment from official circles. Their union inevitably became public many years later with the death of Catherine. Naturally some fuss was then made about it, and Owen did a spell in Newgate. In the end the mild and forgiving young Henry VI condoned the offence – if offence it was – committed by the attractive Welshman. Owen finally retired to Wales where he held the office of Keeper of the King's Parks in parts of Denbighshire. As Professor Chrimes wittily puts it, 'At last Owen ap Meredith ap Tudor had unquestionably become Owen Tudor, Esquire.'

His two elder sons did even better. Henry VI was tender towards his half-brothers to whom he had so unexpectedly found himself related. Edmund, the eldest, was created Earl of Richmond at the same time as his younger brother, Jasper, became Earl of Pembroke. A third brother, Owen, vanished into obscurity, and we only hear of him in the household accounts of his nephew, Henry VII, when a suitable sum of money was paid for the burial of one, Owen Tudor, a monk, in Westminster Abbey. A cloister was the safest place in the turmoil of the Wars of the Roses, in which both of his brothers soon found themselves engaged.

In 1455, Edmund made an important marriage, when he wed a great heiress, the Lady Margaret Beaufort. She was descended from Edward III's third son, John of Gaunt, through his mistress, Catherine Swynford. The liaison had been made respectable and the Beaufort line legitimized. Margaret was the great-great-granddaughter of Edward III, but in the blood-letting and head-chopping of the Wars of the Roses, claimant after claimant was forcibly removed. Margaret had survived to become the heiress of the Lancastrian claim to the throne. Her marriage to Edmund was short-lived. In 1456 Edmund, who had been fighting in Wales, died in Carmarthen Castle. He was buried in the Grey Friars church of that town but, in 1536, his remains were removed to a tomb in St David's Cathedral. His widow, not yet fourteen, put herself under the protection of her relative, Lord Herbert. Three months after her husband's death, in January 1457, she gave birth to a son in Pembroke Castle. This son was Henry Tudor. His early days were spent in Pembroke, but his uncle Jasper was always watching him from afar. When the Yorkists were temporarily overthrown in 1470, Jasper brought the boy up to London to receive the blessing of the hapless Henry VI. No doubt he hoped that an aura of Lancastrian legitimacy would fall on the boy, which would be of value in the future. Jasper was nothing if not far-seeing. When the Yorkists returned to win the battle of Tewkesbury, Jasper whisked the lad to safety overseas. The first years of Henry's life had, however, been spent in Wales. Patriotic Welsh historians of the past have pictured him as a Welsh-speaking Welshman, devoted to his native land. This is certainly over-doing it. We cannot be sure that Henry spoke Welsh, for he was brought up in South Pembrokeshire, which, for three hundred years before Henry's birth, had been settled by immigrants from Devon and Somerset. To this day the area is known as 'Little England beyond Wales'. Henry did not return to Wales until he landed to claim the throne many years later.

His early manhood was all passed in exile in Brittany, where the wily Jasper saw to it that he was always one jump ahead of his enemies. In Brittany Henry lived the life of an exile, always ready to slip over the border if the mood of his host should change, and always looking hopefully across the water towards England. He also used his exile, as so many men have done before and after him, to educate himself. Henry was well-read, with an interest in the New Learning. Even more than Edward IV, we can think of him as our first Renaissance king. He could be ruthless when needed, but he was open to new ideas and could turn on the charm when it was politically useful. Jasper performed one other vital service for his nephew. He kept him unmarried. He already had a far-sighted wedding plan for him when the moment came. Henry should marry the Yorkist heiress, Elizabeth of York. In the words of the Tudor propagandists, the red and white roses should intertwine to ensure the peace of the realm.

All this might have seemed a pipe-dream to the exiles before the usurpation of Richard III, and the murder of the Princes in the Tower. It was Richard's own conduct that made Henry's claim to the throne viable. If Richard had not ruined the Yorkist cause in the public eye, Henry might never have been heard of. He might have faded out in exile, a mere footnote to history. Fortunately for Britain, Henry took a gamble which came off at Bosworth Field.

Posterity's impression of the new King may have been influenced by the remarkable bust by Pietro Torrigiano in the Victoria and Albert Museum. This shows Henry as he appeared around 1505 when he had already reigned for twenty-five years. The face is somewhat ravaged and careworn but the deep-set eyes are still shrewd and observant. Here is a man skilled in reading other men's minds, a natural politician, the very type to bind up the wounds and soften the memory of the bloodshed of the last thirty years. Henry, like his uncle Jasper, was a natural survivor. The important thing about his assumption of the throne was that he stayed on it.

The prematurely aged face that looks at us from the Torrigiano portrait does not give us a fair impression of the youthful Henry, who, according to Polydore Vergil, was 'slender, well-built and strong. His height was above the average. His appearance was remarkably attractive, especially when speaking.' He was obviously no extrovert like Edward IV, and he certainly did not possess that monarch's amorous propensities. He lived comfortably with his wife Elizabeth. Henry was hardly the man for sexual passion, even if the fortunes of the House of Tudor had been founded on his grandfather's amorous prowess. Francis Bacon, in that carefully worded prose of his, notes that 'towards his queen he was nothing uxorious, nor scarce indulgent; but companionable and respective and without jealousy.' Not a picture of an exciting married life. Henry was no great lover. But at least he was respectable, and the public approved. More important still, Elizabeth and Henry produced a family. They ensured the continuation of the dynasty, and they did it early.

Four months after Bosworth Field Henry married Elizabeth, and on 19 September, 1486, their first son was born. He was christened Arthur and the choice of name was significant. It was a gesture to Henry's Welsh supporters, to whom – more than to any other supporters – he owed his crown. After the failure of the Glendower revolt, the Welsh had to find some new symbol of their hopes and dreams of the future. There were moments of despair when they felt that any man of power with Welsh connections would fill the bill, someone who would be a new Arthur and restore the ancient glories of the Principality. Even Edward IV, when he was Earl of March, was the subject of Welsh prophetic verse. Henry Tudor was the ideal hero-saviour. He was of Welsh descent, born in Wales and fought under the Red Dragon banner of Cadwallader. He had acknowledged his supporters generously after his success. The great territorial magnate, Sir Rhys ap Thomas, had been instrumental in rallying South Wales to the cause. The story goes that Rhys had sworn that Henry should only advance over his (Rhys's) body. As soon as Henry had landed at Dale in Milford Haven, Rhys is supposed to have hurried to meet him and fulfilled his promise by crouching under Mullock bridge, while Henry rode over it. Again, one of those pretty stories that have no basis in fact. Rhys only joined Henry at Welshpool some time after he had landed. Still, he was rewarded by being made Chamberlain of South Wales and with a host of other lucrative offices.

The Stanleys, whose change of side had turned the fortunes of the day, soared in the aristocracy, but Jasper Tudor outsoared them all. He became Duke of Bedford and collared all the important available offices in Wales. Humbler Welshmen also did well. They joined Henry's new corps of Yeomen of the Guard, wearing the splendid uniform the Yeomen still sport today. Among the Yeomen Sergeants was a David Seisyllt of Altyrynys in modern Gwent. He had marched with Henry to Bosworth. Seisyllt was obviously a difficult name for Englishmen to pronounce, so the ambitious Yeoman Sergeant changed it to Cecil. His grandson was that wise and astute William Cecil who, as Lord Burghley, was Queen Elizabeth's famous minister. Henry had opened the road of opportunity to all Welshmen. There was something like a Welsh job-rush to London. So many Welshmen came to London to seek their fortune that the somewhat atrabilious poet John Skelton circulated a story that St Peter, tired of the clamour for better jobs from the Welshmen in Heaven, arranged for an angel to shout 'Caws pobi' (toasted cheese) outside. Whereupon the Welshmen rushed out in a body and St Peter slammed the golden gates behind them.

Henry must have felt that the golden gates had opened for him with the birth of Arthur. He gave orders that the church bells should be rung throughout the land. Bonfires blazed and Te Deums were sung. Henry had every right to be pleased. Bosworth Field had put him on the throne but conspiracies were already forming to push him off it. He would have to face the pretenders Lambert Simnel and Perkin Warbeck and even fight a battle at Stoke as serious as the one at Bosworth Field before he could finally feel safe. Arthur was a pledge that it would all be worthwhile.

As soon as he felt his son was old enough, he hurried to make him Prince of Wales. In February, 1490, the appointment was confirmed in a splendid Investiture ceremony. The young prince, now a solemn little boy of three and a half, came down the Thames from Kew to West-minster in a splendid procession of boats, accompanied by the Lord Mayor and acclaimed by the crowd on the banks. A similar procession was to take place a hundred years later, when Henry, the eldest son of James I, also came down the Thames in an equally splendid procession to prepare for his investiture as Prince of Wales. Henry, like Arthur, was destined never to come to the throne. Was there some tempting of providence in staging such pageantry on the waters? Garter King-of-Arms compared Prince Arthur's arrival by barge at Westminster to the return of King Arthur from the island of Avalon. No one could see into the future on that wintry but happy day in 1490.

But first the new Arthur had to be educated. His governor was Reginald Bray and the Prince was early introduced to the business of government. He went to live at Ludlow Castle on the Welsh border. Henry VII was following the precedent set by Edward IV when he established a council to exercise general control over Wales and the Marches. Young Arthur was to be introduced to the peculiar problems of his Principality. But even before he had been sent to Ludlow, his father was already busy planning his marriage. Sons and daughters of royalty were always important pawns in the diplomatic game almost as soon as they were born. Henry was to use the marriages of his children to safeguard his throne and to gain European prestige. He proved to be a master of cunning diplomacy.

He married his daughter Margaret to the King of Scotland and through that marriage the Stuarts eventually came to the English throne, and united the two kingdoms. For Arthur's marriage he looked to Spain, where Ferdinand and Isabella had united the states of Castile and Aragon, and the country was basking in the prospects of wealth from the New World discovered by Columbus. From this marriage Henry clearly expected not only prestige but cash. He was a king who knew the value of money. He acquired a reputation for meanness towards the end of his reign, but he was determined to make his monarchy solvent. A solvent government was an efficient and therefore a successful government. From the opening of the negotiations with Spain the size of the dowry figured prominently.

These negotiations began astonishingly early. The little prince was scarcely two when his father started to look around Europe for a wife for him and settled on Spain. The bride was Catherine, one of the five daughters of Isabella of Castile, who was thus brought up from an early age to call herself Princess of Wales in her father's court. At last a formal betrothal was agreed to after a meeting at Woodstock in 1497, and the two young people were allowed to write to each other. We have a letter from Arthur to his bride, written in Latin, paying her formal compliments and saying in elegant, classical phrases how much he longed to be with her. There is no reason to doubt that it is the work of Arthur himself. Tudor princes and princesses were all highly educated and precocious.

At last, in 1501, the bride actually arrived in England after a stormy voyage, a foretaste of the storms that were to await Catherine later in her life. Arthur journeyed down from Ludlow and joined his father to meet the long cavalcade of the bride that was making its slow way through the Berkshire countryside. When the two parties met at Dogmersfield near Odiham, Henry and Arthur had a mild shock. Catherine was accompanied by a large escort of Spaniards, a troop of formidable duennas, an archbishop and a bishop. The Spaniards insisted that the strict rule of Spanish etiquette should be observed. Neither the bridegroom nor his father should see the bride before the wedding day. Henry was astonished and alarmed. This was not the way things were done in the familiar north. We remember the detailed account of Edward III's bride compiled by Bishop Stapleton. Was there some hideous physical defect in Catherine that the Spaniards were trying to conceal? Henry rode over to Catherine's headquarters and demanded to see her 'even if she was in her bed'. The Spaniards had to yield. Catherine was produced, not in her bed but fully clothed, and Henry found her charming. That evening he and Arthur were gracefully entertained by the bride.

The wedding took place at St Paul's amid scenes of great splendour. Henry may have been tight about money, but he knew how to spend it when it came to impressing the crowd. The spectators noted one disturbing thing about the bridegroom. He didn't seem to enter into the proceedings with quite the same gusto as they had expected. He did not take part in the tournament in the barriers outside Westminster Hall, and at the wedding banquet he was outshone by his younger brother, Henry, who flung off his doublet and partnered his sister Margaret in a spirited romp around the room, to the King, and Queen's 'right great and singular pleasure'. Arthur danced sedately with his little sister Cicily. Was the Prince of Wales already overtaxing a weak constitution?

The couple were put to bed on their wedding night with the usual traditional horse-play, in a room in the palace of the Bishop of London which had been richly decorated for the occasion. But was the marriage actually consummated? This delicate matter became of national importance twenty-five years later when Henry VIII was trying to divorce Catherine. Then old courtiers racked their memories and came up with the usual salacious gossip. The Prince is supposed to have remarked to a friend on the morning after, 'I look well for one who has been in the midst of Spain'. The Prince also wrote a letter in Latin to his bride's parents, saying with obvious affection, 'never in my life have

I felt such joy as when I saw the sweet face of my bride.' Bride and bridegroom were both fifteen, an age regarded as perfectly suitable for intercourse in the sixteenth century. Henry VII's own mother, the Lady Margaret Beaufort, who retained a powerful influence upon him as long as she lived, had borne him when she was barely thirteen. Catherine strongly maintained that she had been untouched on her wedding night, and that she had come as a virgin to Henry VIII. But in the words of Miss Mandy Rice-Davies, 'Well, she would, wouldn't she?'

There remains, however, the curious reluctance shown by the King and Queen to allow Arthur and Catherine to set up house together. Were they already aware that Arthur was ailing? When at last the couple moved to Ludlow, Arthur fell ill and soon died. At this lapse of time, it is impossible to diagnose the nature of his illness. The chroniclers call it 'a consumption'. In the end, the body of the Prince, after lying in state in Ludlow Castle, was taken through atrocious weather to a tomb in Worcester Cathedral.

King Henry was desolated. He had been proud and fond of his son. His wife tried to comfort him: 'My Lady, your mother', she said, 'had never more children but you only, and God, by his grace, ever preserved you.'

In addition to losing his son, Henry might also have to lose Catherine's dowry. This gave a double edge to his grief. Ferdinand and Isabella might demand the return of the hundred thousand crowns they had already paid and would certainly withhold the balance due. To add to Henry's problems, his wife, Elizabeth of York, died in 1503. In the same year he had lost his wife and his son and heir. But Henry was a man of iron will. He forced himself to look at the problem of what to do with Catherine with a clear eye. Obviously she must stay in England, and to make certain of her presence, he toyed with the idea of marrying her himself. Queen Isabella, however, would never hear of it. This was pushing the principle that marriage was simply a question of diplomacy a little too far. The negotiators finally settled on a more sensible alternative. Catherine should remain in England and at a suitable time marry Arthur's younger brother, Henry, Duke of York. They were betrothed in June, 1503, and were pledged to marry when Henry reached the age of fifteen. The King characteristically insisted on two further points. The marriage would only take place if a papal dispensation could be obtained, and more important still, if the balance of the dowry was paid. There remained a little confusion over titles. Catherine was Princess of Wales and the twelve-year-old Henry still Duke of York. The King settled the matter by making his son Prince of Wales by letters patent. There was no flamboyant Investiture ceremony. The King felt that here, at least, he could save some money.

The ordinary people of the country now had a chance to look at the new heir, and they liked what they saw. In place of the anaemic Arthur they found a handsome, vigorous youth, a 'young Apollo', who excelled at games of all sorts, from tilting to real tennis, and who was highly cultivated into the bargain. There had been no such acceptable Prince of Wales since the days of the Black Prince. Royal education, however, had changed profoundly over the hundred and fifty years that separated Prince Henry from Edward of Woodstock. We have reached the Renaissance. Princes were now expected to be highly literate as well as proficient in arms. Castiglione's 'Courtier' would become the model for the perfect aristocrat. Prince Henry's future subjects would not look askance at him – as they had at Edward II, Richard II and Henry VI – because of his interest in the arts. Indeed they now expected him to be proficient in music and poetry, the proper arts for a gentleman. Henry more than fulfilled the bill.

He may have owed these accomplishments to his father's somewhat surprising choice of John Skelton as one of his early tutors. Skelton was a strange man. A brilliant Latinist, he had swept the board at Oxford, Cambridge and Louvain. He was a remarkable poet in his own language and had charm enough when he wanted to exercise it. He was also vain and quarrelsome. While he could write one of the most touching of our early poems on the death of a pet sparrow, he could also spill out his venom in verse, as in his flaying of Cardinal Wolsey in *Speak, Parrot* and pour out brilliant bawdry in *The Tunning of Elinour Rumming*. A priest who was also a mass of contradictions. Yet he could boast with justice:

> The honor of Englond I lernyd to spelle,
> In dygnyte roialle that doth excelle . . .

Skelton did marvels for young Henry's scholarship but one wonders what he did for his morals!

For behind the charm of the 'young Apollo' lay darker features, a temper inherited not from his mild Lancastrian forebears but from the more violent Plantagenet strain, a wilfulness that could break out into a disconcerting selfishness. Did the King feel some unease about his new heir? He certainly gave him a lavish settlement when he became his heir, but Skelton was dismissed from his post as tutor. In his *Bowge of Court*, a scurrilous satire on the manners of the courtiers, he had gone too far even for the tolerant Henry VII. He went off to become Rector of Diss in East Anglia, and to dip his pen still deeper into political venom. His place was taken by a more colourless and sober tutor, William Hone, but the Prince's intensive studies still continued. The King kept a close eye on young Henry for he may already have started his amorous career at this early age. The Prince had made a close friend of an elder boy, Charles Brandon, who he was later to create Duke of Suffolk. Brandon was everything young Henry admired – handsome, witty, athletic and amorous. Not a youth to meet with the King's approval. He did not send Henry off to preside over the Council of the Marches at Ludlow, as he had his quieter brother. Instead, he kept the high-spirited Henry conveniently near him at Westminster. The Duke de Estrada, the Spanish ambassador, reported: 'It is not only for love that the King takes the Prince with him. He wishes to improve him.'

Catherine, meanwhile, was also to be kept in close bounds. She was becoming increasingly worried about her position. She was not often invited to court. She heard rumours that the King was planning to use Prince Henry as a pawn in a new diplomatic game, and this caused her pain. She already regarded Henry as hers and he, too, fretted at the delay in carrying out the marriage. Catherine at this time was still beautiful and graceful and had grown into maturity ahead of Henry. She knew how to attract him. When the time came, she was more than willing to go to their marriage bed. That time arrived when, on 21 April 1509, Henry VII died. Barely two months later, Henry VIII had married Catherine.

The country greeted the beginning of the new reign with rapture, as if a new era had dawned, but before we share their somewhat premature delight, we should pay tribute to the old king. He had done well for his country. Professor Chrimes sums up his real achievements:

> If it be true that England showed a greatness and a marked flowering of her spirit and genius in the course of the sixteenth century, such a development would have been inconceivable without the intermediation of Henry of Richmond's regime. Not for him the egoism of his son Henry nor the glorifications of his granddaughter Elizabeth. But without his unspectacular statecraft their creative achievements would have no roots. His steady purposefulness saved England from mediocrity.

After him, there were no further Princes of Wales for over a hundred years. Henry VIII's daughters, Mary and Elizabeth, were occasionally addressed as Princesses of Wales but this was probably court flattery. The King never gave the title to them by letters patent and there is not the slightest evidence that he ever thought of doing so. He probably felt that his only son, who became Edward VI, was too young to be given the honour. Henry died in 1547. Fifty-three years later, James VI of Scotland became James I of England, and the sequence of the Princes of Wales begins anew. James owed his presence on the English throne to the far-sighted vision of Henry Tudor, who had married his daughter Margaret to James IV of Scotland. He thus laid the foundation of the ultimate union of Great Britain. Not the least of the benefits we owe to that strange victory on Bosworth Field.

NEAR THIS SPOT
WAS KILLED
OUR PRINCE
LLYWELYN
1282

Memorial to Llywelyn the Last,
Cilmery.

Effigy of the Black Prince,
Canterbury.

Left *George I, our first Hanoverian king, 1714–1727.*
Right *George II, the first Hanoverian king who was also Prince of Wales.*

Nell Gwynn and the infant Duke of St. Albans, by Peter Lely.

The State Barge of Frederick, Prince of Wales.

'The Lover's Dream', satirical cartoon of the Prince Regent by Gillray.

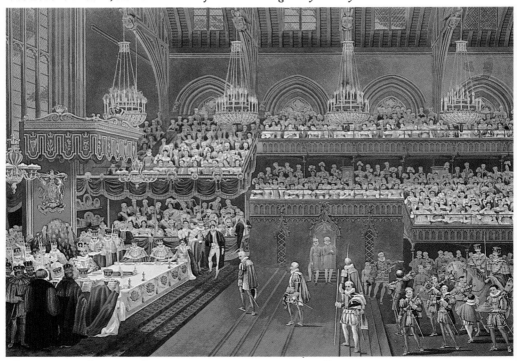

The Coronation banquet of King George IV at Westminster Hall.

Princess Charlotte, daughter of George IV with her husband, Prince Leopold of Saxe-Coburg.

Edward VII, as Prince of Wales, 1859. Painted by Franz Winterhalter.

Above left *Prince Charles with Prince Philip.*

Above *Prince Charles as cellist.*

Left *The Full Achievement of Arms of the Prince of Wales.*

Prince Charles and Princess Diana returning from St. Paul's Cathedral, 1981.

Prince Charles and Princess Diana leaving St. Mary's Hospital, Paddington, with Prince William.

5

The Stuarts and Tragedy

'Methinks the proverb should not be forgot
That wars are sweet to those that know them not.'
                                    JOHN TAYLOR

On 24 March 1603, Queen Elizabeth of England, so rightly called
Gloriana by her subjects, turned her face to the wall as she lay on her
pile of cushions in the withdrawal chambers of her palace and quietly
died, 'as the most resplendent sun setteth at last in a western cloud'.
An ambitious young courtier, Sir Robert Cary, had already placed
horses in relays on the road to Scotland. He lost no time in riding
post-haste to bring the news to the eagerly waiting James VI of Scotland
that he was now King of England, too. Sir Robert reaped his reward
in promotion and, three days later, Sir Robert Cecil sent off the draft
of the Proclamation – 'sweet music it sounded to the King's ear'.

James also lost no time in setting off for London to claim his rich
inheritance. He was in that mood of euphoria that overtakes modern
winners of the pools. As he journeyed south he received lavish hospitality and entertainment and scattered honours equally lavishly in
return. So eager was he to take possession of England, and what must
have seemed to him its fabulous wealth after his lean years in frugal
Scotland, that he left his family behind. That family included his two
sons, Henry and Charles, who were both, in the event, destined to
become Princes of Wales.

A hundred years had passed since the title had last been granted.
Edward VI had never borne it, Henry VIII's daughters, Mary and
Elizabeth, were only referred to as Princesses of Wales by poets or
courtiers anxious to flatter and please. As women they were never so
entitled by letters patent, and neither had sons to succeed them. We
remember the touching cry of regret Elizabeth is supposed to have
uttered to her ladies when she received the news of the birth of James:
'The Queen of Scotland is lighter of a fair son, and I am but a barren
stock!' Now that fair son of the Queen of Scotland was safely on the

throne once occupied by Gloriana, he planned to make his son Henry Prince of Wales as soon as he reached mature age.

The new king of the newly joined kingdoms was a remarkable character who also left a deep impression on the minds and characters of his two sons. The common picture of James as a careless dresser with a rickety gait, slobbering over his food and drink and lolling on the necks of his handsome male favourites, while he neglected his administrative duties for continual hunting, comes from his later years, when he had been living long in an England which must have seemed to him a land overflowing with milk and honey after the stern, Calvinistic atmosphere of his northern kingdom. James in his early years presented a more pleasing aspect. He dressed neatly and was by no means unhandsome. His passion for hunting had kept him fit and given him a healthy, ruddy complexion. The celebrated description of him as the 'wisest fool in Christendom' does less than justice to his very real learning and certainly not to his wit and readiness of speech. As might be expected of a Scot, he was a formidable theologian and wielded an eloquent pen. His books, including his celebrated diatribe against tobacco, are far more readable than many of the more pretentious productions of his learned subjects. In his prime he was no mean figure, able to hold his own with the most skilful of debaters.

True he presented a less attractive picture when it came to personal courage. He wore absurdly padded clothes to minimize the danger from an assassin's dagger thrust and had a series of beds in his room to baffle attempts on his life as he lay asleep. He also betrayed an almost comic horror of naked steel. It is difficult to blame him for all this. From his earliest youth he had lived in the dangerous atmosphere of deadly plots and counter-plots and had repeatedly saved his life by constant cunning.

On one point we can give James our unreserved approval. He was determined that his two sons should be as educated as he was and luckily they both proved eminently educable. The King went to great trouble to see that they had the best of tutors and he himself wrote special instructions for them on a whole variety of subjects, from statecraft to the best ways of preserving their health. Constant letters passed between them and we can still sense as we read them that concern for his children's welfare which was one of James's most commendable qualities. We forget the slobbering James, doting on his unworthy minions, when we read his little note to his growing family advising them 'to keep up their dancing privately though they whistle and sing to each other for music'. The children sent back equally charming letters in return. Many are extant, including one of the earliest written by little Charles in his own careful, childish hand, giving his father, with a certain pride, news of his progress in English grammar: 'Sweete, sweete Father, I learne to decline substantives and adjectives, give me your blessing, I thank you for my best man, your loving sonne, York'.

Henry, the eldest son, was born in Stirling Castle in 1594 to universal rejoicing. One observer described the Scottish people as being 'daft for a month'. He grew up a healthy, active child. He was trained in the usual aristocratic sports and outdoor activities by the celebrated expert, Richard Preston, and did not neglect his academic studies. As he came to maturity he began to attract universal admiration. Clearly he possessed what is now the fashion to term 'charisma'. He was also a solemn young man who did not totally approve of the somewhat spendthrift and even profligate life of his father's court. James had coarsened the old Elizabethan splendours. His Queen was Anne of Denmark and the Danish connection might have brought in a taste for deep drinking that would never have been countenanced by Gloriana. When Anne's brother, Christian IV, was entertained by James at his country palace of Theobalds in Hertfordshire a notorious scene occurred, when the guests got so drunk that the entertainment arranged by the unfortunate Earl of Salisbury collapsed in chaos, the royal personages rolled under the tables, and an actor vomited over King Christian himself.

Yet there was another side to the court life in which Henry, his enchanting sister Elizabeth and the little Charles were now expected to play an increasing part. No less than fifteen of Shakespeare's plays were presented before King James and his court and some of his greatest tragic masterpieces were written not in the reign of Elizabeth but in that of James. The King and his family would have seen the earlier performances of *King Lear* and *Othello*. Ben Jonson created his elaborate masques for the court, in which the Queen and her children took part on special occasions, and Inigo Jones invented marvellous scenic effects that revolutionized stagecraft in Britain.

All the children eventually had their own company of actors, and a group of men of distinction gathered around Henry. His household included Corryat, the traveller, Chapman, the translator of Homer, and Joshua Sylvester, the lyric poet. Better poets, too, were under his patronage including Michael Drayton and Samuel Daniel. Musicians and painters were also part of the same group. Henry excelled at physical activity of all kinds but he yet found time for cultural pursuits. Small wonder that the whole nation began to expect great things of him.

When he reached the age of sixteen Henry was made Prince of Wales with all the ceremony, pomp and feasting so dear to the heart of King James. It is worth while looking at the details of the ceremony for it served as a model for the Investiture when it was revived in our own day. The letters patent presented to our Prince Charles took the same form as those presented to Prince Henry. King James was not the man to let such an occasion pass without loading it with splendour, not only for pleasure but also as a matter of policy. He had elaborated his strange doctrine of the Divine Right of Kings, the assertion that the power of the monarchy was not in the gift of such mundane bodies as elected parliaments but emanated from the Almighty himself. It followed that great princes should be careful to surround their public proceedings with such splendours that would mark them as no ordinary people.

Thus Prince Henry, before that important day in 1609, came by water from Richmond to Whitehall, escorted down the Thames by a splendid procession of boats. The King awaited him in the Great Hall, surrounded by his faithful Commons. His Majesty fairly glittered with jewellery of almost barbaric richness. We know, from the inventories of the Great Wardrobe, the names of some of the choicer pieces that the King and Queen wore on these great state occasions – 'the faire greate pearle called the Bretherin, the Portugal Dyamond and the greate table diamond sette in gould called the Mirror of France'. The peers of the realm then entered, all in their state robes and in strict order of precedence. At the end of the procession came the Prince himself escorted by the Earl of Northampton and the Earl of Nottingham.

They led him to the throne, where he knelt on the topmost step as the Earl of Salisbury read out the letters patent. Two noblemen then girded Prince Henry with his sword and clad him in his ceremonial robe. The King now rose and took his son by the hand, kissed him and placed his gold circlet on his head. He then delivered to him his staff, ring and the richly illuminated letters patent. The trumpeters sounded a fanfare and, no doubt, at this point Prince Henry glanced up at the special box where his younger brother Charles, who hero-worshipped him, sat with his sister Elizabeth and a group of high-born and excited little boys and girls – 'a very goodly sight it was', noted a spectator, 'to behold so many little infants of such noble parentage'.

That night the King retired to his own apartments and allowed the Prince to dine in the Great Hall with full royal honours. We can be sure that the sober-minded Henry never allowed that dinner to

84

degenerate into the drunken revel that ended the entertainment of the King of Denmark. Next day a special masque was performed to celebrate the investiture. *Thetys Festival* was written by Samuel Daniel; the Queen herself took the party of Thetys, Elizabeth was the Nymph of the Thames and little Charles, now aged nine and Duke of York, appeared as Zephyr, clad in a green robe embroidered with golden flowers. As usual the greatest admiration and praise was reserved for Master Inigo Jones, now – to the unrepressed fury of the irascible Ben Jonson – showing his full genius as a stage designer. Nothing seemed beyond him to reproduce on the stage, from the motion of the stars to that of full-rigged ships riding at anchor on a restless sea. These were halcyon days for the newly created Prince of Wales, his radiant sister Elizabeth and the young Charles. None of them on that happy occasion so full of pomp and paternal pride, of music and poetry, could have foreseen the strange fates that the malign luck of the Stuarts had in store for them.

In the years that immediately followed his Investiture Prince Henry gave evidence of steadily increasing maturity, and seemed to be taking his own line in public affairs, not always in accord with that of his father. He was turning into a serious-minded young man who was reacting against the lavish expenditure and profligacy of much of court life under the ageing James. He maintained a sober, almost frugal, household, dressing in a cloth described as 'Welsh freeze', and frowning on swearing and immoral conduct. He even kept boxes handy in the various rooms of his apartments where courtiers who swore were expected to place fines for the support of the poor.

If all this smacks of a solemn, almost ostentatious Puritanism, it was noted with approval by large sections of the community, and it was redeemed by Henry's furious physical activity, his skill at all the aristocratic sports from fencing and tennis to golf and riding. Altogether a man of promise with a gift for leadership. Inevitably the men who were discontented with the royal policies – and they were many – turned towards the Prince. The classical pattern of the opposition hoping to build a party around the Prince of Wales was taking shape again, as it has done throughout our history.

The rising Puritan element in the country noted with approval Henry's strong Protestantism and his steady attendance at sermons. The old school of merchant-adventurers, who still hankered after Eliza-bethan enterprise in exploring for new markets, were happy that Henry was the 'Protector' of the Company of the Discoverers of the North-West Passage. The anti-Spanish party, who were worried by

James's attempts to come to terms with Spain and condemned the King's imprisonment in the Tower of the old hero, Sir Walter Raleigh, to please the Spanish ambassador, applauded Prince Henry's comment, 'Only my father would keep such a bird in such a cage.' Inevitably the King betrayed some impatience with the attitude of the Prince of Wales. He may even have been slightly jealous of his son's popularity and the obvious ease with which he could make contact with people in all walks of life. When he had reached the age of seventeen Henry requested that he should be allowed to preside over the Council. This may have been going a bit too far too soon. James had no desire to put his heir into the very centre of state power. He curtly refused the request. Henry was obviously not going to be an uncritical supporter and admirer of the British Solomon. As he grew older and weary of the troublesome cares of office, James started to depend more on his favourites like the personable Scot, Robert Carr. Henry registered his disapproval. Who could say how the situation might have developed, but for that perverse fate that always seemed to lie in wait for the Stuarts when they seemed set fair for success.

On 13 February 1613, Henry's beloved sister Elizabeth was to be married to the Elector Palatine of the Rhine, a staunch Protestant who was also known as the Palgrave. This marriage alliance with a well-known champion of Protestantism was part of James's ambitious schemes for a series of marriages for his sons and daughter which would bring him into the very centre of European politics. He had, of course, been carefully considering Henry's own marriage. His envoys had travelled extensively to check on all the available princesses, for everybody, including the Prince and princesses themselves, accepted the fact that royal marriages were an essential part of high diplomacy and romance never entered into the business. If love came later – or even mutual respect – that was just a lucky bonus!

Princesses from France, Spain, Savoy and Tuscany were all considered for the Prince of Wales, and James and his counsellors anxiously pondered over the advantages and disadvantages of each alliance with the meticulous attention to financial details worthy of modern business tycoons carrying out a gigantic company take-over. For the moment all the princesses on offer were rejected and Prince Henry could only murmur, with his usual clear-sighted realism: 'My part, which is to be in love with any of them, is not yet at hand.'

Elizabeth's marriage, however, was very much at hand and Henry was in the centre of the festivities. He and Elizabeth had always felt a special affection for each other, and in common with everyone who met her he had always been charmed by her beauty and vivacity. The young courtiers were at her feet, and the poets were untiring in celebrating her charms. Sir Henry Wotton's tribute finds its way automatically into every anthology of English poetry.

You meaner beauties of the night,
That poorly satisfy our eyes
More by your numbers than your light
You common people of the skies,
Where are you when the Moon shall rise?

Although Elizabeth's marriage had, as usual, been arranged for diplomatic reasons, she was lucky in her husband. Frederick was handsome, lively and charming. The marriage was to turn into a true love-match, and Prince Henry prepared to welcome Frederick to England, not only as the Protestant champion, but as the man who was bound to make his beloved sister supremely happy. But unhappily for himself, he began suddenly to feel unwell. He had to abandon his intention of greeting Frederick at Gravesend. As the wedding preparations proceeded he struggled to regain his health. He seemed to have thought that violent exercise would cure his indisposition. He played tennis, plunged into the Thames and walked through the night. All in vain. His vomiting and weakness continued and he was compelled to take to his bed. The doctors tried all the strange and lurid remedies they then applied to their hapless patients. Sir Walter Raleigh, still in the Tower, sent a special and 'sovereign specific' from his prison. Nothing took effect and in November, 1612, the Prince of Wales died. He was nineteen years of age.

This being the seventeenth century, the rumours immediately started to fly that Henry had been poisoned; there was even a suggestion that the poisoner was James himself. The most likely cause seems to have been typhoid, although modern investigators have felt that some of the symptoms were suspiciously like those of the rare disease of porphyria from which Henry's grandmother, Mary Queen of Scots had suffered and which appeared later in the royal family in a spectacular way with poor George III. Whatever the cause of death, the funeral was staged with the same sense of significant royal pageantry as the investiture and the wedding. All the traditional ritual for a royal funeral had to be followed and some of the details of that ritual were as strange and complicated as at the burial of a pharoah of ancient Egypt.

First of all the doctors had to open the body to be sure of the cause of death. Then the Prince lay in state in his death chamber, guarded by members of his household day and night for four weeks. The walls were draped with black cloth while the craftsmen took the death mask and then made a wax effigy of the dead man which was clothed in his robes and decorations as Prince of Wales. A crown was placed on its head, the glittering effigy of St George was hung around its neck and his golden staff of office placed in its right hand.

On the morning of 7 December the funeral procession left for Westminster Abbey. The King declared himself too overcome to attend. The young Prince Charles, so suddenly and unexpectedly become the heir apparent, had to act as chief mourner. Two thousand fellow mourners all dressed in black marched before him through dense, silent crowds. The hearse, with its coffin and the strange image of the dead prince on top, was drawn by eight horses in black trappings. This river of black woe flooded silently through London to the Abbey where Dr Abbot, the Archbishop of Canterbury, preached the funeral sermon on the text; 'But ye shall be as a Man, and ye Princes shall fall like others.'

The text had a prophetic ring about it. The principal royal mourners who walked in that sombre procession were certainly princes who were all eventually 'to fall like others'. Frederick, the Elector Palatine, married his Elizabeth with slightly muted festivities but he had to take his bride back to a Europe in the opening throes of the Thirty Years War, in which Catholics and Protestants were finally to decide their religion by the sword. Frederick unwisely accepted the offer of the crown of Bohemia from the Protestants of that deeply divided state. Within a year the Catholic forces, led by the Emperor, had driven him from his new kingdom and eventually from his own Palatinate as well. Poor Elizabeth became the 'Winter Queen' and her husband a dependant on the bounty of James. She was not to return to England, the scene or her early triumphs and happiness, until she had become a widow saddened by war and misfortune.

A sterner fate was reserved for Prince Charles. He did indeed succeed to the throne but also to the troubles which his father had begotten in his realm during the twenty years he had ruled both England and Scotland. Prince Charles was eventually to lay down his comely head on the executioner's block in vindication of his father's theory of the Divine Right of Kings.

Fortune even had an unpleasant surprise in reserve for the Archbishop of Canterbury who had pronounced the funeral oration. Dr Abbot was a bachelor, a staunch but not a fanatical Puritan, a kindly, tactful man who King James had felt to be a companionable figure to have at Lambeth, a priest who was virtuous without being ascetic. In short, the perfect Jacobean bishop. Unfortunately, in July 1621, Dr Abbot was out shooting wildfowl on the marshes with Lord Zouche – a somewhat surprising activity for an Archbishop of Canterbury. More surprising still, he missed his bird and shot and killed one of Lord Zouche's keepers, thus becoming the only Archbishop of Canterbury who had killed a man during his episcopate. It is a record unlikely to be challenged. The poor Archbishop had to hide his head under a shower of disapproval from court and Puritan circles alike. For him, too, the funeral text had been prophetic. He had proved that primates as well as princes 'could fall like others'.

The grief of the crowd at Prince Henry's funeral was undoubtedly more genuine than the conventional tears shed over many a departed royal personage. Large sections of the community had placed their hopes in him for important changes in many directions. He had shown that he had powers of leadership and an early grasp of public affairs. That shrewd, perceptive statesman the Earl of Salisbury, the King's chief minister, was conscious of Henry's growing importance in the state. He wrote to the tutor of his son, Lord Cranborne, 'The comparison holds not between our boys and the sons of Kings: they are like feathers as like as things of naught: Princes are things of weight and consequence and eminent expectation ...'

Certainly 'eminent expectation' had gathered around Prince Henry from the very moment he had come south in the wake of his father's triumphant rush to grasp his inheritance. His very name of Henry set eager spirits hoping that, although he was Scots born, the future Henry IX would revive the martial glories of English-born Henry V.

Immediately after his death Prince Henry became almost a cult figure, a symbol of the nation's real hopes for its future. The Dorset knight, Sir Simonds d'Ewes was a Parliamentarian of wealth and position, a man critical of the royal establishment, but when he came to write his autobiography he looked back on the announcement of the death of the Prince of Wales as a moment of national dismay.

The first public grief that ever I was sensible was at Wambroe, after the death of England's joy, the inestimable Prince Henry ... a true lover of the English nation, and a sound Protestant, abhorring not only the idolatry, superstitions and bloody persecutions of the Romish synagogue, but being free also from the Lutheran leven ... He esteemed not buffoons and parasites, nor vain swearers and atheists, but had learned and godly men, such as were John Lord Harrington of Exton and others, for the dear companions of his life; so as had not our sins caused God to take from us so peerless a prince it was very likely that Popery would have been well purged out of Britain and Ireland by his care ...

Strong stuff, indeed; but the men of the seventeenth century used their pen as a sword when it came to defending any cause to which they were committed.

The Puritan interests were not the only ones who lamented the passing of this 'peerless prince'. Henry had taken an intense interest in naval and maritime affairs. He was a friend of Phineas Pett, the brilliant shipbuilder and designer who was revolutionizing ship construction in Britain. He was in contact with the mercantile circles in the City of London. He was, in fact, accessible – a vital quality in an heir to the throne. His death deprived a whole younger generation of their chance of getting their foot on the ladder of promotion. The ageing king turned to his favourites for support in his government, for Henry's young brother Charles was still too young to fill the gap in court circles left by the death of the Prince of Wales.

Again we enter the fascinating area of the might-have-been and yield to the temptation in spite of the serious historian's disapproval, of speculating on what could have happened if Prince Henry had become King Henry IX. Would he indeed have altered James's Spanish policy and become the Protestant champion in Europe, another Gustavus Adolphus as Sir Simonds d'Ewes clearly hoped? Would he have redirected the nation's energies back towards the Elizabethan concern with exploiting the New World? Above all, would he have been able to adjust the monarchy to the rising claims of Parliament and thus avoid the anguish of the Civil War? Or would he, with his obvious power of leadership, have taken the reverse course and, like Louis XIV in France, established a successful and efficient absolute monarchy? We cannot tell, for the future now belonged not to Henry but to the puzzled and distressed youngster who followed the dead prince's coffin to Westminster Abbey. We can only echo the words of Prince Fortinbras of Norway over the dead body of Hamlet at the end of Shakespeare's tragedy:

... Let four captains
Bear Hamlet like a soldier to the stage;
For he was likely, had he been put on
To have prov'd most royal ...

Unfortunately it was Henry's younger brother Charles who was 'put on', and who perhaps proved far too royal!

The two brothers presented a striking contrast. Henry had been open, athletic, approachable and eloquent; Charles was delicate, bookish, reserved and far from ready in his speech. Charles was just twelve when his brother died and was deeply distressed at his loss, for Henry had been his admired hero and Charles, throughout his life, felt the need of a stronger personality on whom to lean. This tendency, and many of the other traits that strongly marked the man, was present from his earliest years, and we need not resort to the more extreme theories of psychoanalysis to admit that the circumstances of Charles's upbringing in his early youth had a profound effect on his character in maturity. In the first place, there was the matter of his health. From the day he was born he had to struggle against a daunting series of childhood ailments. Charles was born at Dunfermline Castle, about fifteen miles from Edinburgh and looked so sickly that emergency arrangements were hurriedly made to christen him before he faded away. Even the announcement of his birth sent to England by George Nicolson, the English Ambassador, had a sinister note in it, for Charles had been born when James had just crushed the mysterious Gowrie conspiracy:

On Monday last the King rode to the Queen to Dunfermline returned yesternight. They never loved better. This night at 11 of the clock the Queen was delivered of a son and word thereof this night about 3 hours brought to the King. Whereon the King this morning is gone to the Queen and 3 pieces of ordnance shot by this castle in joy of the same.

The Earl [of Gowrie] and his brother were yesterday hanged on the gibbet in the market place here and after quartered by the hangman.

The baby survived, although the inevitable rumours ran about Edinburgh that James was not the father. Anne, indeed, was a light-hearted, rather fluffy blonde who may have been a little indiscreet when she first arrived in the Calvinist and repressive Scotland of the time. One body, a Dane, claimed long afterwards that he was the father of Charles. There is no evidence at all to support this story, but Princes of Wales, throughout our history, have been subject to similar imputations whenever the dynasty was unpopular or the succession disputed. It was a common technique adopted by unscrupulous politicians in opposition. We have seen Richard III declaring that the children of Edward IV were illegitimate and James II was accused of arranging with the Jesuits to smuggle a new-born child into his wife's bedroom in a warming pan to ensure the succession. James VI of Scotland was himself the victim of such scandal. His enemies put it about that he was really the son of David Rizzio, the Italian favourite of his mother, Mary Queen of Scots. As a boy he had heard shouts from the crowd hailing him in the streets as 'Jimmy Davidson'. It was one of James's better qualities that he refused to countenance such stories about his wife for a single moment and always treated her openly with honour and affection. Baby Charles had plenty of other troubles to face in his early years without being saddled with illegitimacy.

Charles was so sickly that his parents were compelled to leave him behind when they moved down to England. His weakness was such that he did not succeed in walking or even talking until he was two-and-a-half. The joints of his knee, hips and ankles were loose and he had to be helped to stumble even a few yards. He might possibly have suffered from rickets, a common disease in the seventeenth century when the consequences of a monotonous diet and lack of sunlight were not understood. This condition was only diagnosed some years later when, as John Aubrey, that genius at collecting gossip and odd scraps of curious information, noted in his delightfully inconsequential way that the name came from 'one Ricketts of Newberye, a Practitioner in Physick, [who] was excellent at curing Children with swoln heads, and small legges ...'. Ricketts arrived on the scene too late to cure Charles and the little boy remained so weak that it was some years before his guardians, Lord and Lady Fyfie, could risk bringing him down from Scotland to join his parents. This was his first royal procession, for he travelled in a litter, accompanied by a troop of horses, with trumpeters sounding his arrival at every town. From his earliest moments Charles was thus made conscious of the pomp and splendour that then surrounded the monarchy.

In England the enterprising Sir Robert and Lady Carey took over as guardians from the Fyfies and Charles passed wholly into English hands. He also slowly got stronger, rather through his own will-power than any doctor's administrations. He had a narrow escape from seventeenth century medical expertise when James actually considered the suggestion that the string under Charles's tongue should be cut to help him to speak. Luckily Lady Carey protested and Charles turned to the old, classical method by which the great Greek orator, Demosthenes, was supposed to have cured himself. He practised with a pebble in his mouth. His speech slowly improved but he always remained hesitant and even stammered. He thought carefully before he uttered a word and this made people feel he was proud and unapproachable. It was part of the tragedy of Charles that the only occasion on which he spoke with fluent and persuasive power was at his trial. He was never more eloquent and his words never had more poetic force than before his execution.

We have to admire the determination and courage of little Charles. When he was first brought to England, he was still suffering from all the handicaps he had acquired at birth. Even when he was made Duke of York at the age of four, following the now established custom of vesting the dukedom in the king's second son, Charles had to be carried into the ceremony by an attendant. But he gritted his teeth, rode every day, struggled to improve his speech and slowly conquered his disabilities. His stammering remained and he never grew tall. His armour, still preserved in the Tower of London, shows him to have been 5 ft 4 inches tall. The average height of people in the past was certainly lower than it is today, but Charles, like many other prominent people in his position, was always conscious of his lack of stature. He preferred his painters to depict him on horseback, seated or on a dais. Napoleon did the same thing and Mussolini had his photographers well under control. Both were also small men.

Young Charles was now better able to take part in the activities of the court. He was deeply attached to his mother and she took care that he participated in all the artistic activities of Whitehall. James's own interests were mainly literary as far as culture was concerned, and he certainly enjoyed good living. To be a 'lusty reveller' was no bar to his favour. The Queen was more concerned with music, painting and all the arts associated with the masque. Charles grew up in a court which may have been profligate in some matters but which encouraged the arts. His taste for great painting in later life was firmly laid in his youth.

Charles was also lucky in his tutor. Thomas Murray was an earnest young Scot who had come south with the King. He was an excellent classical scholar whose Latin verses were much admired. He gave his young pupil, who still felt it a struggle to practise the usual outdoor sports and activities expected of royal children, a taste for reading and study. Charles became an enthusiastic letter-writer. The first letter of his that has been preserved was to his brother. The handwriting may be Murray's, but there is no mistaking the voice of young Charles as he pours out his hero-worship for his beloved Henry.

> I will send my pistolles by Master Newton. I will give anie thing I have to yow, both my horses and my books and my pieces and my crossbowes, or anie thing that yow would haive. Good Brother love me, and I shall ever loove yow.

The letter gives proof of young Charles's generous heart, but it also betrays another quality which showed itself in the mature man – the need that he always felt for the support of more positive characters than his own. This was the reason why, as Prince, he later fell under the spell of Buckingham, and as King, turned to Wentworth and Archbishop Laud for his political and ecclesiastical policies.

The premature death of Henry had made Charles the heir apparent. He was immediately granted the Duchy of Cornwall so that his future financial position was guaranteed. He was next formally invested as Prince of Wales. Contemporary accounts of the ceremony indicate that its splendours were somewhat muted. The Queen was deeply affected by Henry's death and James may have allowed his slight jealousy of Henry's popularity to influence his outlay on the proceedings. But Charles, nevertheless, was escorted in style down river a few days before the ceremony. He was received at Chelsea by the Lord Mayor, the aldermen and members of the City companies. For the final stage of his journey to Whitehall stairs, Charles's barge was surrounded by the gaily decorated boats carrying the aldermen and the liverymen, trumpets blowing and banners flying, and in the midst of the flotilla came floats carrying a representation of London riding on a sea-unicorn, flanked by the rivers Thames and Dee, and surrounded by tritons enthusiastically sounding their conches. The spectators crowded the river bank to see the procession pass. Masques and pageants were an important method of propaganda in the days before newspapers and when the majority of the working population could not read or write. They emphasized the importance of royalty and the successes of the regime, although it required some courage for the lady who represented London and the gentleman got up as Neptune to play their parts in the icy November weather! Still, everyone cheered, and Peace, sitting on her pet dolphin, bravely delivered her poem of welcome. Again we who, from our vantage point in history, know what was to happen to the sixteen-year-old Prince, cannot read the words of that address without some sense of ironic pity.

Welcome, oh welcome, Spring of Joy and Peace!
Borne to be honour'd, and to give encrease
Welcome, oh welcome, all fair joyes attend thee,
Glorie of life, to safety we commend thee!

On the Monday following, Charles went through all the appropriate ceremonies, receiving his letters patent as Prince of Wales at the hands of his father and dining in regal state in the Great Hall, watched by the King from the balcony. This time there was nothing muted about the arrangements. The Venetian Ambassador noted that 'the King had spent money by handfuls'.

The Prince was now to have his own household and Sir Robert Carey succeeded, by using those back-stairs manoeuvres at which he was a master, in getting the post of Chamberlain. Charles now stepped out onto the wider stage. His marriage would soon become a matter of importance. The courtiers and the ambassadors of the European courts all began to take a closer look at him and assessed his qualities with minute care. Through their eyes we see the new Prince of Wales as a serious young man, not without charm and with a grace of manner which was combined with dignity. He was well educated by the standards of the day. He understood Greek and Latin and later spoke French, Spanish and Italian. He was deeply interested in history and had a good understanding of the principles of mathematics. Like most of the young princes of his day, he was an active student of the military arts. His portrait appears as the frontispiece to the English translation of the most celebrated military manual of the time *The Civil and Military Aphorisms of Guicciardini*. He would not have been the son of James if he had not also become a keen, even a learned, theologian. In short, Charles was developing into an intelligent and cultivated 'all-rounder'. But his manner still made him slow and deliberate in speech and therefore somewhat obstinate in maintaining the opinions that he had formulated with such difficulty.

Physically, he still gave an impression of delicacy. He was something of a Puritan in his general conduct and rather held himself apart from the grosser pleasures of the court. This led to some suspicion among the ambassadors about his virility, a matter of some importance in the seventeenth century when it was a monarch's patriotic duty to produce a large family and ensure the succession. The Venetian Ambassador was a keen collector of all the court gossip about the Prince of Wales. He noted that the young Charles blushed easily and did not exactly enjoy the lewd jokes that delighted his father. In 1616 the ever-watchful representative of the Serene Republic reported that Charles's constitution was still too delicate to allow him to take a wife unless he waited many years. By the time such reports found their way to Germany it was widely assumed that Charles would be incapable of fathering a child. Later, in 1622, the Venetian Ambassador wrote that, although Charles was now a grown man, 'as far as one knows, he has not tasted certain youthful pleasures and has not felt love except for some show of poetry'. The Duke of Buckingham put it more bluntly. He declared that Charles 'was slow enough to be eager after feminine prey'. This dilatoriness was most certainly not characteristic of George Villiers, Duke of Buckingham, who was destined to play such an important part in the lives of both the Prince and the King.

The King himself was naturally the most powerful influence on the growing Prince. James had the gift of pithy exposition of ideas that Charles must have envied. The Prince was bound to absorb every detail of the theory of the Divine Right of Kings when it was put so persuasively by James. 'First of all things, learne to know and love that God, whom-to ye have a double obligation; first for that he made you a man; and next, for that he made you a little God to sit on his Throne, and rule over other men.' What young prince, at an impressionable age, could resist the temptation to prepare himself seriously for his future role as a little god? Least of all, Charles! But as he took his rightful place beside his father as Prince of Wales, he found to his dismay and annoyance that the position was already occupied. George Villiers had become James's new favourite, displacing Robert Carr, Earl of Somerset, whose career was soon to end in disgrace and tragedy.

Villiers came from comparatively modest stock. His father had been a small Leicestershire landowner, but his mother was a formidably ambitious lady who was not dismayed by her husband's early death but pinned all her hopes on George, her second son who, she realized, had every quality that would make him successful at court – especially at the court of King James. She sent him to Paris for three years, and he returned an accomplished courtier, graceful, elegant and, above all, handsome. All observers agree on this last quality. Some, John Aubrey among them, went so far as to maintain he was the handsomest man in Europe, combining masculine strength with feminine charm to an unprecedented degree. 'From the nails of his fingers, nay, from the sole of his foot to the crown of his head, there was no blemish in him. And yet his carriage and every stoop of his deportment more than his excellent form were the beauty of his beauty.' He combined this beauty with a ready wit and a quick intelligence. His mind had no real depth to it, however, and this proved a drawback in his later career. It hardly mattered when he was introduced to the court with the deliberate design of displacing Carr, one of his backers being George Abbott, the Archbishop of Canterbury.

Villiers was early famed for his amorous nature. Arthur Wilson noted: 'He affected beauty where he found it, and if his eye cull'd out a wanton beauty he had his setter that could point a meeting.'

King James was now, in 1616, entering his fifties, and was becoming elderly by the standards of the day. The British Solomon was losing his pristine vigour. He was becoming tired and negligent of business. He was losing his teeth and therefore bolted his food and slobbered his wine. His general health was bad. He suffered from arthritis and was impatient of pain. He grew reluctant to wash. A courtier noted 'His skin was as soft as taffeta sarsnet, which felt so, because he never washed his hands only rubbed his fingers' ends slightly with the wet end of a napkin.' And again the same observer; 'By his good will he would never change his clothes until worn out to the very rags, his fashion never, insomuch as one bringing to him a hat of a Spanish block, he cast it from him, swearing he neither loved them or their fashions.' A sad picture of a once vigorous and intellectually gifted man entering on the long decline of the last decade of his reign. James had lost his eldest son. In a few years his wife would also die. He was fond of young Charles but the Prince's reserved and dignified manner was not what he required. Handsome George, with his gusto for life and his endless fund of high spirits, went straight to his heart. Villiers's rise was rapid. In next to no time he was created Viscount Buckingham and had the ear of the King. The King declared to his Council in 1617 his affection for his new favourite in extraordinary terms: 'You may be sure that I love the Earl of Buckingham more than anyone else, and more than you who are here assembled. I wish to speak in my own behalf and not to have it thought to be a defect, for Jesus Christ did the same and therefore I cannot be blamed. Christ had his John, and I have my George.' No wonder Arthur Wilson wryly comments in his memoirs, 'No one dances better, no man runs or jumps better. Indeed he jumped higher than ever Englishman did in so short a time, from a private gentleman to a dukedom.'

Charles was bound to contrast himself with this radiant personality, and inevitably the two men fell out. James was distressed. He almost forced them to stage a reconciliation. Then, as might be expected, Villiers's charm was all conquering and Charles, himself, fell permanently under the spell. From now on, their careers were to be strangely intertwined.

James became even more affectionate to both of them as he felt the infirmities of age creeping on him. Buckingham became 'Steenie' from his fancied resemblance to a painting of St Stephen; the Prince of Wales was 'Baby Charles'. In his letters, James fairly let himself go in terms that would certainly have raised eyebrows if they had been written by Oscar Wilde. Steenie was his 'Sweet child and wife', 'Sweet Heart', 'Sweet Stevie gossip'. The King signed himself as 'Your dear Dad', and 'Thy dear Dad and purveyor'. James pictured himself as a modern Plato instructing his two young pupils in the arts of government, and indeed they seem to have profited from his precepts if not from his example. Says Walton of Buckingham he 'yet had learned at court, first, to sift and question well, and to supply his own defects by the drawing or flowing unto him of the best instruments of experience and knowledge, from whom he had a sweet and attractive manner to suck what might be for the public or his own proper purpose.'

The ever watchful Venetian Ambassador gives us an attractive picture of the growing Charles. He now obviously thought more of him as a marriageable proposition. He said that the Prince was 'very grave and polite, of good constitution as far as can be judged from his appearance. His hair is light and he closely resembles his royal mother. He was dressed in scarlet and gold lace, with a gilt sword and white boots, with gold spurs according to the fashion of the country.'

Charles's marriage was now becoming important. He had obviously conquered all his early physical disabilities. He was a graceful dancer and a fine horseman. Even his stammer was under control. He was playing an increasing part in public affairs as his father became older and more negligent of his royal duties. The rumours about his virility ceased to circulate. But James's diplomacy had become ever more fumbling and lacking in direction. He had begun his reign in England with confidence in his dual role as the great Protestant champion and the peacemaker with Spain. As the years passed this dual role had become increasingly difficult to play. Early marriage plans for Prince Henry had envisaged a Spanish alliance, but this had broken down when James discovered, to his anger, that Philip III was offering Henry, not the Infanta but her younger sister. Lord Salisbury, the great minister who James had inherited from Elizabeth, consoled his master: 'Our brave Prince will find roses elsewhere instead of this olive.'

In 1613 there arrived in England Diego Sarmiento de Acuna, Count Gondomar, one of the most astute and influential ambassadors ever to be accredited to our court. He soon established a remarkable control over James's foreign policy to the dismay of the King's advisers and, indeed, of the nation. James's son-in-law, Frederick, having rashly accepted the crown of Bohemia from the Protestant rebels, had been thrown out by the Imperialists in less than a year. His own principality of the Palatinate was soon to be overrun and with the help of Catholic Spain. Poor James, the peacemaker, found his prestige melting away. His Protestant country clamoured for him to do something about the unhappy fate of his son-in-law and his daughter, Elizabeth. Gondomar cunningly insinuated that a marriage with the Infanta, together with a handsome dowry, would lead to better treatment for the displaced ex-king of Bohemia. The King of Spain was known to be uncertain about the advantages of the match, alternating between approval of its advantages and fearful of its disadvantages. The Pope's dispensation had to be obtained. The Infanta herself was deeply worried about marrying a heretic. Yet Gondomar persisted in planning the alliance. The negotiations went on for the incredible time of eight years. By February 1623, Charles and Buckingham were getting restless. Gondomar was still suggesting that the Spanish match was the only way to give help to the Palatinate and James was still dithering, still as uncertain as the King of Spain about the wisdom of the marriage.

But during that February, James was at his favourite hunting lodge at Royston, near Cambridge. He was in better spirits than usual and delighted when he was joined by Steenie and Baby Charles. They took advantage of the King's good humour to propound one of the most curious, even crack-brained, schemes ever connected with the marriage of a Prince of Wales. Why should not Buckingham and Charles disregard the niceties of protocol? They would go in disguise across Europe, arrive at Madrid, and sweep the Infanta off her feet. The Spanish authorities would be bound to give their consent when they saw Charles before them in person. They would bring back the Infanta in triumph to England.

At first James was delighted. He remembered his own romantic journey to Denmark to bring back his Queen. And if Buckingham went with Charles, surely his charm would prove as irresistible to the Spaniards as it was to James. They celebrated the idea with gusto that night. But next day, the King suddenly thought of all the drawbacks and the dangers. He rolled on the bed crying out that he was undone, that he would lose Baby Charles in the dangers of a journey, incognito, through France. Buckingham did his usual reassuring act, and Charles pleaded eagerly for permission to depart. Steenie might have made the original suggestion but now it was Charles who pushed the plan forward. This was to be his first trip abroad, his own personal adventure, his first break-out from the rather restrained pattern of his life hitherto. James changed his mind, gave his consent, and the two adventurers lost no time in setting off, calling themselves, somewhat improbably, John and Thomas Smith.

They had a narrow escape from early discovery. They crossed the Thames at Gravesend and showed their inexperience as conspirators by tipping the ferryman with a gold coin. The ferryman suspected that they were young aristocrats going to France to fight an illegal duel. He reported them to the local magistrates who hurriedly set out to arrest them, for James had issued stern edicts against duelling in Britain. Luckily Buckingham had arranged for fast horses to be waiting on the other side and Tom and John Smith got safely to Dover.

Charles revelled in all the incidents of the journey through France. Buckingham showed him the delights of Paris. They bought heavy peri-wigs, and thus disguised joined the crowd to watch the Queen Mother dine in public. On they went, staying at humble inns and maintaining their disguise, in spite of some narrow shaves. They sent secret letters back to the King reporting their progress, and James senti-mentalized over the daring of his 'sweete Boys and dear ventrous Knights, worthy to be put in a new Romanco'.

Charles, it was reported, danced with joy when the party crossed the frontier and actually stood on the soil of Spain. Within four days they had reached Madrid and were knocking at the door of the surprised and incredulous Earl of Bristol, the English Ambassador. Gondomar was then in Madrid. He had an excellent intelligence service. In a matter of hours he was hurrying into the presence of the Conde d'Olivarez, the King of Spain's most powerful minister. Olivarez was at supper and was surprised to see the excited Gondomar. 'What's the matter?' he asked, 'you look as if you have the King of England in Madrid.' Gondomar replied, 'if I have not got the King, at least I have the Prince.'

But why had he come? What was to be done with him? The Spanish court buzzed with excitement. The crowds gathered outside Bristol's house, and the rumour raced through Madrid that Charles had come to be converted to Catholicism. This seemed to the average Spaniard the only possible explanation of Charles's madcap journey. Buckingham first conferred with the King of Spain and his ministers. The Spaniards realized that, with Charles actually in their hands, they could raise the 'ante' in the great poker game of the treaty with England. For them, the marriage and the treaty went together. Charles should not have the Infanta unless James signed the treaty – and the terms of that treaty got more onerous the longer Charles stayed.

Spanish court etiquette was stiff and formal. Charles had been allowed to glimpse the Infanta as she passed in her coach in the Prado, but there could be no question of an intimate interview in which Charles might plead his cause in person. In the meantime Charles went hunting with the young Philip IV, gifts were exchanged and the King of Spain sent a present of animals to the King of England, including camels and one 'ellefant'. The Prince was overwhelmed by the splendour of the Spanish art collections and gave a sitting to a promising young painter named Velasquez.

Back in England James went ahead with the expected reception of the Infanta. Apartments were prepared for her, Inigo Jones designed a special chapel and the fleet was put in readiness to escort the new Princess of Wales to her future home. As usual on these occasions, James ignored his financial embarrassments and 'spent money in handfuls'.

All looked bright on the surface but soon the negotiations started to run into difficulties. Charles had to state firmly that he would never become a Roman Catholic as so many Spaniards had expected. The Infanta, in turn, declared that, rather than marry a heretic she would retire into a convent. The Pope's dispensation had to be obtained. To and fro passed the drafts of the treaty and nothing seemed to be finalized. Charles was granted one formal interview with his projected bride but when he expressed himself in the warm terms of a lover, the Spanish ladies were scandalized and the whole feminine troop withdrew in indignation. This was not how Charles had pictured his wooing when he had first decided on the adventure. He resolved to take a desperate step, 'worthy to be put in a new Romanco'.

The Infanta was wont to go and gather flowers in the May dew in a royal garden called the Casa da Campo, near the river. A high wall surrounded it and Charles got his servant to give him a lift-up to the top of the wall. He then jumped down on the other side but unfortunately went tumbling at the very feet of his beloved. The Infanta gave a shriek and fled. Her duenna turned on Charles and then pushed him out through the door in the wall. An episode from a farcical comedy not from a romanco!

Charles began to be discouraged. His position was humiliating. The Pope's dispensation might take months to arrive – if ever. The Spanish negotiators went on changing the terms and the Infanta withdrew into an icy silence. Charles's letters home betrayed his growing irritation and James wrote tearfully back. He advised Charles to cut his losses and come home immediately, otherwise 'never look to see your old Dad again, whom I fear ye shall never see, if you see him not before Winter: Alas, I now repent me sore, that I ever suffered you to go away. I care for Match for nothing, so I may once have you in my arms again: God grant it, God grant it, God grant it, amen, amen, amen.'

By August Charles had had enough. He left his proxy in the hands of Bristol, the English Ambassador, had a last formal audience with the Infanta, made his farewell to the King and went by coach to the coast. As he rode on he had a sudden spasm of fear. The Infanta might still insult him by retiring to a convent even after the Pope's dispensation arrived. He sent a message hurrying back to Madrid and told Bristol to cancel the proxy, but not to announce the cancellation to the Spaniards until after the Pope's dispensation was in the King of Spain's hands.

He thus left a time bomb behind him which would explode at the right embarrassing moment for his Spanish hosts. The Infanta might take English lessons and the Spanish courtiers might address her as Princess of England. Charles by his actions had made certain that she would never be Princess of Wales.

He and Buckingham sailed for England from Santander and Charles found himself in the great cabin of the battleship the *Prince*, which had been sumptuously redecorated for the expected reception of the Infanta. He had been in Spain for exactly six months – six months of frustrated hopes and personal humiliation. He would never forget them. When the party reached home, bonfires blazed in the London streets. Charles must now look elsewhere for a wife, and he did not have far to look. When he passed in disguise through Paris and had stood in the crowd to watch the Queen Mother dine, he had noticed a small, vivacious, dark-haired girl of fifteen dining at Marie de Medici's side. Henrietta Maria was the daughter of Henry IV, the jovial monarch who had become a Catholic in order to become King of France. The French were thus not likely to be so bigoted when it came to an alliance with a Protestant prince. They would certainly want to strike a hard bargain, but to the sorely wounded Charles, even the most complex diplomatic exchanges with the French sounded sweet.

His envoy was an accomplished courtier, Viscount Kensington, who was a fluent French speaker and who had also previously distinguished himself as a lover in the highest aristocratic circles in Paris. In his reports to Charles he described Henrietta Maria as 'the sweetest creature in France'. She was somewhat 'petite', but Kensington assured Charles that 'her growth is very little short for her age and her wisdom is infinitely beyond it'. Moreover, this 'sweet creature' was willing and even eager to marry Charles. She knew all about the Spanish wooing and gaily commented, 'The Prince need not have travelled so far to find a wife.'

All this was balm to Charles's wounded *amour propre*. As for Henrietta Maria being small, was he not on the small side himself? He waited impatiently for the professional diplomats to work out all the details, and when the contract was at last signed, felt that he could sit down and write his first love letter. Being Charles, he made several rough drafts before he was satisfied, and the final version has a certain stiffness. This starts to disappear in the final sentence. Charles could never have written that to the Infanta!

> I have not dared to take the liberty of testifying to you, by a single line, the great impatience with which my spirit has been tormented, during my long waiting for the happy accomplishment of this treaty, until I received good tidings of it, begging you to be assured that, besides the renown of your virtues and perfections, which is everywhere spread abroad, my happiness has been completed by the honour which I have already had of seeing your person, although unknown to you; which sight has completely satisfied me that the exterior of your person in no degree belies the lustre of your virtues. But I cannot, by writing, express the passion of my soul to have the honour of being esteemed . . .

Through the long convoluted sentences we can sense that the young, rather priggish Charles was becoming human. Not only in his affairs of the heart. He now felt more confidence in his ability to handle public affairs. Poor James was starting to crumble and both Charles and Buckingham knew it. They began to take control. It was Charles who really handled affairs in James's last Parliament. James had admitted in his speech at the opening ceremony that he was 'an old king'. Charles by contrast had a youthful vigour and a new dignity that surprised the House. He had grown a beard in Spain, that elegant, carefully shaped and pointed beard which appears in all his celebrated portraits by Van Dyke. The painter has made it the most memorable part of the royal image he handed down to posterity. We cannot think of Charles without it.

Charles was now ready to rule and wanted to have his future Queen at his side. The question now was – would James survive long enough to see Charles united with his bride? In the spring of 1625 it was clear that the King was failing. He was in a high fever. The doctors clustered around his bed. Buckingham and his formidable mother bypassed the doctors. They apparently plied the King with a remedy of a country doctor, John Remington, which had cured Buckingham in one of his recent illnesses. The doctors protested, led by a Dr Crappe – according to the account published many years later in the safety of Frankfurt by another of the physicians, a Scot named John Englishmen, James certainly had problems with the nomenclature of his doctors – Buckingham drove them from the sick-room with a drawn sword. Immediately the suggestion was made that Buckingham had poisoned James.

Gondomar was returning to England. Once he got near to James he would surely use his overpowering influence to restore the Spanish match. Away would go the chance of Henrietta Maria becoming Princess of Wales. So, said Buckingham's enemies, he removed James. Again there is no proof that Buckingham did any such thing. Rumours of this sort would, however, continue to gather around every royal death-bed until well into the eighteenth century.

On the morning of 24 March 1625, James died, or as one historian put it with the florid phrasing that would have delighted James, he left this earth 'with his lords and servants kneeling on one side, his archbishops, bishops and other of his chaplains on the other side of the bed, without pangs or convulsions at all. Solomon slept'.

Charles was king at last. Almost his first step was to complete the arrangements for his marriage. The ceremony took place on May Day outside the west door of Notre Dame in Paris, with the Duc de Chevreuse acting as proxy. Buckingham went to France to bring back the bride, and apparently used the opportunity to make amorous approaches to the Queen of France herself. The handsome Englishman was certainly a believer in machismo! Nothing is certain about the incident, but Alexandre Dumas made rich use of it in his best seller, *The Three Musketeers*.

So Britain never had a Spanish Princess of Wales, and Henrietta

Maria missed becoming Princess of Wales by a few short months. Perhaps it was just as well. The other French bride who also narrowly missed the title was Isabella, who married Edward II. Henrietta Maria proved a devoted and loving wife to Charles, but at first the royal pair went through a strange period of misunderstanding. The Queen clearly thought that her marriage contract allowed her to bring up her children as Catholics until the age of thirteen. If this had occurred, the reaction in the country can be easily imagined. Charles naturally rejected this interpretation of the document. Tension mounted between the two. It lasted for some years and led to an extraordinary episode. After Buckingham had warned the recalcitrant Henrietta Maria that 'Queens of England have had their heads cut off before now', Charles forcibly flung out her attendants from Whitehall, 'like so many beasts'! There could be no sign of the desired heir under such circumstances. As the Venetian Ambassador noted sadly, 'The King of England has married for a successor, as is only reasonable, but children come from love and not from anger.' But things changed dramatically after the assassination of the Duke of Buckingham. The favourite was stabbed by a half-pay officer with 'a poor, ten-penny knife', and the duke who had dazzled and infuriated half Europe with his splendour expired on the dining-table of an inn in Portsmouth. Charles instinctively turned to Henrietta Maria for support. In the same month as the murder of Buckingham, the Queen became pregnant.

The pair remained devoted for the rest of the strange, troubled and eventually tragic remaining twenty years of the reign. Their love is enshrined in the moving letters they wrote to each other. At the lowest point of the King's fortunes, when Henrietta Maria had gone to seek help overseas, she wrote to him, 'If I don't turn mad it shall be a great miracle, but provided it shall be in your service, I shall be content – only if it be when I am with you, for I can no longer live as I am without you.' Charles might have replied in exactly the same spirit, for the Queen established a powerful influence over him.

In this, the Prince of Wales foreshadowed the King. In Charles's deep need for a stronger character to lean upon – a Henrietta Maria, a Wentworth, a Laud – we see again the lonely little boy, who fought his disabilities and hero-worshipped his elder brother. In his formal manner and frosty dignity we trace the youngster who struggled so hard to conquer his stammer. In his obstinacy and deviousness, which brought him into such conflict with Parliament, we can detect the young man's humiliation over the Spanish match and his subsequent determination never again to wear his heart on his sleeve, but to keep his counsel as close and as secret as possible. No wonder that his opponents declared that Charles's mind was 'as full of schemes as a warren is of rabbits, and like rabbits they all went underground'.

We can enumerate his defects, and they eventually brought their own punishment; it is now more important for us to dwell on his virtues and prominent among them was his concern for his family and his determination to bring up his heir in the best possible environment. But when would that heir arrive?

Charles's first son was born after many years of wedlock and unfortunately died at childbirth. The doctors turned to Charles in the emergency. Should they save the mother or the child? Charles replied that he would rather the cast were broken than he should lose the mould. As usual in royal births there were tensions around the bed. Henrietta Maria's religious advisers were present, determined to get the child baptized as a Catholic. Charles had almost to lock them in the ante-room while messengers sped hurriedly to bring Laud. He arrived while the child still lived, and was able to christen him Charles, in the Anglican faith.

An unhappy business. But in the year that followed Charles and Henrietta Maria recovered their spirits. The King had dissolved a troublesome Parliament and was beginning his long period of personal rule. True, Buckingham had been assassinated, but the great painter Rubens had arrived at his court, acting not only as an artist but as a diplomatic representative of Spain. Charles was thus happy on three counts. He had got rid of Parliament for the moment. He was delighted to have Rubens at his side. And the Queen was pregnant again.

This time Charles was determined that all should go well. Madame Peronne, the celebrated French 'accoucheuse' was again invited over from Paris. The skilful lady was captured by pirates when she was crossing the Channel, but Charles happily paid the ransom. The boy arrived safely – a large, dark and healthy baby. The Queen was delighted. She was soon writing about him light-heartedly to her friend, Madame de St George: 'He is so ugly that I am ashamed of him, but his size and fatness supply the want of beauty. He is so fat and so tall that he is taken for a year old, and not only 4 months! His teeth are already beginning to come; I will send on his portrait as soon as he is a little fairer.'

Charles remained dark and tall for the rest of his life. A few months after he was born, the King's sister Elizabeth, now in exile from both Bohemia and the Palatinate, also gave birth to a child – a daughter name Sophia. She was the little girl who was to marry the Elector of

Hanover. By a strange twist of fate, it was the princes of her line and not those of the direct Stuart line, as represented by the dark boy of whom Henrietta Maria was so proud, who would eventually inherit the throne of Britain.

Prince Charles was the first male heir born to a reigning monarch since the days of Henry VIII. The baby was baptized on 27 June 1630, in the public chapel of St James's Palace, which was decorated with royal splendour for the occasion. There was damask cloth on the altar, taffeta curtains on the walls and Turkey carpets on the floor. The peers, the heralds, the ambassadors, the aldermen of the City of London, almost everyone of consequence was there, and Laud officiated at the font. If the baby cried during the service no one heard him, for there were two organs accompanying the choir. From his very first moments the young Charles was surrounded with pageantry and ceremony. King Charles was so pleased with the whole affair that he presented Madame Peronne with £1,000.

Following the custom of the time, the little Charles soon had his own household, with his tutors, his guards and his private servants. He was brought to court at frequent intervals, and appeared with his brother and sisters at many of the formal occasions. We hear of him, at the reception of the Venetian Ambassador, being gently reproved by his father for the offhand way he had acknowledged the Ambassador's kissing of his hand. This was a mistake in courtesy that he never repeated. We also hear of the King rapping him on his head with his cane at a service in the Chapel Royal, when he caught the Prince paying more attention to the ladies than to the sermon. A mistake the young Charles was destined to repeat only too often!

The atmosphere of the royal court had certainly changed from the boisterous days of James. King Charles liked to think of his surroundings at Whitehall and in his other palaces as oases of elegance and decency in the midst of the growing chaos of the outside world. A stricter etiquette had been introduced. On state occasions, when the King and Queen dined in public, they were served on bended knee. Everything moved with studied grace. The very dress of the courtiers reflected the change. Out went those heavily padded doublets, those stuffed pantaloons and those monstrous farthingales that swathed the men and women who look out at us from the paintings of Daniel Mytens and the miniatures of Isaac Oliver. Their place is taken by the elegant personages pictured by Van Dyke, in their silks and fine lace, with their decorations placed with artistic restraint and not with barbaric profusion.

The same formality and elegance prevailed in the miniature court that now surrounded the Prince of Wales. He, too, was served on bended knee, and ate off gold and silver plate, waited upon by a whole host of attendants who carved and tasted his meat, proffered him water and handed him his napkins. The menus of those meals are still preserved in the household accounts and make strange reading. How a growing boy could have got through them without permanent indigestion baffles our modern comprehension. What are we to make of a breakfast that consisted of bread and buttermilk, mutton, chicken and beer? Or a lunch, or rather dinner at two o'clock of wine, game, rabbit pies and sweet tarts. On to supper with fish, custards, and a ragout of pigs' and chickens' livers fried with ginger and hard-boiled eggs. And so to bed!

The Prince may have been offered all these delicacies on bended knee, but he probably didn't tuck into them on an excessive scale. He was a modest eater in later life, whatever he did with wine. In this he was probably following the advice of his governor, the Earl of Newcastle. Newcastle joined Charles when the Prince was eight years old, and brought a refreshing change into the somewhat restraining atmosphere that had characterized the princely household hitherto. Charles was clearly growing up a lively and intelligent boy, and the kindly Irish bishop, Brian Duppa, had been in charge of his formal education. Charles needed a slightly more worldly approach, and Newcastle was exactly the right man to give it to him.

The Earl was a great nobleman, an experienced courtier as well as a member of the Privy Council, and famous throughout Europe for his skill at horsemanship. He wanted to make Charles an elegant all-rounder and not an over-educated pedant. As for Latin, he advised the Prince 'I would rather have you study things than words, matter than language!' He maintained that 'the greatest clerks are not the wisest men', and he continued, 'Neither have I known bookworms great statesmen. The reason is plain; for divinity teaches what we should be, not what we are.'

Newcastle was a devoted royalist but he was not blind to the grave flaw in the character of King Charles I – his inability to communicate with the majority of his subjects, the icy air of disapproval he could assume when anyone presumed to offer him advice. Newcastle said to the Prince; 'Though you cannot put on too much King, yet even there, sometimes a hat or a smile in the right place will advantage you.'

Such advice was honey to little Charles. Through Newcastle's guidance, he became an excellent horseman, a graceful dancer and a ready speaker – 'but not [warned Newcastle] a living dictionary'. He may not have made much progress in his Latin, but he certainly began to win high marks in the kingly arts of tact and graceful compliments. When John Farrer came from the famous Anglican retreat to present him with a magnificently transcribed copy of the Bible, richly bound, the Prince, who may not have been as keen a theologian as his father or grandfather, knew exactly what to say. 'Here is a gallant outside,' he exclaimed as he took the volume. Then he added, as he turned the pages, 'Better and better.' Mr Farrer was overwhelmed by the royal condescension.

He still had to write between carefully ruled lines, but even if his penmanship was backward, the material the prince placed between the lines was well advanced in charm. He wrote a delightful letter to his absent governor after he himself had been scolded for not taking his medicine. 'My lord, I would not have you take too much physic; for it doth always make me worse, and I think it will do the like for you. I ride every day, and am ready to follow any other direction from you. Make haste to return to him that loves you.'

King Charles may have regarded his royal circle as a charmed and cultured Arcadia, but outside the storm clouds were gathering. The rift between King and Parliament widened. The Prince became aware that his father was running into deep trouble. Some members of his household told him that King Charles might even lose his crown. The little Prince was deeply upset, and went crying to bed at nights. At last, his father asked him what was the matter. 'Your Majesty should have asked me that sooner,' said Prince Charles. The King insisted, 'Tell me,' and the tearful boy cried out, 'My grandfather left you four kingdoms – and I am afraid Your Majesty will leave me never one.'

This seemed only too probable as the King began his bitter battle with the Long Parliament. The Prince had to start learning about politics at an early age and in the hardest way. We can imagine the feelings of the young boy, aged eleven, when he was sent to face the stern leaders of Parliament and deliver a letter pleading for mercy for the condemned minister, the Earl of Strafford. The Queen hoped that the youthful charm of the Prince would melt their hearts. The boy was sent back with the letter unopened.

Few of our Princes have had such a hard, troubled, and dangerous preparation for their public duties. Although he was always addressed as Prince of Wales, Charles was never formally handed his letters patent, as his father had been. The times had become too unsettled for ceremony. When, at last, the inevitable Civil War began, young Charles and his brother, James, Duke of York, became important pawns in the grim game. They could not be allowed to fall into the hands of the Parliamentarians, who might have set up the Prince as an alternative to the King. From the moment the royal standard was raised at Nottingham, and then blown down in a gale, the two young princes had to trail along with the royal armies, or to help in rallying support for the royal cause. This last task took Charles on his first visit to his Principality as Prince of Wales. With the Earl of Worcester, he came to the Earl's stronghold of Raglan Castle in Gwent. This castle now lies in impressive ruin but in 1642 it was a fairy castle, crammed with treasures and curiosities, for the Earl was one of the richest men in Britain. He eventually ruined himself in the royal cause, but, when Charles came to Raglan its glories were still intact, including the curious water works and mechanical marvels created by the Earl's son, Lord Herbert. Charles enjoyed himself inspecting them, for all through his life he was attracted to scientific affairs.

He had, however, come for a sterner purpose. The gentry and countryfolk responded to his appeal for support for the King. They poured out their silver plate and the local farmers and peasantry brought their humbler offerings of pigs and cattle. Charles was deeply moved and made his first public speech in thanks. With his inborn sense of the occasion he did not forget that he was in Wales.

'Gentlemen,' he said, 'I have heard formerly of the great minds, the true affections and meanings of the ancient Britainies – but my kind entertainment hath made me confide in your love, which I shall always remember. I give you commendations, praise and thanks for your love, your bounty and liberal entertainment. I know you desire nothing but thanks. You may be sure of that, and of my favour as long as I am Prince of Wales!'

Surely a remarkable effort for a boy of thirteen. But Charles was developing fast in the hot-house of war. His formal education was perforce neglected. He could never become a scholar, but he made precocious progress in the royal art of reading the minds and motives of men. He was soon to see uglier aspects of life when he and his brother James were present at the first great battle of the Civil War at Edgehill. The King had placed the two boys in the hands of his physicians, Dr Harvey and Dr Hinton for safety, but in a confused battle like Edgehill, safety was a relative term. We turn to the account of John Aubrey, that marvellous gossip who collected all the best stories and scandal of the seventeenth century. Dr Harvey had made his name by his discovery of the circulation of the blood and seems to have an absent-minded approach to the problems of warfare. Aubrey says of the doctor,

> When Charles I by reason of the tumults left London, he attended him, and was at the fight of Edge-hill with him; and during the fight, the Prince and the duke of Yorke were committed to his care: he told me that he withdrew with them under a hedge, and tooke out of his pocket a booke and read; but he had not read very long before a bullet of a great gun grazed on the ground neare him, which made him remove his station.

Charles was determined to dodge the good doctor and get into his first fight. He managed to mount his pony and rode towards the enemy. As a troop of Roundhead horse approached the youngster levelled his pistol, and rode towards them, shouting 'I fear them not'. He would probably have been killed or captured had not Dr Harvey's fellow medico, Dr Hinton raced up, grabbed the bridle of Charles's pony and pulled him back to safety. For this, Hinton was knighted by the King, but Charles proved his courage. The next three weary years were to test not only his physical courage but his faith, resourcefulness and resilence as well. Charles and his brother moved around the parts of Britain that still remained faithful to the King, or stayed at Oxford as long as it remained the royalist capital. The fortunes of war slowly turned against the King. The better organized New Model Army of Parliament closed in for the kill. On one depressing day, the King sat with his two sons on the side of the road. The younger boy asked him, 'When do we go home?' King Charles gave him the sad reply, 'We have no home.'

In the aftermath of the crushing defeat of Naseby, the Prince of Wales finally separated from his father. He would never see him alive again. Inexorably, the Parliamentary army forced the Prince and his ever diminishing entourage to move, first to the West Country, then to the Isles of Scilly, then on to the Channel Islands. His father became a prisoner in the hands of his enemies, and the Prince began his life as an exile. This was to last for fourteen long years.

His mother had already preceded him into exile. She was at the French court, busy with endless schemes for raising money to help her husband. These schemes now required the urgent presence of Prince Charles. The powerful, cunning Cardinal Mazarin now controlled French policy in the name of the nine-year-old king, Louis XIV.

Mazarin was watching affairs in England with care. He might not give full support to the fading royalist cause. Henrietta Maria turned to the idea of a lucrative marriage for Charles, for it so happened that there was now a rich plum waiting on the matrimonial market, the wealthiest heiress in France.

Anne Marie Louise d'Orleans, Duchesse de Montpensier, *petite fille de France* (and granddaughter of Henry IV) was always called 'La Grande Mademoiselle'. She was, indeed, a very great lady. As she admits in her lively, candid and egotistical memoirs, she never for a moment doubted that her destiny was marriage with an emperor or at least a king. She, herself, scanned Europe for likely royal prospects and even set her sights at Louis XIV, as he grew to manhood. In the meantime, she was prepared to consider Prince Charles as a sort of 'back stop' in case her imperial plans failed.

Charles was sixteen when he came to Paris and his wandering life during the Civil War had hardly allowed him time to become fluent in French. La Grande Mademoiselle, in her memoirs, noted that Charles 'was tall for his age, with a fine head, black hair, a swarthy complexion and quite agreeable presence'. But his want of French was a drawback. Henrietta Maria kept on singing her son's praises and she almost stage managed the courtship. The Duchesse remained a little doubtful. 'I don't know what success he might have had if he himself had spoken to me; but I do know I can never put much stock on what others tell me on behalf of a man who can say nothing for himself.'

The strange courtship pursued its course through many years, like some stately but out-of-date gavotte. Charles's French improved but the improvement was hardly due to the circle around Mademoiselle. The two sons of the assassinated Duke of Buckingham, George and Francis, had descended upon Paris. They had been old school fellows of Charles. Now they appeared before him with all the inherited fascination of their father and the added glamour of wealth and worldly experience. They had left their studies at Cambridge to fight for the King, although the Parliamentary Commissioners still paid their allowances from their father's estates. Inevitably they dazzled young Charles. They had money and panache. George Villiers was already an accomplished rake. He had also inherited the sexual appetite of his father, the first Duke of Buckingham.

We turn again to John Aubrey for the scandalous but revealing anecdote. Henrietta Maria was anxious to capture Mademoiselle, but was equally anxious to remedy the obvious gaps in her son's

Henry VIII in old age. He became Prince of Wales after the death of his brother, Arthur.

Henry, Prince of Wales, died, at the age of nineteen, before his father, James I. He was succeeded by his younger brother Charles.

Sophia, Electress of Hanover, daughter of Elizabeth, wife of the Elector Palatine.
Through her the Hanoverian kings inherited the throne of Britain.

George III as a young man. He was the son of
Frederick, Prince of Wales.

Frederick, Prince of Wales, playing the cello
with his sisters.

Queen Charlotte,
wife of George III,
painted by Zoffany.
With her is the Prince of Wales,
later the Prince Regent,
and eventually George IV.

The Prince of Wales, by Stubbs, in his early youth, when his conduct alarmed his father, George III.

High life under the Regency. 'Sporting a toe at Almack's'.

education. The great English philosopher and mathematician, Thomas Hobbes, was also an exile in Paris and the Queen of England succeeded in enlisting him as one of the Prince's tutors. Hobbes was a bold, original thinker who was suspected of atheism and he may have confirmed Charles's innate scepticism in matters of politics as well as religion. Hobbes was a powerful political writer and while he was tutoring Charles, he was completing his master-work, *Leviathan*, a full-blooded defence of the all-powerful state. Charles probably never read it, although he would certainly have chuckled over Hobbes's description of algebraic signs as the scratching of hens upon paper. Buckingham joined Charles as a pupil of Hobbes, and many years later the indefatigable Aubrey persuaded Hobbes, now a venerable old gentleman, to regale him with a most improper piece of gossip about the young Duke.

> Mr Hobbes told me that G. Duke of Buckingham at Paris when he was about twenty years old desired him to read geometrie to him; his grace had great natural parts and quickness of wit; Mr Hobbes read and his grace did not apprehend which Mr Hobbes wondered at; at last Mr Hobbes observed that his grace was at mastrupation (his hand in his codpiece). That is a very improper age for that reason for learning.

A very improper age indeed! Charles may have benefited by the teaching of Hobbes, but he also gladly followed the example of Buckingham. It is difficult to blame the young man who found himself suddenly transported from the grim scene of the Civil War in England to the gaiety and glitter of the most pleasure-loving capital in Europe. It therefore comes as no surprise to find that when Charles found himself at The Hague, where he had gone to get Dutch aid for a descent on Britain, he immediately took his first, officially acknowledged mistress. This was the celebrated Lucy Walter. She may also be regarded as his second connection with his Principality, and a slightly more agreeable one than his first. Her father and mother came from Haverfordwest in south-west Wales, and her father would have lived in the romantically placed family castle of Roche if he could have afforded it. The Walters quarrelled and Lucy found herself an exile with her mother at The Hague. She had already plenty of sexual experience before she met Charles and the story goes that she was handed over to the Prince by one of his courtiers with the statement, 'Let who will have her, she's already sped'.

The somewhat prim Evelyn described her in a celebrated comment as 'a bold, brown, beautiful but insipid creature'. This may simply mean that Lucy was not intelligent but Charles was hardly looking in Lucy for the qualities he had found in Hobbes. At any rate, by the time he left The Hague, Lucy Walter, now known as Mrs Barlow, was with child by the Prince. Her son grew up to be Charles's favourite among his numerous illegitimate offspring. He was created Duke of Monmouth and came to a tragic end after his invasion of England in the reign of James II.

All that lay in the uncertain future, but Charles's present was equally uncertain. In England his hapless father was now being brought to trial by his enemies. Charles and Henrietta Maria had to watch with powerless horror as the trial proceeded to its inevitable verdict of 'guilty'. Charles was back in Holland and in January 1649, dispatched three pieces of paper, each with his signature, and an accompanying letter asking Parliament to put any terms they desired over his name. One went to Charles I himself, who burnt it because he feared it might compromise the Prince. Another was handed to Cromwell, who brushed it aside. One copy survives and this tragic relic is now in the British Museum.

On 4 February, William of Orange had gone for a yachting trip. His yacht was hailed by an English fishing smack, the captain came aboard and gave William the news that King Charles had been executed outside his palace of Whitehall on 30 January. William hurriedly returned to The Hague and debated how the terrible news could be broken to Charles. Finally it was decided that one of the Prince's chaplains, a Dr Goffe, should have the unenviable task. The unhappy Dr Goffe entered the royal apartments and found it difficult to speak. He stumbled on over a string of pointless sentences and then, almost by accident, addressed Charles as 'Your Majesty'. He broke off hurriedly but it was too late. There was a sudden silence, then Charles burst into a torrent of bitter sobs and tears. He turned on his heel and fled to his room. He bolted the door and remained by himself, alone with his own grief, for several hours. His anxious entourage remained in suspense. At last Charles emerged, again master of himself and now King of England.

King, indeed, but destined to remain the King in Exile for the next eleven years; increasingly bitter years as he went from court to court with his poverty increasing as his chances of return decreased. His first attempt to return as king had failed. He had been crowned in Scotland but was crushingly defeated by Cromwell at Worcester. He made his celebrated and romantic escape after the battle, to reappear in Europe surrounded by the same glamour that later surrounded Bonnie Prince Charlie after his escape following the '45. Even Mademoiselle was impressed. Here before her was an attractive and assured figure, far removed from the awkward boy of sixteen who had first been produced for her inspection. The amorous gavotte continued, but Charles was not destined to marry Mademoiselle. She had realized that her money was his main interest in wanting to marry her, and that was hardly conducive to a successful romance. Besides she herself was turning from marriage plans to politics. She became deeply involved in the aristocratic revolt against Mazarin known as the Fronde. As a result she was destined to die a spinster, but even in her death she remained original and still capable of drawing attention to herself. She died in 1693 at the age of sixty-six, thus outlasting her old suitor Charles. Her funeral was the sensation of Paris. The Duke of Saint-Simon, whose memoirs give us a fascinating account behind the scenes in the court of Louis XIV exercised his acid pen with gusto on the scene.

Mademoiselle, as a *petite fille de France*, was given the full treatment. Her body lay in state for a week watched over by relays of duchesses, princesses and ladies of quality, all draped in black veils and specially appointed by the King, through his Master of Ceremonies. This guard of nobility was changed every two hours. At the funeral itself, says Saint-Simon,

> a rather ridiculous incident occurred. In the middle of the proceedings, when the ceremony was at its height, the urn which contained the entrails and which had been placed on a pedestal exploded with a terrifying noise and with a sudden and intolerable stench. At once, all the ladies were fainting or rushing in flight. The heralds at arms and the monks who were chanting the psalms, all joined in the rush to the door. The confusion was extreme. The majority of the people got out into the garden or the courtyard. The entrails had been badly embalmed. It was their fermentation that caused the fracas. Everything was sprayed with perfume and restored, and the scare made everyone laugh.

So La Grande Mademoiselle, the original 'poor little rich girl', passed from the scene. What would Charles II have said had he known about it? He would probably have viewed it with a certain cynical and amused detachment, for this had been one of the qualities that he had been compelled to cultivate in exile, and which had been first implanted when he was Prince of Wales. Surely no other Princes of Wales have had such a rough initiation into the business of kingship; his early youth shattered by a civil war, his father executed, his own life risked in battle, his years spent in exile and sometimes in poverty. Small wonder that, when he came to the throne by what his contemporaries regarded as a miracle, he determined to enjoy himself and keep his own counsel. He became all things to all men. As the witty Earl of Rochester put in his celebrated impromptu verse,

> God bless our good and gracious King,
> Whose promise none relies on,
> Who never said a foolish thing,
> And never did a wise one.

To which Charles replied that his words were his own but his deeds those of his ministers. There is truth in this. As Prince of Wales and as King in Exile, Charles II had profited from his trials. He had learned the art his father never acquired – how to bow gracefully before the inevitable. As a result he never had any need to do the one thing he would never face – 'to go on his travels again'.

6

Stuart Tragedy – Act Two

'But you that are a Sovereign Prince, allay
Imperial Pow'r with your paternal sway.'

JOHN DRYDEN

On a winter's evening in 1685, fifteen years after his astonishing
return to the throne of his martyred father, King Charles II held court
in his palace of Whitehall. Lord Macaulay, in his *History of England*,
has given us a celebrated description of the scene. Macaulay may be a
little out-of-date as an historian but what a script writer he would have
been for a film or a TV series! When it comes to historical drama he
doesn't miss a trick.

His palace had seldom presented a gayer or a more scandalous
appearance than on the evening of Sunday the first of February
1685. Some grave persons who had gone thither, after the fashion of
that age, to pay their duty to their sovereign and who had
expected that, on such a day, his court would wear a decent aspect,
were struck with astonishment and horror. The great gallery of
Whitehall, an admirable relic of the magnificence of the Tudors, was
crowded with revellers and gamblers. The King sat there chatting
and toying with three women, whose charms were the boast, and
whose vices were the disgrace, of three nations ... A party of twenty
courtiers were seated at cards round a large table on which gold
was heaped in mountains. Even then the King had complained that he
did not feel well. He had no appetite for supper; his rest that night
was broken ...

The rest of his whole kingdom was soon to be broken. Next morning
no sooner had Charles risen from his bed than he fell back with a cry.
His face turned black, his eyes rolled in his head and he became
insensible. The whole place suddenly became a hive of frenzied
activity. The Queen and the Duchess of York hurried into the
bedchamber and the unhappy mistress, the Duchess of Portsmouth,

hurried out of it in tears. The gates of the palace were closed, and every available doctor of repute in London hastily summoned to the bedside. Soon fourteen practitioners were clustered around the King, all busy blood-letting, purging and plying him with emetics of strange and even revolting composition. The King bore it all with the courage of a martyr. Even as the last moments approached he did not lose his legendary courtesy and charm. He apologized to his courtiers for troubling them by being 'an unconscionable time a-dying'.

Death-bed drama seems to have continually haunted the Stuarts. Charles joined Mary, Queen of Scots, and Charles I in arranging a dramatic departure. When the doctors had clearly abandoned all hope of recovery, the King's successor, his brother James, Duke of York, succeeded in clearing the apartment and secretly introducing a Roman Catholic priest – none other than the Benedictine monk, Father Huddleston, who, at great risk to his own life, had saved the King's life after the Battle of Worcester. Father Huddleston came secretly up the backstairs, received the King into the Roman Catholic Church and administered the Last Sacrament. Then he departed as secretly as he came. The King thus died in a religion other than that for which his father had lain down his life.

The majority of the King's subjects would have been profoundly shocked if they had had the slightest suspicion of what was going on. Britain was officially and firmly a Protestant country, still deeply mistrustful of the Catholic minority, the Papacy and the European powers which supported the Church of Rome. The Lords and Commons had accepted the fact that James would succeed to the throne, although he had become a Catholic convert and was known to have the convert's firm, even obstinate, attachment to his new faith. The monarchial tradition was still deeply embedded in the country's political consciousness – it had even been strengthened by the events of the Civil War. Cromwell himself, faced with all the problems of running an effective administration with restive parliaments, had speculated on the problem of the succession: 'What if a man should take it upon himself to be king?' And in the event, his son Richard did succeed him. Richard was a kindly, well-meaning man, but poor 'Tumble-down Dick' didn't last long. Yet what if Cromwell's son had possessed the fire and iron determination of his son-in-law, Ireton? Again one of those tempting if forbidden 'might-have-beens'! But such speculation can be forgiven at this point for the whole country was busy doing the same thing. Everyone was pondering on the problem, not so much on who would succeed Charles II – James's accession was not disputed

– but on who would succeed James? Would the country again have a hopeful Prince of Wales, and above all a Protestant one?

Crudely put, everything turned on the fertility record of the available kings and queens and princes and princesses. The politicians studied the field with the care of members of a syndicate at the bloodstock sales checking the stud book.

Charles II had, of course, created the problem. Most certainly he was not infertile, for he had quite a brood of illegitimate children. He acknowledged six of them, including his favourite, the Duke of Monmouth, but Charles's partiality for the handsome Duke never went so far as to tempt him to create his bastard a Prince of Wales. As was so often the case with erring royal husbands, Charles treated his wife, Catherine of Braganza, with unfailing courtesy, but Dryden, in his famous satire *Absalom and Achitophel* had another view of the succession problem. In his poem, Charles features as King David and Catherine as his wife, Michal. David, says Dryden,

> ... wide as his command,
> Scattered his Maker's image through the land.
> Michal, of royal blood, the crown did wear,
> A soil ungrateful to the tiller's care ...

Maybe so. At any rate Catherine failed to provide Charles with the longed-for Prince of Wales.

James was in exactly the same position at the moment of his accession. He too had no male heir, a fact which gave encouragement to the Protestant cause. They also noted that James was now fifty-two and his second wife, Mary of Modena, showed no sign of ever producing another child. In the first few years of the marriage Mary had given birth to four children but only one, Isabella, had survived for any length of time. Isabella had died in 1681 at the age of four and a half.

James rivalled Charles as a compulsive womanizer. Charles once remarked to the Duc de Grammont that the Duke of York's chief occupation was adultery, but the Merry Monarch, as a well-known connoisseur, did not admire his brother's taste in women. He declared that James's mistresses must have been imposed upon him by the priests as a penance. James, moreover, totally lacked the charm that excused Charles's transgressions. He was a remorseless but unimaginative copulator. All his qualities seemed to cancel each other out. He was a brave soldier but indifferent to the well-being of his own soldiers. He was a good administrator but impervious to his experts' advice. He became devoutly religious as he grew older but less tolerant of any other religion

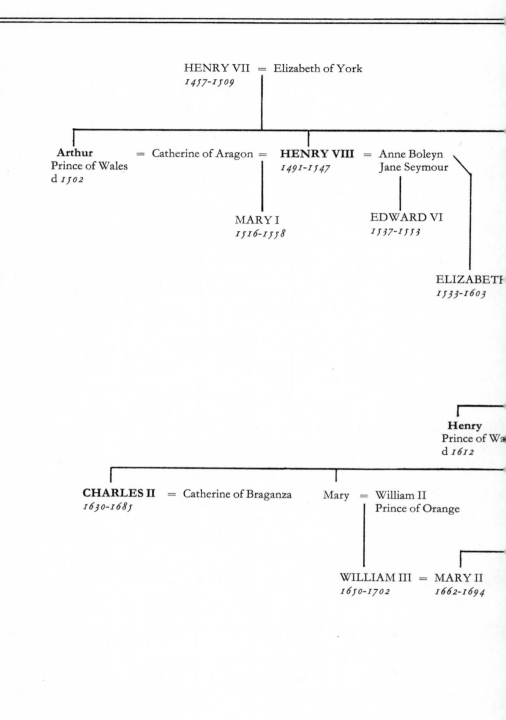

HENRY VII = Elizabeth of York
1457-1509

Arthur   = Catherine of Aragon =   **HENRY VIII** = Anne Boleyn
Prince of Wales   *1491-1547*   Jane Seymour
d *1502*

MARY I   EDWARD VI
1516-1558   *1537-1553*

ELIZABETH
1533-1603

Henry
Prince of Wa
d *1612*

CHARLES II = Catherine of Braganza   Mary = William II
1630-1685   Prince of Orange

WILLIAM III = MARY II
1650-1702   *1662-1694*

Houses of Tudor and Stuart

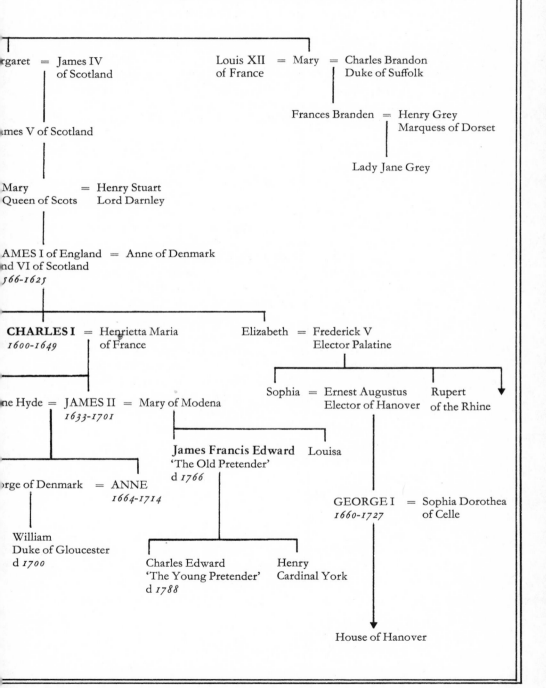

rgaret = James IV
of Scotland

Louis XII = Mary = Charles Brandon
of France | Duke of Suffolk

Frances Branden = Henry Grey
| Marquess of Dorset

ımes V of Scotland

Lady Jane Grey

Mary = Henry Stuart
Queen of Scots Lord Darnley

AMES I of England = Anne of Denmark
ınd VI of Scotland
1566-1625

CHARLES I = Henrietta Maria
1600-1649 of France

Elizabeth = Frederick V
Elect07 Palatine

Sophia = Ernest Augustus Rupert
Elector of Hanover of the Rhine

ne Hyde = JAMES II = Mary of Modena
1633-1701

James Francis Edward Louisa
'The Old Pretender'
d *1766*

orge of Denmark = ANNE
1664-1714

GEORGE I = Sophia Dorothea
1660-1727 of Celle

William
Duke of Gloucester
d *1700*

Charles Edward Henry
'The Young Pretender' Cardinal York
d *1788*

House of Hanover

but his own. James, in fact, was dull and opinionated and therefore a potentially dangerous monarch.

Rumour maintained – again to the comfort of the Protestants – that James was suffering from a venereal disease and was therefore unlikely to produce further offspring. James had two daughters by his first marriage to Anne Hyde, the daughter of Lord Clarendon. Anne had been a Catholic but her daughters were staunchly Protestant. Mary, the eldest, had been married to William of Orange, the redoubtable Protestant soldier who was defending his country through all difficulties against the might of Catholic France and Louis XIV. William was an iron-willed character, a good soldier but ruthless in his devotion to his cause. A cold, able man, yet his wife adored him. Horace Walpole made his usual acid comment: 'Mary contented herself with praying to God that her husband might be a great hero, since he did not choose to be a fond husband.'

It was therefore clear that Mary would not produce a Prince of Wales, although, when James eventually died, she would come to the throne with William as her consort. This left Mary's younger sister Anne for the consideration of the anxious Protestant politicos. She was in an interesting position because she was always in an interesting condition. Her marriage had not been childless. Her husband, Prince George of Denmark, has remained a somewhat shadowy figure in our royal pantheon – if such a description can be applied to a man who was a gargantuan eater and drinker and whose figure, as a result, was anything but shadowy. This was the only substantial thing about him, for his brain seems to have been as small as his stomach was large. King Charles declared that he had tried him drunk and tried him sober and that either way there was nothing in him. He was nicknamed '*Est-il possible?*' – Is it possible? – for he made this comment on every statement put to him. As the old Jacobite jingle put it:

King William thinks all,
Queen Mary takes all,
Prince George drinks all,
And Princess Anne eats all.

The Princess, in truth, rivalled her husband as a mighty trencherwoman, but did not compete with him in the drinking stakes. When she came to the throne, the Jacobites again resorted to scandal and spread the rumour that Anne consoled herself with copious drafts of brandy, which she concealed by drinking out of a tea-cup. They made wry jokes about the Queen's 'cold tea'. There is no evidence for this. The scale of her eating and the strain of continual child-bearing were surely quite sufficient to account for her blotched and red complexion She had been pregnant nearly twenty times but had frequently miscarried, and most of the babies who survived had died of hydrocephalus in their infancy. But in 1688 there was still time for her to produce another offspring, preferably a boy, who might eventually succeed. Her husband, that fat but amiable Prince George, was still following the advice given him by King Charles, when he had consulted him on the best way of controlling his increasing obesity. Said Charles, 'Walk with me, hunt with my brother and do justice to my niece.'

Confident that Prince George was still firmly doing his duty, the Tories, the leaders of the Anglican Church, the staunch Protestants and the merchants of the City of London all felt that, although they now had in James a Papist on the throne, there was no danger of the succession being firmly in Roman Catholic hands. Moreover James, in the first few days of his reign, had made reassuring speeches in which he had declared that he would defend the liberty of the Church of England, which he knew to be pre-eminently loyal. Indeed it was, for the High Anglicans were imbued with the doctrine of the Divine Right of Kings. Even a wicked monarch had to be obeyed, if passively, in the hope of better things. He could not be legally resisted. Even Parliament, where the spirit of the Civil War and the Good Old Cause still lingered in some quarters, proved more than complaisant and voted the new king unprecedented sums. James thus began his reign under surprisingly favourable auspices. When the Duke of Monmouth landed in the West Country and the rebellion was put down with ferocity, the rest of the country remained passive. People were prepared to give James his chance. Yet in three short years he had thrown all these advantages away. His country was on the verge of rebellion.

The reason was quite simply that James was determined that the country should return to the Catholic faith and he set about realizing his object with a dull persistence that finally outraged the most loyal of his subjects. In vain the King wooed the Nonconformists by proclaiming a Declaration of Indulgence and easing the penal laws against them. He placed his own creatures in the Army, the Oxford colleges and on the judicial Bench. There were ambitious people in high places who were prepared to go along with this in the hope of office. Or they were just skilful survivors, like the celebrated Vicar of Bray:

When Royal James possessed the crown,
And popery grew in fashion,
The penal laws I hooted down
And read the Declaration:
The Church of Rome I found would fit
Full well my constitution,
And had become a Jesuit,
But for the Revolution.

The Revolution was indeed very near as the year 1688 unfolded. The Archbishop, Sancroft, had naturally reacted strongly against the first Declaration of Indulgence. When the second one was issued, even more comprehensive than the first, he felt that passive resistance could no longer prevent action. He and six of his bishops sent a petition against the new declaration to the King. James was outraged and determined to bring the Church of England to heel. He would prosecute the bishops for seditious libel. The whole country felt that the breaking point was now fast approaching. It was in this atmosphere of high tension, and even the most loyal of men were debating what they ought to do, when all Protestants felt that they were about to be engulfed by the Catholic tide, that James announced, with pride, that his wife was about to produce a child.

Never had a royal birth seemed more momentous. If the child turned out to be a daughter no one would worry overmuch. But what if it turned out to be a boy? A Prince of Wales, brought up by the Jesuits, to despise – perhaps even to persecute – the Protestant church! To the onlookers, the fate of the whole country seemed to turn on this pregnancy of Mary of Modena. Many of our kings have had large families. It is a patriotic duty for our queens to provide as many heirs to the throne as possible. In the old days this was a sensible insurance against the risks of fever, plague, miscarriage and all the ever-present menaces to health that children then ran. The birth of an heir was celebrated, but not with a feeling that the whole future of the nation depended on it. Her Majesty could be relied on to provide a replacement in case of disaster.

This birth would certainly be different. For the first and only time the vast majority of the king's subjects dreaded the birth of a Prince of Wales. James, naturally, took a different view. As he pushed the Catholic cause forward with grim determination, he knew that he needed a son to complete the good work. In this his church strongly encouraged him. Before she died, his mother-in-law, the dowager

Duchess of Modena, had presented a golden heart to the shrine of Our Lady at Loreto in the pious hope of encouraging her daughter to produce the longed-for heir. Not to be outdone, James himself took his wife to the famous shrine of St Winefriede at Holywell in North Wales. This holy well had been one of the most popular places of pilgrimage in the whole of Britain in the Middle Ages.

St Winefriede – Gwenffrewi in Welsh – was a North Wales princess whose head had been hacked off by a neighbouring prince, intent on rape. Her uncle, St Beuno, luckily appeared and used his power to restore her head to her shoulders. But where it had fallen a miraculous fountain burst forth which soon acquired a reputation for curing almost anything, and which was especially useful in cases of infertility. Even the Reformation could not stop the pilgrimages, and the graceful arches set up by Henry VII's mother, the Lady Margaret Beaufort, are still reflected in the quiet waters.

James made his earnest prayers to the saint, and Mary offered to the shrine part of the shift worn by Mary, Queen of Scots, at her execution. Perhaps they both felt that a Welsh saint would be the appropriate saint to produce a Prince of Wales. Whatever the cause, less than fifteen months later Mary declared that she was pregnant. The long awaited, much prayed-for miracle had taken place. James, sustained by his faith and encouraged by the Jesuits, was sure that the child would be a boy. Immediately the attention of both sides was focused on the embarrassed and perhaps over-modest Queen. The prayers of all Catholics, from the newly converted to the old faithful, went up continually from every available altar, while Protestant spies prowled around the palace ready to pick up every scrap of gossip from servants, pages and footmen.

No one was more anxious for reliable news than William of Orange on whom the Protestant lords had firmly placed their hopes for the future. He had an efficient spy organization headed by a canny Scot, James Johnstone, who seems to have had an excellent source of information in Margaret Dawson, bedchamber-woman to the Queen and a close friend of Johnstone's sister. Through Mrs Dawson we have an unrivalled picture of almost every day in the arrival of a new Prince of Wales.

The pregnancy had been first announced on 23 December 1687, and a Day of Thanksgiving was appointed for 15 January 1688, in London. Immediately doubts and debates over the event swept the country. The Opposition proclaimed that the whole business was a trick. Lord Clarendon dutifully attended the Thanksgiving service and then noted in his diary: 'It is strange how the Queen's great belly is everywhere ridiculed as if scarce anybody believes it to be true. Good God help us!'

Princess Anne was naturally deeply concerned with the affair, for if Mary of Modena produced a son, her own chance of succeeding to the throne would disappear. Portly Anne was not devoid of ambition and was as fervent a High Anglican as James was a Catholic. As a young girl, she had been taken away from her Catholic parents, on the command of Charles II, in order that she should be brought up in the faith of the Established Church. As a result she was rather afraid of her father, and perhaps slightly jealous of her younger mother-in-law. In March she noted that James's wife, no doubt out of excessive modesty, was refusing to let her ladies of the bedchamber see her undressing and did not allow them to carry out the long-practised ritual of touching her belly to confirm the pregnancy. Anne wrote to her sister in Holland, 'Her being so positive it will be a son, and the principles of that religion being such that they will stick at nothing, be it never so wicked, if it will promote their interest, give cause to fear there may be foul play intended.'

Anne became more and more suspicious as the lying-in time approached. Again she wrote to her sister in The Hague, 'Nobody will be convinced it is her child, except it prove a daughter. For my part I declare I shall not, except I see the child and she parted.'

This was just what Anne did not see. Mary of Modena was convinced that her baby would be born in June, while her doctors were equally certain that it would be born in July. James believed the doctors and allowed Anne to go to Bath for a cure, but Mary was right. The King wanted his son to be born in London and had selected St James's Palace as the scene for one of the most important events of his reign. As the time had been officially miscalculated, a room had to be hurriedly prepared. On the morning of Trinity Sunday, 10 June, it became clear that the birth could not be long delayed. The required witnesses were hurriedly rounded up. It had long been one of the duties of the members of the Great Council of State to be present at an important royal birth in order to make certain of its legitimacy. Until the eighteenth century, their lordships did not wait tactfully in an antechamber. They had to be in the bedroom itself and see the arrival of the prince – or princess – with their own eyes. These important officials fairly raced to the palace, for the Queen was now well advanced in labour. They arrived in the nick of time. They were admitted to the bedchamber at nine and the child was born just before ten o'clock.

We have detailed descriptions of the scene. We know the size and shape of the room – it was strangely small for the importance of the occasion and the witnesses were crowded around the bed. The fug in the room must have been overwhelming for, although it was mid-summer, there was a fire burning in the grate and it is probable that the windows were shut. The conception of the baby had been hailed as miraculous but the real miracle was its survival for a minute in such an atmosphere!

We know exactly where every witness stood in relation to the un-happy Queen, as her labour progressed and her distress increased. The King stood at the foot of the bed. He had refused to listen to his wife's natural pleas that the curtains of the four-poster should be drawn. Lady Sunderland was on the left at the head of the bed and next to her were Lady Roscommon and Lady Bellasyse. The midwife, Jane Wilks, was seated and had her French assistant with her. The Queen Dowager, the widow of Charles II, was also seated in a chair specially placed for her at the foot of the bed to the left of the King. Along the right-hand side of the bed was ranged a row of the high officers of the Council of State including Jeffreys, the Lord Chancellor, and Sunderland, the Lord President of the Council. Other statesmen were crowded around them until the small room seemed packed with all the great men of the realm. Lost somewhere among them was the Queen's laundress.

Also present was that intriguing political figure, Sidney Godolphin. Godolphin was one of those people who are essential to every govern-ment. He was a financial expert and no king or queen could do without him. He served in turn Charles II, James II, William and Mary and Anne. He was a sort of political Vicar of Bray on a grand scale. Or perhaps he was Britain's first top-level civil servant. As with everything in his life – even with his horse-racing at Newmarket, where he played a major part in improving our bloodstock – he calculated his exact position in that crowded room. He decided to stay by the fire. He could then claim, in the event of an uncertain future, that although he had fulfilled his duty by being present, he had not been able to see the actual bed. As that shrewd and witty judge of character, King Charles, had said of him; 'Little Sidney Godolphin is never in the way or out of the way!'

There was any amount of impeccable witnesses who had stood close to the bed, men and women whose honour and veracity could not be questioned, but the suspicious Protestants pointed to notable absentees. The Princess Anne, they claimed, had been lured away to Bath by a trick, but where were her uncles, the Lords Clarendon and Rochester? Or the Dutch ambassador to represent William of Orange? The Arch-bishop of Canterbury was also absent but for a very good reason. James had just clapped him and six of his colleagues into the Tower of London preparatory to their standing trial for seditious libel.

There can be no doubt, however, that a child was born to Mary of Modena in that small, stuffy room. But no sooner had the baby appeared than a strange, and in the light of all the suspicion that had gathered around the event, an unfortunate incident occurred. Lady Sunderland and the midwives immediately took the infant and carried it through a door at the head of the bed into an adjoining room. In a few moments, the King followed them leaving consternation behind him. The bedroom had been so crowded that very few persons had seen the child clearly. An excited buzz of questioning filled the stifling chamber, 'What is it? What is it?' In about five minutes the King emerged and announced that the baby was a boy. Members of the Council then followed him back and viewed the child in the next room. With that, the rest of the witnesses had to be content.

Today, after all the evidence has been examined – and James himself supplied much of it through the commission he set up four months later – it is impossible to believe that the King or Queen would be party to such an arrant imposture. No question but that the boy was the son of James and Mary. But the whole atmosphere of the country had now been poisoned by suspicion and by fear of a Catholic Prince of Wales. The wildest rumours were believed. Mary's child had been born dead and a substitute had been smuggled in to the next room from the convent adjacent to St James's. Again, it was claimed that the child was the son of a miller and had been smuggled into the palace in a warming-pan! Absurd as this story seems, it gained strength and eventually held the field. The new Prince of Wales was soon being taunted as 'James o' the Mill' just as his great-grandfather had to put up with the shouts of 'Jimmy Davidson'. That unfortunate carrying of the infant so quickly into the next room, although it may have been done purely to get him out of that incredible fug in the birth chamber, gave the Protestant pamphleteers full scope for their imagination.

James seemed, for the moment, to be blind to all the rumours and insults. He christened his son James Francis Edward with the Francis taken from the Catholic saint, St Francis Xavier. This did not please the Protestants. They were even more outraged when the Pope was invited to be godfather. James immediately proclaimed his son Prince of Wales. He was now certain that Heaven was on his side. In complete confidence he ordered the trial of the seven bishops.

His subjects felt no such surge of confidence in the future. Now there was a Catholic Prince of Wales firmly blocking the path to peace and progress as the Protestants saw it. The time had come to strike a decisive blow at the tyrant. On 30 June, twenty days after the birth of the Prince, the bishops were acquitted and the Army, into which James had so carefully infiltrated Catholic officers, cheered the result of the trial in their camp on Hounslow Heath. On the same day a letter, signed by leading statesmen both Whig and Tory and also bearing the name of the Bishop of London, was secretly dispatched to William of Orange inviting him to come over with an army to insist that James should summon a freely elected Parliament. This would surely settle the grievances of the Protestants once and for all. High among these grievances was the doubt about the paternity of the Prince of Wales. The letter of invitation had no hesitation in claiming that he was not legitimate.

It said, of the birth, that 'the false imposing of that upon the nation, being not only an infinite exasperation of men's minds here, but being certainly one of the chief causes upon which the declaration of your entering the kingdom in a hostile manner must be founded in your part.'

William was cautious and waited to make certain of his support before acting, but on 5 November he landed at Torbay at last. James might have confronted him, and who knows what might have happened if the King had stood his ground. But James had already been shaken by the desertion of leading men all around him. The Churchills had persuaded Princess Anne to leave the cause of her father. Prince George departed too. 'What, is *Est-il-possible* gone too?' said the King. 'After all, a good trooper would have been a greater loss.'

Soon it became clear that James did not have even one good trooper left. William had reached the outskirts of London. The capital was in an uproar and the King was laying his plans for flight. His first thought was to send the Prince of Wales across the Channel to the safety of France. He entrusted the precious child to Lord Dover who immediately carried the Prince down to Portsmouth. There he gave the King's orders to Lord Dartmouth, who was in command of the fleet. To his consternation, Dartmouth refused to take the child. No one had been more loyal than Dartmouth. He had done his best to intercept William's expedition as it came through the Channel, but contrary winds had kept his ships in port. But he was also a zealous Protestant. With sorrow, and after much heart-searching, he explained his dilemma in a humble and honest letter to his king. A Prince of Wales ought to remain in the country to be brought up in the faith of the Established Church. Dartmouth ended by saying he was prepared to lay down his life for the throne but he could not betray his religion by transporting the heir to the throne to a hostile country.

Perforce the seven-month-old child had to be brought back to London, to a city which was now almost completely in the hands of William and his supporters. Clearly James had come to the point when he dared not trust even the most loyal of his subjects. Yet it was now desperately urgent to get not only the Prince but his mother, the Queen, out of England into safety. In this crisis he turned to a remarkable Frenchman who had been living in exile in his court, Antoine, Duke of Lauzun. The life of Lauzun, it was said, had been stranger than the dreams of other people. He had been the favourite of Louis XIV in his youth and had aspired to marriage with La Grande Mademoiselle. This would have brought him into the magic circle of the members of the royal family itself. He had soared too high. He suddenly found himself flung into an Alpine fortress. He never lost his courage or his hope. He went in and out of royal favour as fast as he went in and out of the royal prisons. This gallant and accomplished courtier was now prepared to risk his life in repayment of the hospitality he had received from James. He agreed to convey the Queen and her child through a violently hostile London to a ship moored at Gravesend. He brought with him a trusted friend, M. St Victor.

James brought them secretly into the palace at night. Lauzun gave the Queen his hand and St Victor wrapped the Prince up in a warm cloak. They slipped out of the palace by the back-stairs and walked through the rain to a boat moored on the Thames. The night was wild and stormy. The short journey across the Thames was hazardous in the extreme. The little boat rocked and tossed in the waves, but at last they got to the south bank. Lauzun had arranged for a coach to be waiting at a riverside inn at Lambeth, but Mary was afraid to enter the inn. She feared that her face might be recognized. With the child in her arms she sheltered against the storm under the tower of Lambeth church. The two waiting women with her could not speak English and she feared that their foreign accents might betray them all. Suddenly a light flashed on their faces. Had they been discovered? Luckily it was the ostler who Lauzun had sent to bring them to the waiting coach.

Thankfully the little party crowded into the darkened vehicle and set off through the storm, with St Victor riding behind to protect them. The fury of the storm was an even better protection. At last they reached Gravesend where they found the yacht waiting for them. On board were Lord Powis and his wife and three Irish officers who had sworn to protect the heir to the throne with their lives. The yacht put out into the gale and the rain concealed them from any watcher on shore. As they slipped in the darkness down the Thames, the wind moderated· and the yacht turned towards France and safety.

Rain, storm and darkness may have been the fitting accompaniments for the departure from his native land of a prince whose long, disappointing life was to be full of them! He never set foot in England again for the whole seventy-eight years of his unhappy exile. He became the Prince over the Water and then – to most of the men who might have become his subjects – not the king but the 'Old Pretender'! It was not long before his father, after many adventures which mingled tragedy with farce and excitement with insult, followed his Queen and his son to the safety of France.

The royal fugitives received a most royal welcome from the King of France. Macaulay gave a memorable description of the splendours of the reception of Mary and the little Prince of Wales.

As soon as the news that the Queen of England was on the French coast had been brought to Versailles a palace was prepared for her reception. Carriages and troops of guards were dispatched to await her orders. Workmen were employed to mend the Calais road that her journey might be easy. Lauzun was not only assured that his past offences were forgiven for her sake, but was honoured with a friendly letter in the handwriting of Louis. Mary was on the road towards the French court when news came that her husband had, after a rough voyage, landed safely at the little village of Ambleteuse. Persons of high rank were instantly dispatched from Versailles to greet and escort him. Meanwhile Louis, attended by his family and his nobility, went forth in state to receive the exiled Queen. Before his gorgeous coach went the Swiss halberdiers. On each side of it and behind it rode the bodyguards with cymbals clashing and trumpets pealing. After the King, in a hundred carriages each drawn by six horses, came the most splendid aristocracy of Europe, all feathers, ribands, jewels, and embroidery. Before the procession had gone far it was announced that Mary was approaching. Louis alighted and advanced on foot to meet her. She broke forth into passionate expressions of gratitude. 'Madam,' said her host, 'it is but a melancholy service that I am rendering to you today. I hope that I may be able hereafter to render you services greater and more pleasing.' He embraced the little Prince of Wales and made the Queen seat herself in the royal state coach on his right hand. The cavalcade then turned towards St Germain.

The palace of St Germain now became the new Stuart court. Here James was reunited with his Queen and his son. Louis himself escorted him to the Queen's room. 'Here,' said Louis, 'is a gentleman you will be very glad to see.' The exiles were even gladder to see the princely pensions Louis immediately granted them – forty-five thousand pounds sterling a year, with a further ten thousand more for their immediate needs. Moreover Louis ordered that James and Mary were to receive full royal honours as if they were still in their own country. The courtiers who had followed them into exile soon gathered around. St Germain became a replica of Whitehall.

It is impossible not to admire the magnificent kindness of the King of France to his unfortunate brother monarch. Macaulay noted that European opinion – Catholic Europe at any rate – was deeply impressed: 'in truth his conduct was marked by a chivalrous generosity and urbanity, such as had not embellished the annals of Europe since the Black Prince had stood behind the chair of King John at the supper on the field of Poitiers.'

The country he had recently deserted, and from which he had taken away their Prince of Wales, could not be expected to appreciate all the finer points of the chivalry of Louis XIV. He was now their enemy and the Prince of Wales would be brought up on enemy soil in the religion abhorred in England. Indeed was James Francis Edward still legally the Prince of Wales? He had been so entitled at his christening in October 1688, and that ceremony had taken place on English soil. But now his father had been legally excluded from the throne. This was occupied jointly by William of Orange and James's daughter, Mary. The Prince of Wales was surely excluded, too. No matter how he was entitled in the shadow court of St Germain, he had now no legal standing in England.

The little boy who had been smuggled out of the country he might one day have ruled, wrapped in a thick cloak, grew up in the strange atmosphere of a court in exile, surrounded by plots and counter-plots, hopes excited and disappointed, powerless people given meaningless honours, and always surrounded by courtiers out of touch with the realities of Britain who reassured him that he was the rightful prince and that, one day come what may, he would return to the throne of his fathers in spite of every twist and turn of fortune.

But always there was one irremovable obstacle that stood in the way of the realization of this glittering dream. The young Prince was being brought up as a Roman Catholic. At the age of twelve he went in great state through Paris to make his First Communion. A medal was even struck to mark the occasion. His education was perforce a French education. He might carefully cultivate his English and study his English history and law, but his mind was bound to take a great deal of its colour from the foreign atmosphere that surrounded him and from the French statesmen whose money sustained his father's court.

At St Germain, Mary of Modena presented her husband with a little girl, which rather settles any doubts about the paternity of James Francis Edward. We have a touching picture by Largillière which shows the Prince of Wales, at the age of six, taking his sister by the hand. As was the custom in those days, both children are dressed in formal clothes which are miniature versions of the court dress of their parents. The little boy seems to look out at us from rather sad eyes set in a solemn face. And no wonder! He may have already sensed the trials and tribulations that the future held for him.

In 1700 an event occurred that seriously affected the fortune of the young Prince of Wales in exile. Anne had produced one child who had succeeded in surviving the long procession of miscarriages and deaths in infancy that made up the sad record of her career as a mother. In 1700, the Duke of Gloucester was eleven years old. By all accounts he was a well-disposed child although hardly a brilliant scholar. That could not be expected from the phlegmatic Anne and the torpid George, but the very fact that he was alive had a vital importance in the politics of Britain. Anne would obviously make the Duke of Gloucester her Prince of Wales when she came to the throne. Since 1688 the Tories, who had reluctantly and, as they hoped, temporarily abandoned their theory of the Divine Right of Kings, had consoled their consciences with the thought that, as long as the Duke of Gloucester lived, a branch of the Stuart line – all good Protestants – would occupy the throne. The High Churchmen had also waived their devotion to non-resistance with the same consoling thought. The birthday of the little Duke had been joyfully celebrated at Windsor with splendid parties and a magnificent fireworks display. But in July the Duke of Gloucester died and with him died all the hopes of the Tories. The whole business of the succession became once again a burning political problem.

To the out-and-out Jacobites James II was still their lawful King and his son, James Francis Edward, their lawful Prince of Wales. But not even the most right-wing Tory or firm High Churchman would dream of restoring James and his son as long as they remained Catholic. There was naturally no hope that the exiled King would change his religion. After all, he had abandoned his earthly kingdom in the sure hope, as promised him by the Jesuits, that at least he would inherit the Kingdom of Heaven. The Prince of Wales however, could be certain of the succession only if he turned apostate. There were plenty of precedents for convenient religion conversion. The French Protestant leader, Henry IV, had done it the other way in order to make himself the undisputed King of France. His blithe statement, 'Paris is worth a Mass', throws as much light on the strength of his religious conviction as on his political sagacity. James Francis Edward was no Henry IV. The solemn young boy who had gone in such state to celebrate his First Communion in Notre Dame would never abandon his faith for the sake of a coronation in Westminster Abbey.

Once again the politicians had to study the form-book. The question was; 'Who would succeed Anne, who now had no son?' The Acts of Parliament passed after the Glorious Revolution of 1688 had not envisaged this question. They had debarred any Papist from coming to the throne but had settled the succession on William and Mary and afterwards on Anne. Now the line of the Protestant Stuarts seemed to be running out. Back everyone had to go to look at other offspring of Charles I. Charles had had four surviving children. Charles II and James II are already accounted for. The youngest daughter, Mary, had married William II of Orange, and it was her son, William III who had married James II's daughter, Mary. There were no children by this marriage. This line was obviously sterile.

But what about Charles's youngest daughter, Henrietta, who had married Philip, Duke of Orleans? Their daughter, Anna Maria, had married Victor Amadeus, Duke of Savoy. Savoy was the little duchy that straddled both sides of the Western Alps. The couple had produced a son and he was clearly first in the running. The suggestion had long been mooted that this young prince should be sent to England and brought up as a Protestant. The father was no religious zealot. Victor Amadeus was only too pleased to put his son in for the Succession Stakes. But if he was flexible in religion, he was a little too flexible in politics.

In the great war with France that followed the expulsion of James II, Victor Amadeus had been on the Protestant side, but he had then made one of his crafty political changes and gone over to Louis XIV. He was never forgiven. When peace was signed at Ryswick in 1697, William III set his face firmly against any Savoyard candidate. The heir to Savoy stayed at home, remained a Catholic, was crossed out of the running and England thus missed having her first Prince of Wales who spoke fluent French and Italian!

Where, then, was the desirable Protestant heir to be found. The descendants of James II had been eliminated. So had those of Charles I. There was nothing for it but to go further back still, to James I. And here, once again, the tragic and beautiful figure of Elizabeth of Bohemia, the 'Winter Queen', reappears in our history. In the midst of her trials her daughters turned Catholic – all except one, Sophia. Thackeray calls her 'one of the handsomest, the most cheerful, shrewd, accomplished of women.' He continues that 'she remained, I cannot say faithful to the reformed religion, but at least she adopted no other.' At least she had married a solid Protestant, Ernest Augustus of Brunswick who became the first Elector of Hanover. We shall look again at the character of this jovial and hard-headed prince and at his remarkable wife. For the moment, the important thing to note about them is that they had remained Protestants. Not without temptation to change sides, of course. That was a continuous temptation in the troubled world of the late seventeenth century. But they treated the affair with cool sensibility. Again Thackeray sums it up:

> An agent of the French King's, Gourville, a convert himself, strove to bring her and her husband to the sense of the truth; and tells us that he one day asked Madame the Duchess of Hanover of what religion her daughter was, then a pretty girl of thirteen years old. The Duchess replied that the Princess *was of no religion yet.* They were waiting to know of what religion her husband would be, Protestant or Catholic, before instructing her! And the Duke of Hanover, having heard all Gourville's proposal, said that a change would be advantageous to his house, but that he himself was too old to change.

So it was that the Electress Sophia and her descendants took first place in the race for the succession. King William approved. The Electress had her doubts and professed her unwillingness to accept this potentially dangerous inheritance. William himself pleaded with her to agree. Finally she gave her consent. On 3 March 1701, the House of Commons passed the Act of Settlement which ensured that the crown would, on the death of the childless Anne, go to the House of Hanover. It was this Act that made it possible for George I to succeed without too much difficulty in 1714 and start the long series of Hanoverian Princes of Wales. Whatever may be said about them, they were certainly different from the Stuart and Tudor princes who had gone before them!

Meantime, across the water, the Stuart Prince of Wales in exile was facing another violent change in his fortunes. In the spring of 1700 it was clear that James II was dying. This had certainly drawn the attention of William and the English Parliament to the succession problem and had hastened their determination to prepare the Act. It was also rumoured that William had been determined to push on with it because he was suspicious of Anne's reputed tenderness for the exiled Prince of Wales. She might be tempted to bequeath the throne to him after her death. James II left a paper giving an account of some supposed suggestion of Anne's to him that she should come to the throne and then leave it to James Francis Edward. There is no trace of such a correspondence. William had not been on good terms with Anne. She and her favourite, Sarah Churchill, called him 'Mr Caliban'. The King wanted to make certain that there was no danger of the Protestant succession failing.

By September 1701, it was obvious that James II was on his deathbed. Then ensued the memorable scene so vividly described by Saint-Simon. He paints the picture of the anxieties and anguish that reigned in the court of the exile at St Germain. Says Saint-Simon:

> In these circumstances the King of France made a decision more worthy of the generosity of Louis XII or Francis I than of his wisdom. He went from Marly where he was staying to St Germain on Thursday, 3 September. The King of England was so ill that, when the King was announced to him, he could hardly open his eyes for a moment. The King told him that he could die in peace with respect to the Prince of Wales who he would recognize as King of England, Scotland and Ireland. The few Englishmen present flung themselves on their knees, but the King of England gave no sign of life. Soon afterwards the King repaired to the Queen of England to whom he gave the same assurance. They then sent for the Prince of Wales to whom they repeated it. One can picture the thankfulness and the expression of relief of the mother and the son. When he returned to Marly the King announced what he had done to the whole court. It was received with nothing but acclamation and praise.

There was no acclamation or praise in the courts of Protestant Europe. Saint-Simon relates that William received the news in his palace of Loo in Holland, while he was dining with some German princes. 'He spoke not a word; he turned red, crammed his hat down on his head and could scarcely control the expression on his face.' War was now inevitable – the War of the Spanish Succession, in which Marlborough won such glory and the new King of England in Exile lost all real hope of his restoration. Jacobite sympathizers might toast James under the safe title of the Chevalier de St George. And when King William died in 1702 after his horse had stumbled over a mole hill, they might also drink a toast to the mole as 'The Little Gentleman in Black Velvet', but most of them were more prepared to raise their glasses than rise in rebellion. Anne was now on the throne, 'the Church of England's Glory'. All parties from extreme Whig to high Tory supported her. There were some shadowy attempts to support the cause of James III in Scotland but they came to nothing. James always had the capacity for being in the wrong place at the right time.

On a warm summer night in August 1704, for example, he went with his mother, the Dowager Queen, as a special guest to a splendid fete given by Louis XIV, who at this date was waging war against England, the very country to which 'King James III' hoped to return and rule. The night was warm, the court at Versailles glittered with orders and diamonds; the nobility, beauty and wealth of France made a show of splendour unparalleled in Europe. A triumphal car carried the God of War, surrounded by warriors and nymphs past the Sun King. Then followed a pageant of the rivers of Europe in which the Thames, the Scheldt, the Meuse, the Neckar and the Danube paid tribute to the supremacy of the Seine. The pageant ended with a magnificent display of fireworks and the King of England and his mother drove home through the soft, consoling night convinced of the overwhelming power of their great protector. In the end he would surely restore them to their rightful heritage.

On that same night, the English army under Marlborough, after their astonishing march from the borders of Holland to the Danube, were joining the force of their ally, Prince Eugene, and beginning to take up their position opposite a little village called Blenheim on the banks of the very Danube that had figured as a tributary stream in the great pageant at Versailles. The next day they began their preliminary moves which resulted in the resounding victory that brought undying fame to Marlborough, new power to England and sent the first clouds of failure scudding across the military glory of the Sun King. Again, the Old Pretender had been in the wrong place!

In truth he lacked what it is now fashionable to call 'charisma' – that electric quality that gathers followers around you and which can even lead them to offer their lives in your cause. The Old Pretender's son had it, at least for a brief but memorable period. James III married a Polish princess, Clementina, who gave him two sons, Charles Edward and Henry. Henry, the youngest, became a cardinal in the Church of Rome, but Charles entered history as that 'Bonnie Prince Charlie' who we shall find casting a romantic sunset glow over the dying Stuart cause. He was the last Stuart 'Prince of Wales'.

All that lay in the future. In 1704 the present must have looked more than dismal to the Old Pretender. Anne was firmly on the throne of England and no one was prepared to displace her to put him in her place. Not that Anne had much charisma either. She was now almost an invalid and kept no brilliant court. Those who wanted favours usually went to the tactful Godolphin. The occasional receptions that she held for foreign ministers and diplomats must have been glum affairs. The diplomats sat for an hour in dead silence. One witness states that when visitors came to the palace, Anne never 'cared to have them come in to her, having little to say to them, but that it was either hot or cold'. What little exercise she took consisted in following the hunt at Windsor. Swift, in his *Journal to Stella*, noted – perhaps with tongue in cheek – 'She . . . hunts in a chaise with one horse which she drives herself and drives furiously like Jehu and a mighty hunter like Nimrod.' If she did drive furiously, then this was the only thing she did at speed during her whole career. In everything else she was slow and deliberate but also painstaking and conscientious. She listened to the brilliant talk of her close friend, Marlborough's wife, Sarah, but she did not forget her duty to consult her ministers and work hard at her state papers. She may have lacked glamour but she had honesty and a good heart. Not a bad combination for ruling England. So her reign, in spite of the dowdy Queen, ran a brilliant course. There were triumphs on the battlefield, great names in literature and a steady growth in industry and wealth.

At last, in the summer of 1714, the portly Queen who had done her best lay dying. The exiled court at St Germain throbbed with a new excitement. Perhaps Anne had, after all, made a will leaving the throne to her half-brother's son? The Tories might still take their courage in their hands and proclaim James III in London. The Elector of Hanover might refuse to carry out the terms of the Act of Settlement. The exiles hurried ahead with their intrigues, obscure negotiations and hasty military preparations. As had happened so often in the long history of the Stuart dynasty, all their hopes were destined to disappointment.

7

Hanoverian Horrors

'Th' illustrious house of Hanover
And Protestant succession,
To these I lustily will swear
While they can keep possession.'
From *The Vicar of Bray*

We move from the world of the Stuarts to that of the Hanoverians and immediately experience a sense of anticlimax. Whatever we may think of the Stuarts as statesmen and administrators, they certainly added colour and drama to our history. By contrast, the Hanoverian sovereigns seem dull, unattractive and, at times, positively repulsive. George I could hardly speak English when he landed on our shores in a fog in 1714, accompanied by a horde of German courtiers, two middle-aged mistresses whom his new subjects immediately christened 'The Maypole and The Elephant', and a son whom he soon made Prince of Wales and with whom he constantly quarrelled.

The nation accepted this strange foreign circus mainly because the rival show was more unattractive. Protestant Hanoverian George was preferable to the Catholic 'Old Pretender'. The Jacobite supporters had muffed their opportunity to proclaim James III in London. The leading men in England, and in Scotland as well, carried out the terms of the Act of Settlement, even if they did it in the spirit of the Vicar of Bray:

When George in pudding time came o'er,
And moderate men looked big, sir,
My principles I changed once more,
And so became a Whig, sir.
And thus preferment I procured
From our Faith's Great Defender,
And almost every day abjured
The Pope, and the Pretender.

Faith's Great Defender was a somewhat portly man of fifty-four, who had packed off his wife to life imprisonment in the castle of Ahlden for infidelity, who loved horses, eating, rather fat women and the music of Handel in that order and who was in no great hurry to take up his new inheritance. He was happy in his palace of Herrenhausen outside Hanover. In this miniature Versailles he enjoyed walking with his ladies through the formal gardens and kept his magnificent stables containing six hundred horses. Both our first two Georges felt more at home at Herrenhausen than at Kensington Palace, and it is easy to understand why. In Herrenhausen and the surrounding Electorate of Hanover, the Elector was monarch of all he surveyed. He was a benevolent despot and his subjects enjoyed his absolute yet easy-going rule. He was proud of the success of his ancestors in raising this once obscure part of the sandy North German plain into one of the nine Electorates which had the right of electing the Emperor of the Holy Roman Empire.

It was the father of our George I, Ernest Augustus, who finally achieved the electoral dignity. He also married Sophia, the daughter of Elizabeth of Bohemia, who, by the Act of Settlement, was the named successor to Queen Anne. Her eldest son, George Lewis, was born in 1660. Like most of his brothers he was packed off to the wars as soon as he grew up. He fought for the Emperor against the Turks and brought back two living trophies of his warlike prowess in the shape of two Turkish servants, Mohamet and Mustapha. Their images still look down on the Grand Staircase in Kensington Palace. Unfortunately, his marriage was not as successful as his battles.

In 1682, George Lewis married Sophia Dorothea, the daughter of the Duke of Celle. Ernest Augustus planned the marriage to assist the territorial expansion of his small state. Some diplomatic marriages turn out well but usually only if the wife exercises forbearance and common sense. Ernest Augustus's own marriage had been a success because Sophia, afterwards the Electress, was a highly intelligent and practical woman who turned a blind eye to his infidelities. George Lewis's Sophia Dorothea – how historians must wish that parents in these little German states were a little more imaginative when it came to naming their numerous offspring! – was not so forbearing. She was lively, pretty, intelligent and interested in the arts. She soon found herself at odds with her somewhat unimaginative husband, who later in life, after he had come to the English throne, declared that he 'hated all poets and painters'. He also had an official mistress at the time of his marriage – not a good omen for the success of his union with a spirited bride of sixteen.

The first child, George Augustus, destined to become our first Hanoverian Prince of Wales and afterwards George II, was born in 1683. George Lewis then went off to his Turkish wars and did not return until some years later, when his second child, a daughter, was born. After that, the marriage steadily drifted onto the rocks to end in a scandal and tragedy that became the sensation of the courts of Europe. It is worthwhile looking at the details of this strange affair, because it was probably the cause of hostility between George Lewis and his son George Augustus, a hostility which became almost a family tradition with our Hanoverian kings.

Horace Walpole maintained that it was caused by 'something in the Hanoverian blood'. In the nature of things there was always a tension between the monarch and his heir. We even see it under the Tudors and the Stuarts when the kings took special care over the education of their Princes of Wales, but in their case the tension was always relieved by the genuine affection between fathers and sons that soothed away any misunderstanding. In the case of the Hanoverians misunderstanding is hardly the word to use. Venomous hatred would be nearer the mark in the case of George II and his son Frederick, and there was certainly no love lost between George III and the Prince Regent. Did it all spring from the unhappy collapse of the marriage of George Lewis and Sophia Dorothea?

In 1689 a Swedish soldier, Count Philip von Königsmark, arrived at the Hanoverian court and was appointed a Colonel of Dragoons. Königsmark was everything that George Lewis was not – witty, handsome and elegant. He was also a bit of an adventurer and, by all accounts, a sexual athlete. He was bold enough to pay court to Sophia Dorothea and she soon became captivated by him. She was increasingly indiscreet in seeking his company and was warned by both Ernest Augustus and his wife to be more sensible of the social risks she was running. Did the pair actually become lovers? We cannot be sure, but rumours to this effect began to circulate in the courts of Europe. Königsmark was as indiscreet as Sophia Dorothea and boasted of the relationship in his cups in far too many German towns. Ernest Augustus had reached a critical stage in his scheme for becoming the ninth Elector. He became seriously worried. At this time, of all times, no scandal must be allowed to touch the court of Hanover. It was rumoured that the pair were about to elope and fly the country. They had crossed the borders of tolerance. Ernest Augustus determined to act.

Urged on, some say, by his *maitress en titre* the notorious Countess von Platen, nicknamed '*Die Böse*' – the Wicked One – a close watch was kept on the amorous conspirators. On 1 July 1694, Count Philip von Königsmark was seen by several witnesses to enter Sophia Dorothea's apartments. She herself was not there and George Lewis was out of Hanover, but Königsmark was never seen again. From here on, all is uncertain. Rumours ran like wildfire around the courts of Europe. One lurid story maintained that the Count had been enticed to the door of the apartments by a false message from von Platen and was then hacked to pieces at the door while the Countess watched from her coach. She got out and ground her heel on the dead man's face. The remains were then buried under the floorboards in the apartment. In plain truth, all we know for certain was that Königsmark disappeared and in all probability he was murdered.

The unhappy Sophia Dorothea was brought before the Consistory Court in Hanover, divorced from George Lewis and sent off to imprisonment at the castle of Ahlden. There she remained for the rest of her life. She was forbidden to remarry or to see her children. She seemed to have received a reasonable money allowance, and she could walk in the gardens and even go for short drives in the surrounding countryside, but when it came to any suggestion of her release, George Lewis remained implacable. He became Elector on his father's death in 1696, and then King of England, but he steadily refused to consider his divorced wife's friends' requests for her liberty. There were good political reasons for this. Jacobite agents were reported as trying to get in touch with the 'Queen of England'. But there may also have been deeper psychological motives behind George Lewis's conduct. The intercepted letters of the lovers, according to one account, contained wounding comparisons of George's performances in bed with those of Königsmark's. These comparisons touched George on his most sensitive spot, for he was proud of his prowess as a womanizer.

The effect of all this on his little son, who was nine years old at the time, can easily be imagined. George Augustus had been fond of his mother and now she had been ruthlessly torn away from him. The boy was fair haired like his mother, and every time he looked at him, George Lewis was reminded of memories he would have been happy to forget. Sophia Dorothea remained a forbidden subject between father and son. In his adolescence, the son was said to have tried to swim the moat at Ahlden in order to get in touch with her. He kept a miniature of her around his neck until the day he died.

George Lewis, now Elector, put his son through the usual princely paces of service in the army and then marriage. The bride chosen was Caroline of Anspach and the choice could hardly have been better. She was handsome and possessed a pair of magnificent breasts which she had no hesitation in displaying when the occasion required. Her submissive nature appealed to George. She also possessed what the Electress Sophia had, and which Sophia Dorothea lacked to her undoing – the ability to turn a blind eye to her husband's infidelities. All Hanoverians made unfaithful husbands, with the exception of poor George III. He, poor man, went mad instead!

Caroline established a powerful if carefully concealed influence over her husband, which was never fully appreciated until her death. The outside world was astonished at the extent of her husband's grief. She had borne her last illness with exemplary courage, but even on her death-bed she still thought only of her husband's future. She urged him to remarry as soon as possible. George paid her the highest compliment known to a Hanoverian husband. 'No, no,' he cried between his sobs, '*J'aurais des maitresses*' – I'll only have mistresses.

The Elector, George Lewis, looked with envy on this curious little oasis of domestic happiness in the midst of the formal, heartless and corrupt society of Herrenhausen. Not that young George was a model husband as far as sex was concerned, but the Elector could not help contrasting Caroline's understanding treatment of her erring partner with his own experience with Sophia Dorothea. His resentment grew when Garter Herald Lord Halifax was sent from England to present the Order of the Garter to George Augustus, who, after all, was the future Prince of Wales. The Elector behaved with even more unkindness when poor Caroline was expecting her first child. If it turned out to be a boy, he too would eventually become Prince of Wales.

As soon as the Elector heard that Caroline was in labour he banned everybody from her apartments except the doctor and the midwife. A guard was set on the door and stopped not only the old Electress Sophia from entering but kept out the husband as well. Outside, Hanover was in the grip of the wild Venetian carnival, introduced by the first Elector, Ernest, who had been enchanted with Venice and encouraged his subjects to let themselves go in the Italian style, if only once a year. The ensuing revels were more Breugel-like than Venetian and they were hardly an encouragement to Caroline in her first approach to motherhood. A future Prince of Wales was thus born with the doctor and midwife as the only witnesses. Even James II had done better than this. The husband was only allowed to see his son briefly some hours after the birth. The grandmother was banned altogether after she had suggested that the strange proceedings of the Elector might raise doubts about the paternity of the new arrival. The British envoy was kept in ignorance of the event which had a constitutional importance for his country, and the birth of Frederick Louis was not officially announced until a week later. After all this, it was no wonder that the rift deepened between George Lewis and his son, George Augustus.

Frederick Louis was not a healthy child. He had a slightly yellowish complexion and narrowly escaped the smallpox which had left pits on the face of his mother Caroline so deep that the thickest cosmetics could not disguise them. His parents nicknamed him the Griffin – *Der Greif* in German – from his supposed resemblance to this fabulous beast. When they came to England they referred to him, in their uncertain English, as the Griff. The name stuck. Frederick Louis was better-looking by the time he was two, but he remained the Griff throughout his life.

What a strange ménage it all was at Herrenhausen and Hanover city in the early months of 1714 as the electoral family waited to hear the famous announcement, *'Die Königin Anne ist tot'* – Queen Anne is dead! When the court adjourned to the summer palace of Herrenhausen, the Elector lived in its centre surrounded by his mistresses and their numerous offspring. Banished to a remote wing, far apart from the magnificent stables, the baroque theatre, and the Venetian gondolas floating on the moat, lived George Augustus, Caroline and the Griff, for whom his parents were beginning to feel the same Hanoverian revulsion as the Elector had felt for George Augustus. Then, away in London, on 1 August 1714, Dr John Arbuthnot, Queen Anne's personal physician and friend of Pope and Swift, announced that Queen Anne was really dead, or as he put it more elegantly, 'Sleep was never more welcome to a weary traveller than death was to her.'

The Elector had become King. George Lewis of Hanover was now George I of England, Scotland and Ireland. He spent a leisurely month making arrangements for the good government of his beloved Hanover in his absence, and appointed a Privy Council which included his younger brother Ernest Augustus the Prince-Bishop of Osnabruck. But he reserved all major decisions for himself. He felt it important, however, that a direct descendant of the family should still remain in Hanover as the formal head of the state.

His son was now almost automatically Prince of Wales, for the Hanoverians never attached any ceremony to the assumption of the title. Gone were the days of James I when the eldest son became Prince of Wales with all available splendour. George I declared that he disliked

Victoria, Albert and family.

Victoria, 'Bertie', the future Edward VIII, and his wife, Alexandra of Denmark.

Mrs. Keppel.

Lady Brooke.

Below *Sandringham, bought and rebuilt for 'Bertie' and Alexandra.*
Right *Queen Alexandra.*

*The Prince of Wales wins the Derby with
Persimmon in 1896.*

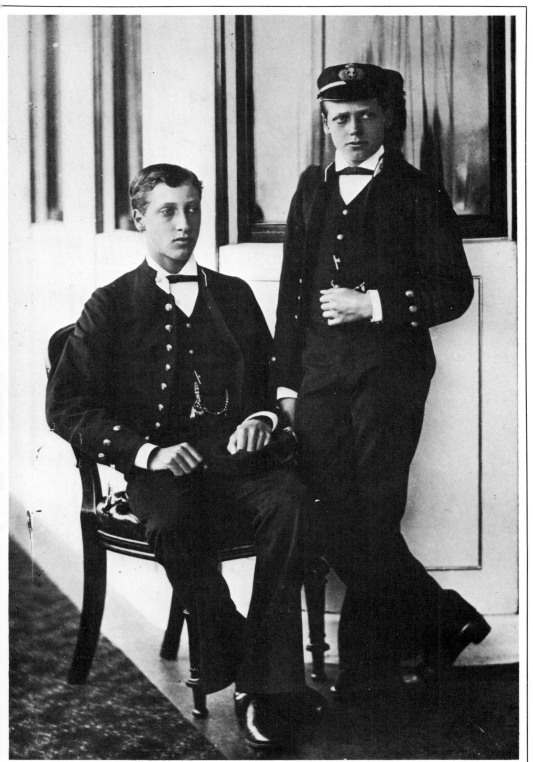

Prince Albert Victor and Prince George. 'Eddy' died in 1892, leaving George as heir to the throne.

Revival of the Investiture Ceremony. Queen Mary with Edward, Prince of Wales, at Caernarfon.

Edward, Prince of Wales, later Duke of Windsor.
Left *In Investiture robes.* Above *The Dancing Prince.*
Below *Another fall at steeplechasing.*

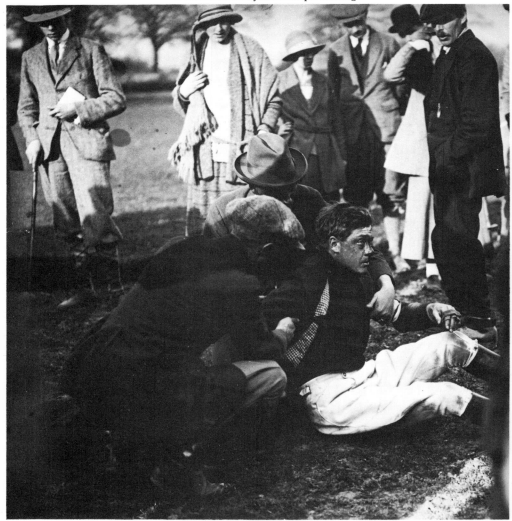

unnecessary expense. But the Prince of Wales, whether George liked it or not, had to accompany him on this first voyage to his new realm, and the Princess of Wales would follow with her daughters. But not with her eldest son. George I had made the harsh and extraordinary decision to separate the Griff from his mother and make this boy of seven the symbol of the dynasty's devotion to the Electorate. Little Frederick Louis, suitably escorted, would preside at all formal occasions, while a portrait of George I in his electoral robes would be placed on the throne. This strange arrangement might have suited the new king; it had a disastrous effect on the Griff.

Meanwhile, the long procession of coaches carrying George's mistresses, the new Prince of Wales, the hordes of Hanoverian courtiers, Mustapha and Mohamet, fourteen cooks and one washerwoman rumbled across Europe into Holland, to embark, for the first time for many of the reluctant travellers, on the uncertain waters of the North Sea. Their voyage ended at Greenwich on 18 September, when they found England wrapped in a dense fog – which was exactly what the King and his Hanoverians expected.

George I may not have had the graces of Charles II or the domestic virtues of Charles I, but he was no fool when it came to the study of man. He knew well enough why he had been invited to occupy the English throne, and he did not court or expect popularity. His English was not as sparse as had been suggested although the Prince of Wales could speak the language better than his father. This was one of the sources of the irritation that possessed the King about his son. A stronger irritant was soon supplied. Parliament had voted the Prince of Wales a surprisingly generous income, which was further increased by the revenues of the Duchy of Cornwall. The Prince was financially independent and could therefore take an independent line with his father. Inevitably the Prince of Wales became the centre of those discontented with the new regime, especially after the collapse of the Jacobite causes after 1715.

The Jacobites had raised the standard of revolt in Scotland under the irresolute Earl of Mar, known as 'Bobbing John', Stuart history had a habit of repeating its ill omens. When Charles I had raised his standard at Nottingham at the start of the Civil War it was blown down. When the Earl of Mar raised his standard at Braemar, the golden ball at the top of the flagstaff fell off into the mud. An ill-managed attempt at invasion of England was defeated at Preston and Mar himself fought an indecisive battle at Sheriffmuir, after which his Highland supporters went off home. The Old Pretender, as usual, was in the wrong place at the wrong moment. By the time he had landed at Peterhead in Aberdeenshire the Jacobite cause had been lost. He was not the man to revive it. As one Scot wrote, 'When we saw the man whom they called our king, we found ourselves not at all animated by his presence; if he was disappointed with us, we were ten-fold more so with him.'

The English could have said the same about George I. They saw their new Hanoverian ruler as cold, tight with money, totally lacking in charm and surrounded by rapacious courtiers with 'cacophonous, out-landish German names'. But, after the failure of the rising, the Pretender could no longer be a safe rallying point for discontent. The Whigs held all the places of power and were to retain them for the whole period of the first two Georges. Politics thus developed into a game of intrigue between the 'ins' and the 'outs'. The 'outs' naturally turned to the Prince of Wales.

Tension began to show itself between King and Prince when George I, in 1717, decided that it was now safe for him to risk a visit to Hanover, after the fading of the Jacobite threat. Normally, the Prince of Wales should have been his first choice as Regent. George was quite prepared to give his son extensive powers in his absence, and drew up elaborate instructions for him. This would be a useful exercise in government for the man who would one day inherit the throne. But the title of Regent was another matter. It smacked too much of setting up a rival power to the throne. The lawyers obligingly ferreted in the dusty files of our past history and discovered that, in similar circumstances, the Black Prince had been entitled Guardian of the Realm. This antique title temporarily soothed the feeling of both Prince and King.

As usual in every family quarrel, there are two sides to the dispute. In the matter of the Regency the King had common sense on his side. On the next occasion of friction, the blame cannot be attached to the Prince. This celebrated explosion of fury between father and son fascinated high society in 1717. The Princess of Wales had given birth to her second son. The Prince dutifully invited the King to be one god-father and notified him that he proposed asking his uncle, Ernest Augustus, Prince-Bishop of Osnabruck, to be the second. George immediately overruled the Prince and ordered him to invite the Duke of Newcastle to undertake the duty. Newcastle was Lord Chamberlain and, by a long established custom in Britain, the Lord Chamberlain was always asked to be one of the godfathers to royal children of importance.

Newcastle was one of the curiosities of British politics in the first half of the eighteenth century. He wasn't a man of outstanding intellectual gifts and his eccentricities of speech and behaviour in later life made him a favourite for that supreme gossip, Horace Walpole. Walpole's picture of the Duke at the funeral service of George II gives you the full flavour of this curious man.

> The grave scene was fully contrasted by the burlesque Duke of Newcastle. He fell into a fit of crying the moment he came into the chapel, and flung himself back in a stall, the Archbishop hovering over him with a smelling-bottle; but in two minutes his curiosity got the better of his hypocrisy and he ran about the chapel with his glass to spy who was or was not there, spying with one hand, and mopping his eyes with the other. Then returned the fear of catching cold; and the Duke of Cumberland, who was sinking with heat, felt himself weighed down, and turning round, found it was the Duke of Newcastle standing upon his train, to avoid the chill of the marble.

Yet this somewhat ludicrous figure was a key man in the political life of Britain for nearly forty years. The reason was simple. Thomas Pelham Holles was a very rich man who controlled any number of pocket boroughs, but he brought more to politics than his riches. He was prepared to go to endless lengths to cultivate his fellow members of Parliament. He had a prodigious memory and could assess the interests of every man in that strange world of secret compacts and family loyalties uncovered by the researches of Sir Lewis Namier. He became the king of patronage in Britain. Not even bishops could hope to get appointed without a word from Newcastle to the King. Such a man was not likely to forget his privileges as Lord Chamberlain.

The Prince had perforce to agree to Newcastle's presence, but as soon as the ceremony was over, he turned in fury on the trembling Newcastle, among whose qualities personal courage did not rank high. He shook his fist under the nose of the Duke and apparently shouted, 'I will find you out.' The Prince's English might still have been a little guttural and Germanic, for Newcastle thought that he had said 'I'll fight you out', and that the Prince was challenging him to a duel. He immediately ran to the King and bumbled out his story. The King was furious and, after elaborate inquiries, he stopped short of his first intention of flinging the Prince into prison. Instead he banished the Prince and Princess from their apartments in St James's Palace, while ordering their three children to remain. This was harsh punishment indeed for a trivial offence, and unwise as well. The Prince and Princess of Wales set up house in Leicester Fields, Leicester Square, which immediately became the centre of a little court, frequented not only by the dissatisfied but by the lively and intelligent who would have found the official court at St James's dull and unsatisfying. By his own act, the King had created a rallying point for the Opposition.

People were not wanting who carried to the King's ear all the malicious gossip about the court of the Prince of Wales. George I, like all the Hanoverians, delighted in bawdy talk, and relished the story, related by his Hanoverian court official Schulenburg, of the unfortunate predicament of one of the ladies-in-waiting at a levee of the Prince of Wales. Etiquette demanded that she should stay firmly in her place in the circle around the Princess of Wales, until at last overcome by necessity, she was forced to relieve herself where she stood. Whereupon, says Schulenburg, 'a puddle the size of a table to seat ten' spread almost to the feet of the Princess and made compulsory viewing for the guests. The eighteenth century could always be relied on to mingle coarseness with splendour!

Some curious constitutional consequences followed from the quarrel between the King and the Prince. The Prince of Wales ceased to attend the Cabinet meetings, where he had acted as interpreter for his father. Modern historians have modified the old, simple view that it was George's lack of English that forced him to leave the business of government in the hands of his ministers – hence the beginning of our modern Parliamentary democracy. It is true that George gradually withdrew from the meeting of the Cabinet. But he always received his ministers in his private closet and all measures still had to be approved by him. The King remained a very powerful part of the governmental machinery.

Yet the very fact that he was no longer present when the measures were first discussed in detail meant that the ministers not the King were imperceptibly moving towards the centre of the stage. They were the people who would have to steer those measures through Parliament. Throughout the eighteenth century, our modern system of cabinet government steadily took shape.

No one played a greater part in this process than Sir Robert Walpole, the squire from Norfolk. This extraordinary man, a master in the art of managing Parliament, a total realist in his attitude to human nature – his favourite phrase was 'Every man has his price' – set himself out to achieve power with a ruthless determination to employ all his skill in intrigue. His policy was peace abroad, prosperity at home. Not an ignoble programme. Not for him the high drama and romance of the Stuarts. The matter-of-fact Hanoverians suited him perfectly.

He had a long and devious way to travel before he came to power. In the opening years of the reign, Sunderland and Stanhope were the leading lights, both brilliant statesmen of aristocratic lineage. Walpole was a parvenu compared to them, even after he had become the brother-in-law of his Norfolk neighbour, Viscount Townsend. Townsend's title was also a recent creation. Together they formed what we might now call 'The Norfolk Mafia'. They succeeded in worming their way into the Government, but neither the King nor the Prince of Wales really liked them. The Prince regarded Walpole as a designing rascal. This did not disconcert Walpole for a moment. Confident that his time would come, he paid his court instead to the Princess of Wales. A strong bond was established between Walpole and Caroline. Walpole liked lively, witty and intelligent women, and she, with her growing interest in politics, appreciated his skill in managing men. This understanding between princess and politician was to be of prime importance in our history.

Walpole decided that his first step to power would be facilitated if he could stage a reconciliation between the Prince and the King. The King may not have cared less if he never spoke to his son again, but the country would approve of the healing of the breach. Walpole could rely on the Princess of Wales to put pressure on her husband, but the King presented a more difficult problem. Walpole cleverly dangled an irresistible temptation before him. George's Civil List was £600,000 in debt. Only one man could get Parliament to agree to clear it – Walpole. The King accepted the offer and the reconciliation scene was duly staged. Lady Cowper, a lady-in-waiting to the Princess of Wales, has left us a description of the scene after the Prince had gone in to see the King alone in his private closet. The courtiers clustered around the door and tried to overhear the conversation. They heard the King's voice raised, crying '*Votre conduite, votre conduite* . . .' But quite what the King had said about the conduct of the Prince no one could discover. Later on, says Lady Cowper, 'it was nothing but kissing and wishing of joy, and in short, so different a face on things, nobody could conceive that so much joy could be, after so many resolutions never to come to this.'

It could not last. The very next day, Lady Cowper reported, the King did not speak to the Prince when they came out of the private apartments and the Prince looked grave. This uneasy truce lasted for the rest of the reign. No further open breach occurred, but affection hardly blossomed between father and son. The real gainer by the exercise was Walpole. He became Paymaster-General and Townsend was appointed President of the Council and Comptroller of the Household.

Walpole's great moment came in 1720, when Britain was seized with that strange monetary madness known as the South Sea Bubble. This wild explosion of speculation had its basis, curiously enough, in the increased prosperity of the country, but the techniques of money management were still in their infancy. Speculation ran off the rails. Historians have always had a certain malicious pleasure in recording the names of some of the companies that were foisted upon a public going crazy for easy money. They ranged from a plan for breeding silk-worms in Chelsea Park and another for importing jackasses from Spain, to the celebrated prospectus 'For carrying on an undertaking of great advantage; but nobody to know what it is'. The Jacobites lost no time in hinting that royalty itself had been touched by the investment fever, and it was certain that some members of the Government were involved. Inevitably the Bubble burst, bringing dismay, chaos and a crisis in the very structure of society.

By luck, more than the judgement he was afterwards credited with, Walpole escaped being seriously involved in the Bubble. With his uncanny political sense, he retired to Norfolk, thus avoiding the immediate aftermath of the catastrophe. Soon Parliament and the City were clamouring for his return as the one man who could save the country. Of course, he wasn't alone in proposing the measures that calmed the panic. Many of the best ideas did not come from him. No matter, the Bubble had given him his chance to get a firm grip on affairs, a grip that he was not to relax for the next twenty years.

George I had never really liked Walpole, although they had the same taste in bawdy talk and women. But the Bubble affair had shown him that Walpole was now indispensable. Walpole was the one man who could make the machinery of government run smoothly, and George appreciated that skill. With all his lack of charm, the King was efficient, broad-minded and tolerant. He may have quarrelled with his son, but he was determined never to quarrel with his subjects. When we cast up the balance sheet on George I, we must come down firmly on the side of success. Could we have done the same on the Old Pretender?

George died in 1727 on a visit to his beloved Hanover. In those days the political scene was expected to change completely with the death of the sovereign. The 'outs' expected to be the 'ins'. Sir Robert Walpole shared this expectation. The Prince of Wales had never forgiven him for that staged reconciliation with his father, which Walpole had so skilfully engineered, and he had a group of out-of-office politicians around him who would certainly demand Walpole's post – if not his head!

As soon as he received the news, Sir Robert raced down to Richmond Palace where the Prince of Wales was then in residence. It was just after dinner and the Prince was already happily in bed with his wife. Sir Robert insisted on his being disturbed in his domestic pleasure. The Prince eventually appeared, half dressed and holding his breeches on his arm. The portly Sir Robert fell on his knees and broke the news. The story goes that the astonished Prince could only gasp out, 'Dat is one big lie'. The new King obviously did not trust his father's old minister.

The political world now waited with relish for the downfall of the once all-powerful minister. As soon as he was convinced that what Sir Robert had said to him was not 'one big lie', the new King gave the kneeling statesman one curt command, 'Go to Chiswick and take your orders from Sir Spencer Compton'. Sir Spencer was treasurer to the Prince and Speaker of the House of Commons. He was clearly going to be Walpole's successor. Lord Hervey, in his brilliant *Memoirs*, sums him up in one damning sentence. 'He was a plodding, heavy fellow with great application but no talent, and vast complaisance for a court, without any address.' And he adds that Compton's 'only pleasures were money and eating; his only knowledge forms and precedents; and his only insinuation bows and smiles.'

But he now was the man of the moment. Hervey gives us a vivid account of the events that followed the return of the new King and Queen to London.

Walpole had called on Sir Spencer and had told him 'Everything is now in your hands ... all I ask is that I am not abandoned to the enmity of those whose envy is the only source of their hatred.' Sir Spencer had then carried him up to town in his coach and they had attended a meeting of the Council of State at the house of the Duke of Devonshire. The question arose of the speech the King would have to make to the Council, and Sir Compton asked Walpole, as a favour and 'because he was more accustomed to this sort of composition than himself', to draw the draft out for him. As Hervey remarks, 'If Sir Spencer Compton had had common sense or foresight he would have known the better it was done the worse it would be for himself.'

The new King and Queen had now arrived at their old house in

Leicester Field. The house was besieged by a mob of place-hunters, all eager to protest their loyalty. After he had seen the King, Sir Spencer, says Hervey, 'returned to his coach through a lane of bowers in the ante chambers and on the stairs, who were all shouldering one another to pay adoration to this new idol, and knocking their heads together to whisper compliments and petitions as he passed'.

Back at the Duke of Devonshire's he found that Walpole had completed the draft. Sir Spencer Compton swore Sir Robert to secrecy, copied it out in his own hand, got it approved and carried it round to the King. The King wanted a few alterations made, which flustered Sir Spencer. He then committed the folly of asking Walpole to go to the King and beg him to leave the draft unaltered. Sir Robert naturally complied, and the new Queen was at hand to remind her husband of Sir Robert's superiority in this sort of work. The first nail had been struck into Sir Spencer's coffin.

All was still uncertain in the days that followed. Although Leicester House was crowded, Hervey continues, 'Nobody but Sir Robert Walpole walked through these rooms as if they had been still empty. His presence, that used to make a crowd whenever he appeared, now emptied every corner he turned to, and the same people who were officiously a week ago clearing the way to flatter his prosperity, were now getting out of it to avoid sharing his disgrace.' They moved too soon. As the weeks went by, Sir Robert's star began to shine a little more brightly. The King and Queen noted that he had given them a generous Civil List through his power in Parliament. George I had been given £700,000 and the Prince of Wales a separate £100,000 a year. Walpole arranged that the King should have the lot and the extent of the Prince of Wales's allowance was left in the royal hands. When the King had to give his speech to the new Parliament he asked both Walpole and Sir Spencer to prepare a version of it. He approved of Walpole's and shook his head over poor Sir Spencer's effort as 'poor stuff'. The Queen was at hand to whisper her advice into the King's ear and within days it was clear that Walpole was back in power. Sir Spencer Compton was kicked upstairs into the Upper House as Lord Wilmington. Hervey finishes the story. Wilmington, he says, 'seemed just as well satisfied to be bowing and grinning in an antechamber, possessed of a lucrative title without credit and dishonoured by a title which was the mark of his disgrace, as he had been dictating in the closet, sole fountain of court favour at home and regulator of all national transactions abroad.'

When all the hurry and scurry in the ante-rooms and on the palace back-stairs were over, there, once again in the centre of the stage, was the solid impressive figure of Sir Robert Walpole. He was to remain there for the next fifteen years and his actions were to have an important effect on the career of the new Prince of Wales as well as on that of the new King.

George II was in his early forties when he came to the throne. Like his father before him he had waited impatiently in the wings too long, and his character had already been formed during his time as Prince. He was small, dapper and extremely vain. He took after his father in his love of bawdy talk, in which his wife freely joined. He lived his life by the clock. Even his intercourse with his numerous mistresses was regulated by the watch. Stranger still, he discussed them fully with his remarkable consort, Caroline of Anspach. She was an exceptional woman, as capable of governing Britain on her own as she was of controlling her irascible husband. There were moments when he flew into ungovernable rages with his ministers and shouted at them. 'Puppy' and 'Rascal' spluttered from his lips. Caroline made certain that no offence was taken. George, says Hervey, was a man 'who it was easier to hate than to love'.

But on the credit side, George, like all the Hanoverians, was physically brave. He was the last British king to lead his troops into battle. He behaved with courage at Dettingen, encouraging his men with a fine if occasionally slightly comic display of valour. He had enough political sense to listen to Walpole and his wife, and the elder Pitt brought glory to the end of his reign. He was no intellectual and hated to see a book in his wife's hands. His only interest in the arts was in music, where he continued the royal patronage of Handel.

He inherited another trait from his father – a total inability to establish good relations with his son. Frederick Louis had become Prince of Wales when George II had become king. He was a young man of twenty who had spent his whole life in Hanover and never visited England. Furthermore he had never seen his parents after the age of seven, when they had been ordered to accompany George I to England, leaving the little boy behind to represent the Electoral dynasty in Hanover. His education had been neglected and he acutely disliked his governor and chief tutor, a Frenchman named Neibourg. In return Neibourg gave a damning report on his charge to the parents when the time came for Frederick to come over to England. 'His was the most vicious nature and the most false heart that ever a man had; nor are his vices of a gentleman but the mean, knavish tricks of a thieving footman.' Hardly an unbiased view of the new Prince of Wales! The young man had his better points. As Frederick grew into adolescence he took an interest in the arts. He enjoyed French literature, played the cello and developed superficial graces which had been entirely lacking in his father. He was no dullard and was reported to be generous to his friends. But his isolation from his parents in Hanover led him into certain immoral ways which surprised his friends when he came to England.

He had been rather sickly in his early youth and his mother had even expressed an anxiety about his future sexual potency. She strongly supported the fashionable diet of asses' milk as recommended by Dr Arbuthnot. Frederick however took steps to assuage his mother's doubts at an early age. In common with all courts in the eighteenth century, the court at Hanover was lax in its sexual standards. Amorous adventures were expected from an heir to a throne. After all, the mother of Louis XIV had herself selected the lady who was to conduct her son's sexual initiation. The woman who performed the same service for Frederick Louis was well qualified for her task. She had been the mistress of both George I and George II, and she made no demur about taking on the Griff. When a friend was talking about the affair to the wit, George Selwyn, and remarked that there was nothing new under the sun, said Selwyn 'Or under the grand-son.'

Such aristocratic liaisons surprised nobody at court, but the Griff shocked society by his low taste in his subsequent amorous adventures. With no strong influence to guide him in Hanover, he struck up friendships with his footmen and servants who took him with them on their amorous forays into the stews and brothels of the city. As a result, the Griff lost all sense of his place in society. He had none of that aristocratic hauteur which was then expected of a man in his position. He got into the habit of wandering through the streets, chatting easily to everyone he met. This would have been regarded with approval today, and we can regard the Griff as the real inventor of the modern 'royal walkabout'. It upset the governing classes in England, who were not prepared to accept their Prince of Wales in the role of a democrat. He became the darling of the London crowds however, as soon as he arrived in the city, but the despair of his political advisers.

Frederick's arrival in England had been delayed. His parents were in no hurry to bring him over, for George II already scented a rival in his son. The Griff was not invited to the coronation. Instead, William, Duke of Cumberland and the apple of his parent's eyes, became the centre of the celebrations. The King and Queen only changed their minds when they found that Frederick was plotting to make a romantic, runaway marriage with Wilhelmina, the daughter of the King of Prussia.

The new Prince of Wales received a warm welcome from the English populace when he did at last arrive. They were delighted to meet a Prince who actually walked among them and talked to them, even though his English was still a little stilted and careful. There was nothing stilted and careful about his behaviour. He himself was delighted with the effect he had created. 'Nothing', he said, 'has pleased me so much in my life as their huzzas.' The men of the Establishment were far from pleased. They noted with disapproval that the Prince had also taken to the night-life of London with most unprincely gusto. This led to a curious and disturbing adventure towards the end of the Prince's first year in England.

One night the Prince slipped out through the stables at St James's Palace to sample the delights of the teeming, Hogarthian underworld of London, where the brothels were kept by obliging ladies with the suggestive names of 'Madame Sulphur' or 'Madame Brimstone'. He picked up a girl in the darkness of the park. When she departed, the Griff found, to his consternation, that his watch and his royal seals had also departed with her. He sought the help of a guardsman, who failed to find the vanishing lady. Next morning, however, a member of the public was amazed to find the watch and the royal seals lying on the ground outside the Palace. The lady and her protectors had obviously found the loot too hot to handle. They had no intention of ending their careers on Tyburn Tree. But how were serious statesmen to trust a feckless prince who left the royal seals in the hands of a passing prostitute? The King and Queen now felt that they had every right to disapprove of their son. They resented his popularity. They feared the next step in his career – the forming of an opposition party to royal policies. This was not long delayed.

Among the first people to welcome the Prince and strike up a friendship with him was Lord Hervey, whose *Memoirs* give us an unrivalled glimpse of court life under George II and are the source of most of the more outrageous stories about Frederick. Hervey was a highly cultivated man of the world, who suffered from ill health all his life and was widely suspected of being a homosexual, in spite of the fact that he married one of the great court beauties of the period and had eight children by her. He had the misfortune to run foul of Alexander Pope, who gave him a scabrous immortality under the name of Sporus, the minion of the Emperor Nero.

Let Sporus tremble – 'What, that thing of silk,
Sporus, that mere white curd of Ass's milk . . .
Amphibious thing! that acting either part,
The trifling head, or the corrupted heart
Fop at the toilet, flatt'rer at the board,
Now trips a lady, and now struts a lord
Eve's tempter thus the Rabbins have expressed,
A cherub's face, a reptile all the rest
Beauty that shocks you, parts that none will trust,
Wit that can creep, and pride that licks the dust.

Hervey and Frederick eventually quarrelled over a mistress, Ann Vane, and Hervey took his special talents to court. He became the intimate friend of the Queen, who told him everything. He was constantly giving her gossip in return; as Pope put it . . .

Or at the ear of Eve, familiar toad,
Half froth, half venom, spits himself abroad.

There was certainly enough venom in Hervey to make him a dangerous enemy. He encouraged the Queen's growing hatred of her son, which now rivalled that of the King. Hervey wrote a long philippic on Frederick, which the Queen delighted to have read to her on every possible occasion. It is distressing to read in Hervey's *Memoirs* of some of the things the royal mother uttered about her own son. 'My dear first born', she said on one occasion, 'is the greatest ass, and the greatest liar, and the greatest canaille, and the greatest beast in the whole world, and I most certainly wish he was out of it.' The King joined in the vituperative chorus. 'I have always hated the little rascal,' he cried, and then went on to belabour poor Frederick with every unpleasant epithet at his command, calling him 'a false, lying, cowardly, nauseous puppy.' Walpole naturally followed suit. He said to Hervey one day, as they were travelling together in a coach, that he thought that the Prince of Wales was 'a poor, weak, irresolute, false, lying, dishonest, contemptible wretch, that nobody loves, trusts or believes.'

For the King and Queen the Griff's real offence was his popularity with the London crowds and the general public. For Walpole it was Frederick's ability to form a rallying point for the political enemies of his regime. Hervey had been replaced in the Prince's favour by the egregious George Bubb Dodington, a fat and podgy West Countryman, enormously wealthy and avid to obtain a peerage, who combined lasciviousness with a public piety. With the eighteenth century's capacity for flaying a man alive in verse, Charles Churchill wrote of Dodington,

Bubb is his name and bubbies doth he chase,
This swollen bullfrog with lascivious face.

Men of better quality also rallied around the Prince, including the youthful William Pitt who later became the great Earl of Chatham. For the moment the Prince's hostility to the King showed itself in a variety of petty ways. For example, the Prince, ignoring his accumulating debts, decided to outshine the King on the Thames, where it was fashionable to keep splendidly decorated barges rowed by crews in uniforms rich with gold braid, which made a great show for the ordinary folk who lined the banks. The Prince had his barge built by a great craftsman-artist, William Kent. Between them, for an expenditure of a £1,000 for the hull alone, they created what has been described, with some justice, as 'the most beautiful boat in the world'. It remained in the royal service until the days of Queen Victoria and it can still be admired in the National Maritime Museum at Greenwich. It is 63 ft long, slender and graceful, richly ornamented with golden dolphins and mermaids with an elegant cabin at the stern for the Prince and his guests. Frederick was delighted with it, especially when his barge beat that of the King in a specially arranged race.

Another venture of the Griff's into the world of artistic competition was not so happy. The great composer Handel had long been the favourite musician of the court. George II had continued his salary first paid by George I. Handel had built up a great position for himself in the musical world of London. He dominated the opera, and the crowds flocked to the King's Theatre in the Haymarket where Handel provided the best Italian singers for their delight. The King and his daughter Princess Anne were in constant attendance, and no doubt the nobility and gentry came to Handel's opera, not so much for the music but to see and be seen by royalty. The Prince liked Handel's music but intensely disliked the King's pleasure in it. He and his friends decided to set up a new operatic theatre in Lincoln's Inn Fields which would draw the crowds away from Handel. He engaged Handel's rival, Porpora, in 1733, as composer and impresario and spent money lavishly on Italian singers and richly decorated scenery. The beauty of the ladies in the chorus was also an attraction for the new 'Opera of the Nobility'. The fickle fashionable crowds were lured to Lincoln's Inn Fields and poor Handel was left deserted in the Haymarket. Princess Anne declared:

'In a little while, I expect to see half the House of Lords playing in the orchestra there in their robes and coronets.' The battle raged furiously, especially when the Opera of the Nobility succeeded in capturing Handel's own theatre in the Haymarket, forcing the unhappy maestro to struggle for survival in Lincoln's Inn Fields.

Porpora's triumph was complete when he engaged the celebrated 'castrato' Farinelli, who took London by storm. These strange artistic curiosities, the castrati, had voices of singular sweetness and purity, which, according to all accounts, were artificially produced by operations on unfortunate boys in the slums of Rome and Naples. Not all castrati were appreciated outside Italy. One such unfortunate warbler was pouring out his vocal graces in a Handelian-type aria, 'O my chaste love' when a voice interrupted him from the 'Gods' with the shout: 'In your case, chum, what else could it be?' Farinelli, however, charmed the London critics. One of them wrote, 'What a Pipe! What modulation! What ecstasy to the Ear!', but added, of Farinelli's acting, 'But heavens, what Clumsiness! What Stupidity! What offence to the eye!' Farinelli eventually overreached himself in London society, but not before Handel – the 'Great Bear' as he was called – went down in financial ruin and distress.

The great composer was compelled to go through his Dark Night of the Soul while the Griff and his supporters rejoiced. An episode unworthy of a Prince of Wales. Eventually Handel fought his way through his difficulties, to give the world his immortal Messiah, and finally to rest with honour in Westminster Abbey. Even in the depth of his struggle with the Prince and his Opera of the Nobility, he yet had the strength to produce his glorious setting of Dryden's words for *Alexander's Feast*. London music lovers gave the Great Bear an enthusiastic reception as his newly discovered tenor, the nineteen-year-old John Beard, sang,

Happy, happy, happy pair,
None but the brave deserves the fair.

Clearly it was time for the Griff to get married.

The bride chosen for the Prince by the King was Augusta, from the little German principality of Saxe-Gotha. She was seventeen, innocent with not unpleasing features, although the Queen declared, with characteristic acidity, that the Princess was 'far from beautiful, has a wretched figure, pretty eyes and a good mouth. She is anxious as a good child to please. Her hair is almost the same shade as the Duchess of Devonshire's but rather more of a sheep's colour.' Augusta had little idea of the tangle of family hatreds she was walking into. Through no fault of her own she arrived an hour late for her first reception by the morbidly punctual King and almost collapsed when doing a deep curtsey to him. Luckily the vain monarch took this as a compliment to his impressive presence. All the tensions of the wedding pre-liminaries, when the princesses had made a scene over the order of precedence, and the anxieties of the ceremony itself culminated in the scene at the reception after the wedding. The guests and the young couple came in procession to the royal apartments where the King gave the bride and bridegroom his formal blessing. Whereupon poor Augusta was violently sick. Who could blame her after all she had gone through!

However, she made a remarkable recovery and at the banquet offered by the City of London, she charmed everybody with her grace and affability. 'Now we really have a Prince and Princess of our very own,' the crowd shouted; upon which the Queen remarked to Hervey, 'My God, popularity makes me sick!'

Frederick and Augusta got on well together and this marriage, arranged with such calculated indifference by the King, turned out to be a great success. The new Princess of Wales had more character and intelligence than had first appeared. She gave her husband courage and determination to assert his rights, especially in the vexed matter of his finances. It was after his marriage that the Prince made his most determined effort yet to get the position of his allowance raised in Parliament. He pinned great hopes on the outcome, but the King was furious. He was suffering from piles at the time and was more than usually irascible. He urged Walpole to go to all lengths to defeat the motion. In the end, both Houses of Parliament rejected the motion. The King rejoiced, but the Queen was exultant. 'Look, there he goes, that wretch!' she said to Hervey, 'The Villain! I wish the ground would open up and sink the monster to the lowest hole in hell. You stare at me; but I can assure you if my wishes and prayers had any effect, and that the maledictions of a mother signified anything, his days would not be very happy or very many.'

All this was sad enough, but an event now occurred almost without parallel in the chequered history of our Princes of Wales. In 1737, Augusta was pregnant with her first child, who might well be a future Prince of Wales. The King and Queen had removed to Hampton Court for the summer and ordered the Prince and Princess to join them. The Queen, as usual, was deeply suspicious of the

Griff, and continued to discuss with Hervey her doubts about her son's sexual potency. She was sure he was incapable of begetting a child and actually believed that he might be planning a deception on the lines of James II's 'warming-pan baby'. She vowed that she would watch closely over Augusta's pregnancy. 'At her labour I positively will be, let her lie-in where she will; for she cannot be brought to bed as quick as one can blow one's nose and I will be sure it is her child.'

Frederick and Augusta found the whole atmosphere at Hampton Court profoundly depressing. The King and Queen were casting a gloom over what should be a happy event. This may partly explain the extraordinary behaviour of the Griff when it suddenly became clear that Augusta's baby would arrive far earlier than had been expected. On Sunday 31 July, the Prince and Princess had joined the court and attended morning service in the Palace chapel. Augusta, according to some observers, still looked surprisingly slim and no one expected the imminent arrival of an infant. That evening, after supper, the King and Queen played cards as usual. Everything in the Palace seemed normal and proceeding according to well-established routine. But in the Prince's apartments a strange drama was being enacted. The Princess had suddenly been seized by the first pains of labour. Immediately the Prince was also seized with a sudden wild impulse. At all costs his first child should not be born under the inhospitable roof of his father. He ordered a coach to be prepared and brought secretly to a side door. He and Augusta would escape immediately to St James's Palace. His child should be born in friendly London and not in hostile Hampton.

Despite the protests of her ladies-in-waiting, the helpless Augusta was smuggled down the back-stairs. She was in agony. Her waters broke. She begged to be allowed to stay where she was. The Prince overruled all her protests. 'Courage, courage,' he insisted, and dismissed all opposition with a curt, 'What nonsense. It will soon be over.' Away in the State apartments the King, Queen and the court were playing cards and gossiping utterly unaware of what was taking place almost below them. The labour pains became more intense as poor Augusta was helped into the coach with her attendants. The coach-man whipped up and the ponderous vehicle set off at all possible speed for London.

It was ten o'clock at night when the party arrived at St James's. The Palace was dark and almost deserted. Dust covers were everywhere. No sheets could be found so the Princess was hurriedly put to bed between two table-cloths. The Prince had already sent

176

messengers on ahead to summon the official witnesses who were bound by duty to watch the birth. They knocked at the doors of the Lord Privy Seal, the President of the Council and the Archbishop of Canterbury. The Lord Chancellor was out of London, but the Lord Privy Seal and the President of the Council arrived in time to stand at the bedside with the Griff. They made a strange pair. The President of the Council was none other than Lord Wilmington – the same Sir Spencer Compton that had been kicked upstairs to the Lords by Walpole, while the Lord Privy Seal bore a name not unknown in rooms where there was a doubt over a royal birth – Godolphin! At last the Princess's sufferings ended. She gave birth to a small, undersized little girl. The midwife produced it from under the table-cloths and put it in the arms of the astonished Godolphin. Soon after the portly Archbishop came puffing into the room to give the babe his blessing.

At Hampton Court all was peaceful. The royal pair had retired for the night when, at one o'clock the Queen was awakened by a loud knocking at her door. Mrs Tichbourne, her Woman of the Bedchamber, hurried into the room. 'Is the house on fire?' asked the Queen. Mrs Tichbourne told her that a message had been received from the Prince that the Princess was in labour. 'My God,' cried the Queen, 'I'll go to her this moment.' 'A dressing-gown,' replied Mrs Tichbourne, 'and your coaches, too. The Princess is at St James's.' Cried the Queen, 'Are you mad, or are you asleep, my good Tichbourne? You dream.' The bedchamber-woman assured the Queen that the whole thing was true. Clearly it was no dream, but a nightmare. The King was furious and turned on the Queen, 'You see, with all your wisdom, they have outwitted you. This is all your fault. This is a false child that will be put upon you ...'

At four o'clock in the morning, the harassed Queen with Lord Hervey in attendance, arrived at St James's. The Griff received her in his nightgown. The baby was produced for her inspection. She kissed it, and said in French, 'The Good Lord bless you, you poor, little creature. You have arrived in a very disagreeable world.' Later the Queen returned with her report to the King, whose fury now knew no bounds. Inevitably the flight of Augusta led to the next unhappy stage in this dismal story of family relations, or rather lack of relations – the eviction from the Palace. George II issued an order driving the Prince and Princess from the Palace. They were not allowed to take a stick of furniture with them. All courtiers, and even ministers of state were to have as little as possible to do with them, under pain of severe royal displeasure.

In truth, Frederick and Augusta almost welcomed the move. To them this was no expulsion from paradise but a reprieve from purgatory! They settled happily elsewhere – in the Prince's villa at Kew, in his town residences of Norfolk House and then Carlton House, and most cheerfully of all, at Cliveden. Cliveden was the great mansion created by the Duke of Buckingham and boasted a magnificent terrace looking down on the Thames. The house has been rebuilt several times. In our own day it has been the property of the Astors, and gained a certain notoriety before the last war as the meeting place of the 'Cliveden Set'. It is strange how the Griff had the trick of anticipating events by two hundred years. He invented, as already mentioned, the royal walk-about, he almost married a Lady Diana Spencer, and now here he was creating his own Cliveden Set!

He became ever more active in politics as the gulf widened between him and the King. George II even refused to let his son come to see his mother, when she lay dying in 1737. 'No, no,' he shouted. 'The puppy shall not come and act any of his silly plays here.' In fact, Frederick was now effectively excluded from all sources of political power. When Frederick's son, the future George III, was born, the King received the news with indifference. The son of his own despised son had little importance in his eyes. All Frederick could do was to play at party politics. He had a major part in engineering Walpole's downfall and maintained his opposition to the men in power for the rest of his life. His conduct was bound to seem factious and unprincipled for his father had denied him any chance of learning the practical business of government. He could not even turn to the usual consolation of disappointed Hanoverian Princes in Waiting – the Army. He had received no military training. It was his younger brother, William, Duke of Cumberland, who was taken off to the War of the Austrian Succession and who covered himself with glory after being severely wounded in the battle of Dettingen in 1743. When Frederick stood at the top of the stairs to welcome the two heroes, the King and William, home, his father pushed past him without a word. The fickle London crowd now cheered his younger brother as 'Billy the Bold'.

One last chance seemed to offer itself to Frederick to gain military glory. In 1745, Prince Charles Edward, the Jacobite 'Young Pretender', landed at Moidart on the west coast of Scotland and almost single handed, by his personal magnetism, raised an army of devoted Highlanders to begin his astonishing and eventually tragic adventure to regain the throne for the Stuarts. For the first and only time in our history there were two separate Princes of Wales in the country, both claiming to be the legitimate heir to the kingdom. Eagerly Frederick offered his services to the King. Again they were contemptuously brushed aside. Cumberland received the command, and Frederick was compelled to watch the romantic drama of 'Bonnie Prince Charlie' and the '45 in idleness from the side lines. The Griff would have been less than human if he had not felt deeply hurt at being left unemployed in the most serious crisis of the reign. He tried to cover his disappointment by adopting an air of cynical indifference to the affair. He was sarcastic about his brother's military manoeuvres. He even entertained his friends to a dinner at which a replica of Carlisle castle was produced in icing, and the company enjoyed themselves by pelting it with sugar plums. Bonnie Prince Charlie, meanwhile, was capturing Carlisle with real bullets, and then marching south towards London. The contrast between the conduct of the two rival Princes of Wales was striking – and damning for poor Frederick.

But Prince Charles Edward's army faltered at Derby, turned back to Scotland and eventually met a bloody defeat at Culloden at the hands of the Duke of Cumberland. In the murderous aftermath of the Rebellion, Billy the Bold became the Butcher because of the ferocity with which he repressed it. Frederick showed himself in a better light. He intervened to ask for mercy for the rebels – in many cases with success. He visited the Jacobite heroine, Flora Macdonald in the Tower, and when his wife declared that Flora deserved no sympathy, the Prince replied, 'I hope if I had been in Charles Edward's plight, you would have behaved as Flora Macdonald.'

This concern for the unfortunate Scottish rebels shows a more favourable side of Frederick's character. Hervey and Walpole between them have given us a dark picture of the Prince – his lascivious early life, his weathercock politics, his facile generosity and his undignified publicity seeking. 'He never forgot an injury or remembered an obligation,' says Hervey. Many of Frederick's friends would hotly deny this verdict. They found him a generous host and a loyal friend. He was interested in other arts besides music, and was delighted to invite Alexander Pope and other leading literary men of the day to his table. His children regarded him as an indulgent father, who took pleasure in joining in their childhood games. In sport, he was the complete opposite of his father. He was no huntsman and did not enjoy shooting. While George II delighted in slaughtering specially fattened turkeys which could scarcely flap their way up onto the lower branches of the trees in Richmond Park, the Griff could take pleasure in a country stroll accompanied by his dogs. One of his tastes ought to commend

179

him to modern sportsmen; he was a pioneer and a keen patron of the game of cricket.

Did he have a premonition of his early death? It seems strange that, at the early age of 44, he began setting his papers in order and composed a long treatise of advice to his son on the conduct and policy he should adopt when he became king. Early in 1751 he fell ill with something suspiciously like pneumonia. He had been working and over-heating himself, improving his beloved gardens in Kew. He had little strength to resist the infection. Perhaps his powers to resist infection had been lowered, as Horace Walpole suggests, by the effects of a blow from a tennis ball some time previously. Other authorities say that the blow had been delivered by a cricket ball. It would certainly be in keeping with the Prince's slightly absurd career if he had died the first martyr to our national game.

The Griff's funeral was a muted affair. The King and the members of the royal family were conspicuously absent. The body was laid to rest in the vault in King Henry VIII's Chapel, near that of Queen Caroline. FitzFredrick, his illegitimate son by Ann Vane, was also buried near at hand. But the Prince's reputation has been buried even deeper than his body by the cruel lampoon, concocted by a witty Jacobite, and which is probably all that the average man knows about the Griff.

> Here lies poor Fred
> Who was alive and is dead:
> Had it been his father,
> I had much rather;
> Had it been his brother,
> Still better than another;
> Had it been his sister,
> No one would have missed her;
> Had it been the whole generation,
> Still better for the nation;
> But since 'tis only Fred
> Who was alive and is dead
> There's no more to be said.

No more to be said? Only this; poor Fred's good points were his own, but his bad qualities were surely the result of the unnatural hostility of his parents. No Prince of Wales had been left so totally untrained for his future role as was the Griff. There is a touching story of how, during his last illness, he called out to his eldest son

George, who was passing the bedroom door, 'Come George, let us be good friends while we are permitted to be so.' He then poured out to his son an account of his own early youth in Hanover, about which he had never spoken before. The burden of the story was poor Fred's devastating feeling of loss when deprived of parental affection. Would Frederick's son George do any better with his son, or would the Hanoverian family horrors repeat themselves?

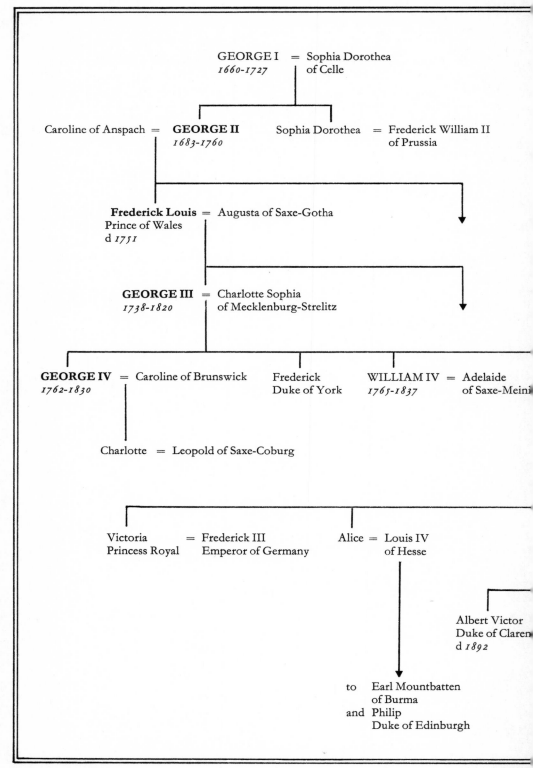

GEORGE I = Sophia Dorothea
1660-1727 of Celle

Caroline of Anspach = **GEORGE II**   Sophia Dorothea = Frederick William II
1683-1760   of Prussia

Frederick Louis = Augusta of Saxe-Gotha
Prince of Wales
d *1751*

GEORGE III = Charlotte Sophia
1738-1820 of Mecklenburg-Strelitz

GEORGE IV = Caroline of Brunswick   Frederick   WILLIAM IV = Adelaide
1762-1830   Duke of York   *1765-1837*   of Saxe-Meini

Charlotte = Leopold of Saxe-Coburg

Victoria   = Frederick III   Alice = Louis IV
Princess Royal   Emperor of Germany   of Hesse

Albert Victor
Duke of Claren
d *1892*

to   Earl Mountbatten
of Burma
and   Philip
Duke of Edinburgh

Houses of Hanover
and Saxe-Coburg

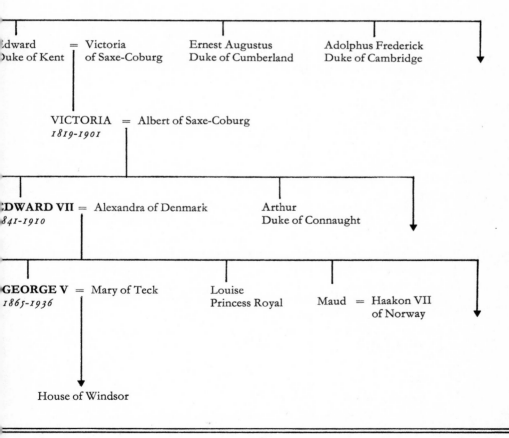

Edward = Victoria   Ernest Augustus   Adolphus Frederick
Duke of Kent   of Saxe-Coburg   Duke of Cumberland   Duke of Cambridge

VICTORIA = Albert of Saxe-Coburg
1819-1901

EDWARD VII = Alexandra of Denmark   Arthur
1841-1910   Duke of Connaught

GEORGE V = Mary of Teck   Louise   Maud = Haakon VII
1865-1936   Princess Royal   of Norway

House of Windsor

8

'Prinny'

'He was the Prince of Pleasure.'
J. B. PRIESTLEY

Prince George was a boy of thirteen when Frederick died. A month after the funeral he was officially made Prince of Wales. He had been deeply upset by the loss of his father. When the news was broken to him, he turned very pale and clasped his hand to his heart as he exclaimed, 'I feel something here, just as I did when I saw two workmen fall from the scaffold at Kew.' His mother, Princess Augusta, had perforce to fling herself on the mercy of the King. He received her with good grace for he had never held her responsible for the breach between himself and his son. As the years passed, Augusta became restive under his somewhat cold and disinterested protection. George II took little interest in the education of the boy who would one day be his successor, and it used to be suggested that, as a result, George III received the worse preparation of any of our princes for his future role. Horace Walpole even declared that, at the age of eleven, George could still not read English!

Recent researches into the extensive archives at Windsor have uncovered letters from the Prince to his father which show that, at the age of eight, he could not only write letters in English but in German as well. While he was alive, Frederick watched carefully over his son's upbringing. He prescribed a schedule of lessons as stiff and intensive as that later prescribed by the Prince Consort for the hapless Edward VII. George and his brother Edward rose at seven and went to their classroom at eight, where they tackled a varied curriculum until twelve-thirty. There was a two hour break for play and dinner. Then more lessons until supper at eight. The dazed royal pupils tumbled bemused into bed at ten o'clock. After such a scholastic battering it was no wonder that Lord Waldegrave, who became Prince George's governor in 1753, declared, 'I found His Royal Highness uncommonly full of princely prejudices, contracted in his nursery, and improved by the society of bed-chamber women and the pages of the back-stairs.' Other observers were kinder to the young prince. Lady Louisa Stuart reported that Prince Edward was his parent's favourite son, and they often cut short George's conversation with a curt, 'Do hold your tongue, George, and don't talk like a fool.' It is not surprising that he seemed a little tongue-tied and shy in company. But Lady Louisa added, 'Pride and sharpness were not in him.'

In truth, George was not badly educated. His essays, still preserved at Windsor, show that he was given a pretty thorough grounding in history and mathematics and that he was the first of our princes seriously to study science. He had a fair command of German and French and developed other interests besides, notably music and astronomy. George's real trouble came from the very nature of his up-bringing. Inevitably a young prince in the eighteenth century was isolated from the company of other boys and from the rough and tumble of everyday life. There was no Gordonstoun School or teaching sessions in Australia or New Zealand for young George.

His lethargy and apparent indolence gave way to application and industry when Lord Bute displaced Waldegrave as the Prince's governor, and it is easy to understand why. Bute was the first man to treat the Prince of Wales with real kindness and understanding. His mother, while deeply concerned with his welfare, was constitutionally incapable of showing him her affection. The King, his grandfather, was too old and selfish to feel any emotion about him. His tutors were more concerned with the training of a model prince than with a growing boy's need for friendship. A recent sympathetic study of George III by the distinguished authority on eighteenth century politics, John Brooke, which has the added advantage of a foreword by our present Prince of Wales, points out that the time has come when 'We can finally scotch the legend that George III as a boy was dull, apathetic, lethargic, unteachable (all epithets which have been bestowed upon him by historians of his reign)'. The Prince's academic exercises, found in seven large boxes in the Windsor archives, are not the product of a youngster with a lazy mind. George would certainly have got an average share of 'A' levels, if he had gone to a modern comprehensive school.

Bute was undoubtedly the man who turned the apparently lethargic boy into the industrious prince, as George approached manhood. This Scottish nobleman, whose political career had been mainly spent in England and who had been a friend of 'poor Fred', played a commendable part in the upbringing of the Prince but a more controversial one in the earlier years of George's reign as king. Bute was a handsome man, with a haughty patrician manner. He was thus a difficult man to get to know intimately or to judge fairly. Contemporaries usually disliked him. Shelburne says of him'He was always on stilts ... He excelled, as far as I could observe, in managing the interior of a court, and had an abundant air of art and hypocrisy.' Waldegrave, who had been displaced by Bute, was naturally even more pointed. 'There is an extraordinary appearance of wisdom, both in his looks and in his manner of speaking, for whether the subject be serious or trifling, he is equally pompous, slow and sententious.' Prince Frederick also noted Bute's pompous manner. He declared that Bute was a fine, strong man, who would make an excellent ambassador to a court where there was no business.

Unfortunately, Bute began to exercise a controlling influence, not only on his new charge but on his mother, Princess Augusta, as well. Later, at the height of Bute's unpopularity in the early years of George III's reign, the ribald pamphleteers had a field day picturing Bute as Augusta's lover. Bute was undoubtedly a handsome man, with a fine leg – an asset much admired by ladies in an age when men still wore breeches; but he was also a happily married man, with strong Scottish moral principles. Any suggestion that there was any physical understanding between him and Augusta is absurd. There was a more serious bond uniting them. Augusta, like many uneducated people, was deeply impressed by Bute's learning, which was far more extensive and genuine than contemporaries allowed. He was deeply interested in the advancement of science, and his encouragement gave George his taste for reading and literature, which eventually resulted in the formation of the Royal Library, which is still one of the glories of the British Museum. He had a second claim to Augusta's regard. He gave her strong support in her anxieties over the Duke of Cumberland.

Here we come again to that strange obsession that beset successive Princesses of Wales – 'The Menace of the Wicked Uncle'. What would happen if the old king died and the young Prince of Wales was left a minor? Augusta had no hesitation in casting the Duke of Cumberland in the role of George's Wicked Uncle.

'Billy the Bold', however, was a man of honour. He profoundly resented Augusta's suspicions, and was horrified that she had passed them on to her son. Horace Walpole tells a revealing story of a visit the young Prince of Wales paid to the Duke.

"Prince George, making him a visit, asked to see his apartment, where there are few ornaments but arms. The Duke is neither curious nor magnificent. To amuse the boy, he took down a sword and drew it. The young prince turned pale and trembled, and thought his uncle was going to murder him. The Duke was extremely upset and complained to the Princess of the impressions that had been instilled into the child against him.

The Princess's suspicions only disappeared when the poor Duke lost favour with the King after his defeat by the French at Hastenbeck in 1757. 'Here is my son,' said the King when Cumberland appeared at a levee, 'who has ruined me and disgraced himself.' But if Billy, now the 'Not So Bold' in his father's eyes, had been removed from Augusta's suspicion list, the old King remained on it. Augusta passed her antipathy to George II on to her son. Prince George had enjoyed a reasonable relationship with his own father, Frederick, but the traditional tension between reigning king and his destined heir now showed itself between grandson and grandfather. The Prince – or was it Bute in the background? – helped to force Pitt into the ministry. Further tension occurred when the question of the Prince's marriage began to become urgent.

Prince George was now entering early manhood, after a somewhat delayed adolescence. As he admitted himself in a revealing letter to Bute;

> You have often accused me of growing grave and thoughtful. It is entirely owing to a daily increasing admiration of the fair sex, which I am attempting with the philosophy and resolution I am capable of to keep under.... When I have said this you will plainly feel how strong a struggle there is between the boiling youth of twenty-one years and prudence.

Would the boiling youth boil over as his predecessors had done? Had he inherited that sexual rage in the blood so characteristic of the Hanoverians? Marriage was clearly indicated for safety reasons if for no other. In November 1759, the Prince fell in love with Lady Sarah Lennox, the sister-in-law of the wily politician Henry Fox. The Prince confessed to Bute that Lady Sarah was 'everything I could form to myself lovely'.

Bute wisely advised the Prince of the dangers of an alliance with a lady who had such clear political connections. 'Think, Sir, in the meantime what you are,' he advised, 'what is your birthright, what you wish to be . . .' The Prince's love had been violent, but it was calf love. He, himself, resolved that the alliance with Lady Sarah would not do. He confessed to Bute that he realized that he 'was born for the happiness or the misery of a great nation, and consequently must often act contrary to my passions'. On his own free will he abandoned any idea of marriage while George II was still on the throne. As he said to Bute, 'I will never agree to alter my situation while this old man lives. I would rather undergo anything ever so disagreeable than put my trust in him for a single moment in an affair of such delicacy.'

The 'old man' obliged the Prince by a departure from the scene which was hardly consonant with the dignity of history. Horace Walpole tells the story:

> He went to bed well last night, rose at six this morning as usual, looked, I suppose, if all his money was in his purse, and called for his chocolate. A little after seven he went into the water-closet; the German valet de chambre heard a noise, listened, heard something like a groan, ran in, and found the hero of Oudenarde and Dettingen on the floor, with a gash on his right temple, by falling against the corner of a bureau. He tried to speak, could not, and expired.

With him expired a whole age. A new and, on the face of it, a more hopeful one began. The new king was young, handsome, eager to serve the country and, above all, determined to live a decent family life. He would be the exact opposite of his grandfather and the whole line of Hanoverian princes, electors and kings. The nation welcomed him with enthusiasm. He was the first Prince of Wales for over eighty years who had been born in England. In one of his first pronouncements to his subjects he declared that he gloried in the name of Briton. The trials and tribulations of his unusually long reign – his tussles with Parliament, his clash with Wilkes, the loss of the American colonies, the desperate war with France and his final, sad descent into madness – all lay in the future. For the moment the young King was occupied with urgent personal business. He was arranging his marriage.

In the light of some of the subsequent explanations of his madness and the suggestion that it was due to sexual frustration officially forced upon him, it cannot be too firmly emphasized that the King's choice of bride was entirely his own. Just as he had given up Lady Sarah

Lennox from a high sense of his duty to the country, so he picked his queen with the same dedication to the service of the nation. He carefully laid down her specifications for his envoys and ambassadors. He did not ask for outstanding beauty or even elegance of figure. He wanted his bride to have a pleasant disposition, a lively intelligence and, above all, to be capable of bearing a large family to ensure the succession. She had also to be a Protestant. That narrowed the field. George was forced to search among the princesses of Germany, and in this limited area, there did not seem to be an obvious choice. Some of the princesses suggested were not exactly attractive. The Princess Frederika of Saxe-Gotha, for example, was reported to be deformed and too much given to 'philosophy'! The final choice rested on a comparatively obscure princess who was not even on the first list, and who came from the small duchy of Mecklenburg-Strelitz. Charlotte of Mecklenburg was no beauty but she had intelligence, character and tact. Things now moved at a fast pace. The seventeen-year-old princess came to England in September and the marriage took place within days of her landing. In the same month of September 1761, the young couple were crowned King and Queen in Westminster Abbey. By August of next year Charlotte had presented her husband with their first child. She had certainly lost no time in fulfilling one of the qualifications that George had demanded of his bride. On the fifth day after its birth the child was created Prince of Wales. He was formally christened George Augustus Frederick. He was destined to be the best known and certainly the most written about Prince of Wales in our history. He would feature in the memoirs of the time under the half-affectionate, half-derisory soubriquet of 'Prinny'.

Prinny was one of our Princes of Wales who held that title for a record period of time. His only rivals are the Black Prince and Edward VII. George Augustus Frederick waited fifty-eight years before he came to the throne as George IV in 1820. He did half-ascend the throne, as it were, when he became Prince Regent as his unhappy father sank into that strange state of mental twilight which his doctors, according to the medical knowledge of the time, roundly diagnosed as madness. During this long period of waiting, the Prince succeeded in stamping his personality and name on a whole period in our history – the Regency. We all have a picture in our minds of this remarkable age, when the eighteenth century gave way to the nineteenth and the long war with France ultimately ended with the triumph of Waterloo. Perhaps we see it through a romantic haze created by lady novelists as the Age of Elegance presided over by the Prince of

Pleasure. Here are the Regency bucks gambling deep at White's, Prinny driving with his latest mistress along the Steyne at Brighton, Beau Brummell carefully supervising his valet as he ties the Beau's cravat before he goes to the ball at Almacks. Far away in Spain, Wellington is winning glory as he routs Napoleon's marshals, and the stage-coaches clatter past the elegant Nash-built terraces of fashionable London, flags flying and horns blowing, as they 'Go Down with Victory' to carry the glorious news to the provinces. Nelson has cleared the seas of England's enemies. Wordsworth, Coleridge and Byron are writing. Scott is recreating the novel. Turner is painting and Lawrence is flinging the faces of the fashionable onto canvas with a flourish dear to the heart of the Prince. We ignore the wage-slaves toiling in Blake's 'dark, satanic mills', the children crawling through the damp, deep galleries of the coal-mines of South Wales, the Yeomanry riding down the crowd at Peterloo. We see only the bright, enticing surface of the picture. We can be excused in this, for the Regency was genuinely one of the most splendid periods in our long history.

In the very centre of it stands the Prince of Wales. What sort of man was he, behind the robes, the ribbons, the orders and the decorations in which he delighted so much? Thackeray, in his celebrated diatribe, written at the height of the Victorian reaction to the Regency, denied that there was a real man there at all.

> I look through his life and recognize but a bow and a grin. I try and take him to pieces and find silk stockings, padding, stays, a coat with frogs and a fur collar, a star and blue ribbon, a pocket handkerchief prodigiously scented, one of Truefitt's best nutty-brown wigs reeking with oil, a set of teeth and a huge black stock, underwaistcoats, more underwaistcoats, and then nothing.

Thackeray goes on piling up the sneers, and then asks sententiously, 'Will men of the future have nothing better to do than to unswathe and interpret this Royal old mummy?'

Alas for Thackeray, that is exactly what the men and women of the future have done; and as they unwrap the sanctimonious swathes that Thackeray wound around poor George, they uncover a fascinating, gifted man, with a mass of faults and foibles, it is true, but with remarkable qualities and talents as well. Joanna Richardson points out that 'as Prince of Wales, as Regent, and as King, he fostered the arts and sciences, he had encouraged scholarship and taste as only the truly civilised could do.' Sir Max Beerbohm declared that George 'was a splendid patron ... Indeed he inspired Society with a love of something more than mere pleasures, a love of the "humaner delights". He was a giver of tone ...' J. B. Priestley calls him an 'easy and affable prince', while Roger Fulford maintains 'He did more than any other man before him, or after, to develop the art of living in England'.

His contemporaries did not quite know what to make of him. The Duke of Wellington declared that George was admitted by all to be the most accomplished man of his age, but he also added that the Prince was a most extraordinary mixture of talent, buffoonery and good feeling. George Augustus Frederick stands out from the rest of the Hanoverians like a flamboyant bird of paradise in a flock of hoodie crows. Whatever he was, he was no ordinary Prince of Wales.

As benefited a man who got such enjoyment out of parties and display, he began life as a sort of royal peepshow. His proud parents literally put him on display in one of the drawing-rooms of St James's Palace when he was only twelve days old. His cradle was separated from the rest of the room by a kind of Chinese screen, and while the nobility and gentry queued up for a glimpse of him, they were regaled with cake and with caudle, a sort of gruel laced with wine and spices and regarded as a splendid tonic for women in childbirth. The frugal king noted unhappily that the display cost him £500 for cake alone, not counting the eight gallons of caudle consumed every day. From the first moment he drew breath the new Prince of Wales showed his talent for making the money fly!

George was a fine, vigorous baby. When his nurse took him for an airing in Hyde Park, Lord Bath relates that the crowd hailed him with shouts of 'Gor bless him, he is a lusty, jolly young dog, truly'. Prophetic adjectives, for that is exactly what the Prince turned out to be. The system of education prescribed by the King for the education of the Prince of Wales and his brother, Frederick, was hardly likely to appeal to a prospective 'lusty, jolly, young dog'. It was exactly the same as George III had undergone himself – early rising, long hours in the classroom, lectures on Christian morals, intensive study of history and the British constitution and little contact with other children of the same age. True the Prince had a plentiful supply of brothers of all ages. Prolific Queen Charlotte eventually presented her husband with nine sons, as well as five daughters. But the royal family tended to spend much time away from London in the rural retreats of Kew and Richmond. George III always preferred country to town life. He gloried in the name of 'Farmer George', bestowed on him by his loyal subjects. His son, however, turned out to be no countryman. Perhaps he had had enough of cultivating the garden plants assigned to the boys at Kew as part of their education! We can hardly picture Prinny as a happy countryman, whistling around his cabbage patches and potato plots.

The King's public duties, however, brought him back continuously to London, and the growing prince naturally attended the drawing-room levees that were an obligatory part of the royal routine. He had performed his first public duty at the early age of two and a half. On 1 March 1765 – St David's Day – he received the governors of the Royal Society of Ancient Britons and solemnly presented them with £100 for Welsh charities. We are told that he delivered the few words, in which he had been carefully rehearsed by his parents, 'with great propriety and suitableness of action'.

This was his first and almost his only contact with the land from which he took his title. It was over thirty-five years later that he made his next contact with the descendants of the ancient Britons. He was still Prince of Wales when he rode over the border near Welshpool. He was greeted by an enthusiastic assembly of the nobility and gentry of Montgomeryshire, planted an oak, drank a toast and then departed hurriedly for the more exciting social scene of Brighton. The Prince's Oak still stands on the side of the road to bear witness that the Prince had actually set foot in his own Principality. He descended on Welsh soil for an equally brief moment as King, when stormy weather forced his ship to put into Milford Haven when returning from his visit to Ireland. A suitably fulsome inscription on the bridge at Milford records the delight of the inhabitants at the unexpected arrival of the king, but makes no mention of the royal fury when a second storm drove the monarch back again to the shelter of the Haven.

Should we blame George III for the flaws in the Prince's character which began to show themselves as he approached adolescence? Was the whole system of his education wrongly conceived? Mr John Brooke rightly maintains that the King was hardly at fault. He draws our attention to the fact that, when it came to education, the eighteenth century was convinced that young people would inevitably get into trouble if left to themselves and that it was the duty of every parent carefully to regulate the lives of their children. Says Mr Brooke,

The King accepted without question the conventional ideas of his age, just as most people do today. He wished his children to grow up with a sense of duty and service, first to God and then to their country; and he tried to set them a standard at which to aim.

192

The standard was, perhaps, too high and was set too early in life. The atmosphere of the family circle around the King, with its regular hours and simple country pursuits, was not exactly exciting for a growing prince with the raging Hanoverian blood in his veins. The inevitable tensions soon began to show themselves. The stage was once again set for the now traditional clash between royal father and princely son. This will be the main theme that runs through the life of Prinny as Prince of Wales, colouring all his actions and always present in the background even in his happiest moments.

Not all aspects of the Prince's education were narrow-minded and restrictive. He was early introduced to the arts. The young Mozart played before the family of George III as an infant prodigy, J. C. Bach, the youngest son of the great Bach, was attached to the court. John Couzens, one of the leading water-colourists of the day, taught the Prince drawing. He was well grounded in Latin, and in the literature of his own country and that of France. In short, he was well prepared for his role as a patron of the arts, and not so well prepared for the serious social and political duties incumbent on a Prince of Wales.

At eighteen, he was given a separate establishment, but his father still kept a hold on the purse-strings. Money was to be a constant source of irritation between father and son. The Prince of Wales was inexperienced in life, naturally generous of heart, determined in his pursuit of pleasure. The King was frugal, devout, chaste and diligent in the business of government. How could they possibly understand one another, especially as the Prince was now embarked upon his spectacular career as our leading royal amorist? His father might scold from the bank, rather like an anxious hen watching her duckling paddle off into dangerous waters; the Prince was not to be restrained. George bombarded his son with advice, complaints and reproaches. The Prince went his own wayward way. All parents who have been in King George III's position will readily understand his feelings.

The Prince had been introduced to the pleasures of love as soon as he was out of his father's supervision. There now began the long procession of complaisant ladies whose names have become inseparably linked with his. The first prominent one was the celebrated, or should we say notorious Mrs Robinson, known as Perdita from her appearance in *The Winter's Tale*. It cost the Prince, or rather his father, £5,000 before the royal Florizel was released from her clutches. The pace quickened when the King, with some reluctance, granted the Prince Carlton House as his London residence. The Prince was delighted with his new house.

He poured out money lavishly on its embellishment. Carlton House was refurnished in exquisite taste and splendid entertainments staged there soon became the talk of the town. The Prince flung himself into the pleasures of London with a furious gusto that recalled his grandfather, the Griff, on his first arrival in Britain fifty years before. The Prince, however, showed more taste. Alongside the actresses, the prize-fighters, the racing men and the ladies of the town, he sought the company of the artists, the literary men, in fact, anyone who had wit, originality and a delight in sheer living. He was handsome and had a captivating manner. No wonder he soon became the Prince Charming of London's high society.

Off stage, the King lamented and threatened, but he himself had left his son footloose and fancy free in London. He had refused to give the Prince a position in the state that might have steadied him. George III's other sons went into the Army or the Navy. The Prince of Wales alone was denied the chance to do anything concrete or creative in the field of service to the nation. He did the only thing he could; he turned the pursuit of pleasure into a fine art.

Of course, he became the centre of the opposition to governmental policy. George III had now found a minister to his liking in the younger Pitt, the son of the great Earl of Chatham. Pitt was a Tory. He was also in his twenties and the youngest Prime Minister in our parliamentary history. The Prince of Wales could not help contrasting his own political position on the sidelines with that of a young man almost the same age but already in the centre of power. The Prince naturally turned to Pitt's rival, the Whig leader Fox. Charles James Fox was a man after the Prince's own heart, a gambler who revelled in all the pleasures of life but who also possessed infinite charm and persuasive eloquence. The Prince was to need all the help that Fox could give him to get him out of the next sensational imbroglio into which he fell.

Prinny was always attractive to women but he also pursued them with a reckless and romantic enthusiasm which sometimes went to the bounds of outright folly. One woman alone seems to have inspired him with genuine love. Unfortunately she was the one woman he should not have pursued on any account. Maria Fitzherbert had been twice widowed by the time she was in her late twenties. She was not formally beautiful but she had an air of elegance and distinction. She was also a little older than the Prince, who all through his life was prone to fall under the spell of mature ladies. There were two fatal drawbacks to the princely pursuit of Mrs Fitzherbert. She was a Roman Catholic and she was virtuous. She had no desire to become another royal mistress. The Prince besieged her with furious intensity. He even tried to stab himself in the anguish of unrequited love. We may take this part of the story with a pinch of salt, for George was a first-class actor, as befitted a keen patron of the drama. Beau Brummell once said that the Prince's powers of mimicry 'were so extraordinary that if his lot had fallen that way, he would have been the best comic actor in Europe'.

In this case, the act succeeded, and the strange play came to an even stranger climax when Mrs Fitzherbert consented to be secretly married to the Prince. He had now committed an act of inconceivable folly. Not only had he married a Catholic and would thus be automatically debarred from the throne if that marriage became public, but he had also broken the Royal Marriage Act. The King had forced this Act through Parliament after the disgraceful marriage of the Duke of Cumberland. It ordered that the King's consent had to be obtained for any marriage within the royal circle. The Prince naturally did not inform his parents of his marriage, but London was soon alive with sensational rumours. The clamour became so great that Fox rose in the House of Commons and solemnly denied that any marriage had taken place. This cost him the regard of Mrs Fitzherbert but saved the public image of the Prince.

His bride tried to bring some order into the increasing disorder of his private life, but as he entered his thirties the Prince continued drinking too much and started to put on weight. He became the favourite subject of the cartoonist in one of the greatest ages of caricature. We talk today of the unpleasant way the Press today intrudes from time to time on royal privacy. It is as nothing compared with the savagery with which Gillray attacked the Prince. Would any paper now print Gillray's drawing of the Prince as a 'Voluptuary under the horrors of Digestion'?

Of course, this secret marriage with Mrs Fitzherbert could not last. Prince Charmings are not made for constancy. She tried to ignore his infidelities, but found it hard to bear with some of his more riotous companions. They quarrelled, reunited and quarrelled again. The Prince felt that she was still the only woman he had really loved, and when he died, a locket containing her portrait was found around his neck. But eventually they were bound to part. For the moment Maria Fitzherbert stood aside with dignity, and the Prince felt free to face the overwhelming, unpleasant fact that he had been dodging for years. His debts were now so enormous that there was only one solution to his financial crisis. He had to get married so that his father and Parliament could both increase his allowances to suit his new station in life.

His debts horrified his father and his financial advisers. He owed money on everything – on Carlton House, on his stables, his carriages, even on his clothes. He was in debt to his tailors to the tune of £31,919, an enormous sum for those days. This was what it had cost to attempt to become the Best-Dressed Man in Europe. There was nothing for it but to look for a suitable princess, and that meant that the search was automatically confined to the Protestant princesses of Germany. The choice fell on Caroline of Brunswick, the Prince's first cousin. The King gave his approval offhandedly, merely inquiring 'Is she good-natured?' The Prince himself had made the final selection, but in a strange mood of detached indifference. As long as his debts were paid that was all that mattered. Christopher Hibbert has summed it up perfectly. 'It seems almost as if he chose the Brunswick princess, hastily, sulkily, and petulantly, as a peevish protest against having to choose any wife at all.'

Whatever the motive, the choice was disastrous. When the subtle and experienced diplomat, James Harris, Lord Malmesbury, arrived in Brunswick to escort the future Princess of Wales to England, he was disconcerted to find a rather plump, hoydenish young lady, who chattered excessively and was extremely free with all and sundry. He admitted that she was 'good-natured', but summed up her other qualities with devastating prescience. 'In short, the Princess in the hands of a steady and sensible man would probably turn out well, but where it is likely that she will find faults analogous to her own, she will fail.' This is exactly what happened.

The Princess landed at Gravesend to find no one ready to receive her officially. She was taken to Greenwich, where she gained an extraordinary impression of life in England. The crippled pensioners of Greenwich Hospital turned out to see her. 'My God,' she exclaimed, 'is every Englishman without an arm or a leg?' Her anxiety increased when she found that, prominent among the people who were to escort her to London, was Lady Jersey, who was now reputed to be the Prince's mistress as well as being a Lady in Waiting. Lady Jersey is reported to have done her best (or her worst) to put the poor Princess in an unfavourable light with her future husband. She made Caroline change into an unbecoming dress and to add rouge to her cheeks, which were naturally high coloured. She was even suspected of putting Epsom Salts in a pasty offered to the Princess.

The account of the first meeting between his bride and the Prince reads like an act from some uproarious Restoration comedy. Caroline tried to kneel in homage before him. He raised her up, but that was all he could bring himself to do by way of greeting. He retired to the far end of the room and called Malmesbury to him. 'Harris,' he gasped, 'I am not well. Pray get me a glass of brandy.' Malmesbury suggested, 'Sir, had you not better have a glass of water?' Whereupon the Prince swore and said loudly, 'I will go directly to the Queen,' and forthwith left the apartment. The Princess looked after him with astonishment. 'My God,' she said to Malmesbury, 'does the Prince always act like this? I think he is very fat and he's nothing like as handsome as his portrait.'

After such a social disaster, it is a marvel that the wedding took place at all. On the way to the chapel the Prince confessed to the Earl of Moira, 'It's no good, Moira. I shall never love any woman but Fitzherbert!' He consumed so many quick brandies before entering the Chapel Royal that he had difficulty in standing. Lord Melbourne who was present said afterwards, 'The Prince was like a man doing a thing in desperation; it was like Macheath going to execution; and he was quite drunk.'

Restoration comedy again took over on the wedding night. The Prince had obviously been getting more and more drunk as the receptions and preliminaries proceeded. The Princess retired to her bedroom to await her bridegroom. He was a long time before joining her, and when he did appear, he was so drunk that he fell into the empty fireplace. There the Princess left him. He did recover at dawn and managed to crawl into her bed. He eventually overcame his repugnance and succeeded in getting her with child, in the spirit of the celebrated royal remark attributed to Henry Tudor as he faced Anne of Cleves in the Korda extravaganza, *The Private Life of Henry VIII* – 'The things I do for England!'

Baby Charlotte arrived in January 1796 and the Prince could sigh with relief. At least he had ensured the succession. Charlotte grew up to be a lively, attractive girl, with strong passions and a will of her own. When she had safely survived her first year the Prince felt that there was now no point in living officially with his wife again. She had become totally abhorrent to him. His language about her was unrestrained. He called her 'the vilest wretch this world ever was cursed with'. How these Hanoverians enjoyed cursing one another! For the rest of her life, he was to regard her as a millstone around his neck. The public and the popular Press, who hardly knew her, might have supported her. Prinny, who knew her only too well, certainly didn't. He early removed his daughter from permanent contact with her mother. Caroline retired to Blackheath, where her conduct became increasingly indiscreet. So indiscreet, indeed, that in 1806, the Prince initiated what was tactfully entitled 'The Delicate Investigation'. The Commissioners unearthed a whole heap of fruity scandal, but nothing that would stand up to investigation in a court of law. The Prince's hope for enough evidence for a divorce was disappointed.

In the ensuing years, Caroline continued to be a source of acute embarrassment to him. She toured the Continent in the most flamboyant way. Her association with Signor Bergami was notorious. George made one final effort to get rid of her when he ascended the throne. Again he failed, and he had the mortification of hearing that she had turned up and demanded admittance to his Coronation. She was turned away from the Abbey. How he longed to see translated into reality the rhyme circulating in London society at the time of the Queen's trial:

Most Gracious Queen, we thee implore,
To go away and sin no more,
Or if that effort is too great,
To go away at any rate.

A month after her attempt to appear at the Coronation, the unhappy Queen actually went away unexpectedly and permanently. She died. Her body was taken back to Brunswick and there was some demonstration of popular sympathy in the streets. But the general opinion was expressed by an Englishman writing from abroad. 'As for the Queen, I cannot help thinking that her death is a fortunate thing for the Nation'. Poor Caroline. Would that her marriage had been equally fortunate for the nation.

The Prince of Wales had been unlucky in his wife. He was tragically unfortunate in his father. For, at the age of fifty, George III went mad. At least, that was the diagnosis of the eighteenth-century doctors. Equally unfortunate for the Prince, the King, as it were, had two preliminary rehearsals for his final collapse into insanity. The Prince was deeply upset, but he would not have been human if he had not also prepared to assume the Regency on each occasion.

The Opposition gathered eagerly around him on the first occasion.

A regency would surely mean the overthrow of Pitt, and office for the Fox-ites. They anxiously scanned every bulletin issued by the doctors. Unfortunately, the doctors could not agree on the King's case. The symptoms were extremely puzzling, seemingly contradictory. The King's limbs became weak. His eyesight and hearing started to fail. He could not sleep. And he talked incessantly, continuing until he was hoarse, and even foamed at the mouth. Most distressing symptom of all – the King, whose conduct and speech had been so chaste, now poured out obscenities and even tried to assault ladies-in-waiting. His behaviour became so unusual that the Privy Council, with the Queen's reluctant consent, decided to bypass the orthodox doctors and call in a self-styled expert in insanity, who had built up a great reputation for treating disturbed patients of high rank in his establishment in Lincolnshire.

The Rev. Francis Willis was a clergyman who claimed that he had turned to the treatment of the insane from motives of Christian charity and compassion. George III distrusted him from the start. As Prince Charles has reminded us, the King was no fool when he was in normal health. When he suggested to Willis that it would have been better if he had stuck to his calling as a clergyman, Willis replied that he was only following the example of Christ, who had also gone about healing the sick. 'Yes,' said the King, 'but he did not get £750 a year for it.'

Willis's methods were certainly not filled with Christian compassion. They involved ordering the patient around with the brusqueness of a sergeant-major. Blisters were applied to his legs. Worse still, the unhappy King was thrust into a strait-jacket and even strapped down in his chair or on his bed. He remained trussed up like this for hours at a time. Willis firmly carried out the usual treatment of mentally disturbed people in the eighteenth century.

Modern medical men have a different picture of the royal illness. It was most likely to have been porphyria, a disease not properly diagnosed until our own century. It occurs when the pigment in our blood cells becomes too rich. The symptoms are exactly those recorded in the case of George III. We have already noticed porphyria in earlier Princes of Wales. It was hereditary both in the Stuarts and the Hanoverians. Its underlying presence could explain the conduct, not only of George III but the Prince Regent and later Princes as well. It is part of the tragedy of the King that his doctors knew nothing of porphyria. They could only tackle his malady within the limits of contemporary knowledge.

As it was, it was a marvel that the King ever recovered after the first dose of the Willis treatment. But recover he did. The Opposition retired baffled. Pitt felt secure again. The Prince returned to the wings and the King received the enthusiastic plaudits of his people. Never had 'Farmer George' been more popular.

The same misfortune again fell upon the King in 1810. Again the Willis treatment was applied. Again the political scene fell into confusion and again the King made a recovery. But by 1811 it was clear that George III would never return to public life. He passed into the long, sad night of the bewildered mind, ever more lonely in his withdrawn, private world. He could still play Handel on the harpsicord but his long, white beard gave him a tragic resemblance to that other bewildered and broken royal figure, King Lear. At last, the Prince of Wales became Regent. With hardly any restrictions, he was empowered to exercise the duties of the king. He was still entitled Prince of Wales, but in practice he had ascended the throne long before his coronation.

Here we leave him. At last he had money to gratify his architectural tastes. The Brighton Pavilion, his private Xanadu, blossomed into that astonishing multiplicity of domes which made it look, according to Sydney Smith, 'as if St Paul's had gone down to the seaside and pupped'. Regent Street, in curving grace, swept up through the heart of London to the splendid park that still bears the Regent's name. He could now entertain lavishly, and he still had a succession of middle-aged, motherly mistresses, but the defeat of France lent an air of military glory to the Regency. In the centre of the scene was the florid figure of the Prince Regent, now distinctly portly and padded but still with 'an undeniable air'. Whatever else Prinny did, he brought style to the royal scene.

In one thing he failed. He did not secure the succession. The daughter, whom he had begotten from a grim sense of duty, eventually married after a certain coldness between daughter and father had happily faded. Her husband was Prince Leopold of Saxe-Coburg but in 1817 Princess Charlotte died in childbirth. The whole succession problem loomed large once again. The poet Campbell might moan in classical verse:

Daughter of England, for a nation's sighs
A nation's heart went with thine obsequies.

The nation's rulers had to take a more practical view. They were back again in the situation that prevailed a hundred years before on the death of Queen Anne. There was no obvious successor to the throne. The Prince Regent would most certainly never marry again, even if he had been capable of producing offspring after the curious life he had led. But there was a vast brood of royal brothers who might be expected to oblige. George III had been a prolific father. Queen Charlotte had presented him with six sons and five daughters, the survivors of fifteen children. Edward III had been his only rival in this respect. The poor daughters had been brought up in a very secluded way and were collectively known as the Nunnery. Three of them eventually married rather late in life and thus had no effect on the immediate succession problem. The public spotlight therefore fell on the royal Dukes, and as it played on them, it lit up a most curious and unsatisfactory state of affairs.

Wellington once dubbed these royal Dukes 'the damnest millstones about the neck of any government that can be imagined'. They were certainly eccentric to say the least, and became the delight of the ferocious cartoonists of the day. Most of them had reacted violently against their father's dull and straight-laced court. They were determined to dodge as long as possible their predestined alliances with unattractive German Protestant princesses. They kept mistresses. They did so not discreetly but openly, and their illegitimate children swarmed on every side. But not a single legitimate offspring was in sight.

The second son, Frederick, Duke of York, had been forced to leave the War Office under a cloud of scandal, when it was discovered that his mistress, Mary Anne Clarke, had been running a nice sideline in payments for promotions. He had, indeed, married a German princess but they had soon separated. He died before George IV in 1827. The next brother was William, Duke of Clarence. He had gone into the Navy and eventually succeeded his brother as William IV, but he also failed to produce an heir. In spite of his eccentricities he was probably the only endearing character in the gallery of royal brothers. He had lived with an actress, Mrs Jordan, who presented him with ten illegitimate little FitzClarences. 'Sailor Billy' was generally hard up and Mrs Jordan had often to return to the stage. When her royal protector tried to economize by cutting down on her allowance, she sent her reply in a playbill, underlining the notice at the bottom, 'No money returned after the rising of the curtain.' She died in 1816 and William dutifully married Adelaide of Saxe-Meiningen. She became Queen Adelaide when her husband succeeded to the throne. But there were no surviving children by the marriage. William was popular with the people. They enjoyed his eccentricities. When he went for a carefree stroll down St James's without any guards, the mob swarmed around him cheering, and he got presented with a series of smacking kisses by an enthusiastic Irish tart. The members of White's Club saw what was happening and descended *en masse* to rescue him. The free and easy sailor carried his seafaring habits into the world of royal ceremony. The Duke of Wellington noted, 'His Majesty has an easy and natural way of wiping his nose with the back of his forefinger, which I fancy, is a relic of his middy habits.' He was good-hearted and, like all our sailor kings, determined to do his duty. But he failed in the most important duty of all. He did not provide an heir.

William's younger brother, Edward, Duke of Kent, was the dark horse in the Succession Stakes. He had served in the Army, but had a ferocious sense of discipline. He had to be recalled from Gibraltar where he had produced a near mutiny. His mistress had been a French-Canadian lady, Madame St-Laurent, but he abandoned her when the death of Princess Charlotte reopened the succession question. Quite deliberately, and rather cold-bloodedly, he entered the race by marrying Victoria Mary Louisa, the widow of the Prince of Leiningen. He romped home the winner when his wife produced a daughter. This daughter is known to history as Queen Victoria.

Behind Edward, Duke of Kent, stood a sinister figure. Ernest, Duke of Cumberland, was important because if Victoria had died as an infant and his elder brothers had died Ernest would come to the throne. The mere thought filled the British public with horror. The Duke was a brave soldier but a fierce reactionary in politics. He was also ugly and had lost an eye in the wars. He was rumoured to have fathered a son on his own sister Sophia. He eventually became King of Hanover but not before he had been inevitably cast in the role of the Wicked Royal Uncle. The actual accession of Victoria exorcised him from the scene like an evil spirit.

Two more royal Dukes remain to be accounted for. Augustus, Duke of Sussex was a pleasant, mild-mannered bibliophile who is described in the Dictionary of National Biography as being, in his latter years, 'in great demand at anniversary dinners'. The last on the list, Adolphus, Duke of Cambridge, was a Hanoverian freak – he never got into debt and he kept no string of mistresses. Neither he nor Augustus entered for the Succession Stakes. The kitty had already been scooped by Edward, Duke of Kent. The curtain had come down on the showy, glittering and rakish world of Prinny, with its Regency 'bucks', its *demi-mondaines*, its gambling at Brooks's and White's, its lavish banquets at Brighton Pavilion and all the fashionable scandals and splendours we associate with the Regency. The stage was set for a totally different play. With Victoria, we leave the Age of Pleasure and enter the Period of Rich Respectability.

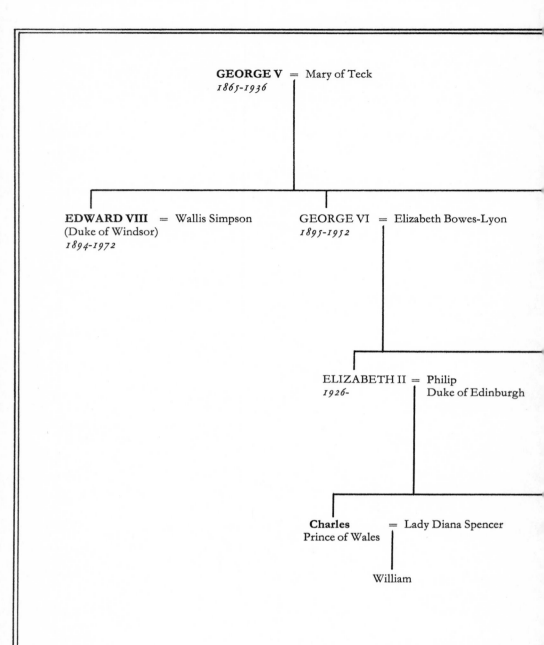

GEORGE V = Mary of Teck
1865-1936

EDWARD VIII = Wallis Simpson
(Duke of Windsor)
1894-1972

GEORGE VI = Elizabeth Bowes-Lyon
1895-1952

ELIZABETH II = Philip
1926-　　　Duke of Edinburgh

Charles = Lady Diana Spencer
Prince of Wales

William

House of Windsor

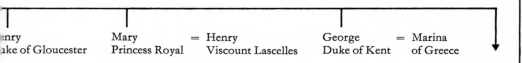

| Henry | Mary | = Henry | George | = Marina |
| Duke of Gloucester | Princess Royal | Viscount Lascelles | Duke of Kent | of Greece |

Margaret = Anthony Armstrong-Jones
Lord Snowdon

Anne = Captain Mark Phillips   Andrew   Edward

9

Retreat to Respectability

'Is it not easy, sir, and is't not sweet
To make oneself beloved?'
LORD BYRON

There can be no question about it. The nation would not have stood for another Prince of Wales like the Prince Regent. As the nineteenth century developed, the whole background to royalty changed profoundly. The Industrial Revolution had made Britain the greatest manufacturing nation on earth. Trafalgar and Waterloo had given her the key to the markets of the world. The middle classes were becoming rich and pushing forward into the political scene, and the Crown had been steadily eased out from the real power centre in the state. Royalty had to find a new role. Queen Victoria and her husband Albert, the Prince Consort, solved the problem by making royalty respectable.

The aristocracy, still retaining happy memories of the Regency, may have found the royal pair a little smug and lacking in elegance, but the general public looked with complete approval at Vicky and her Albert living in domestic bliss at Windsor or Balmoral, surrounded by their ever-increasing progeny and exemplifying everything the middle classes held dear – hard work, devotion to duty, public dignity and a family life of conventional purity. This was how they wished their own family life to be. Royal mistresses might have been tolerated when the Crown also had a difficult job to do. They were not acceptable once the monarch had become the 'great ideal'. Not that Queen Victoria ever became a mere symbolic figure; the mother-symbol set high over a self-satisfied nation. She had vast experience and strong views, and these were respected by her ministers. It was the same with her successors. But the central fact remained. Real power had passed for ever out of royal hands into those of Parliament.

Loyalty to the Crown was as strong as ever among the majority of the population, but it was not unconditional. It was now given to an ideal. Kings, queens and above all Princes of Wales were expected to embody this ideal and to live up to it. Victoria and Albert had no difficulty in fitting into this new role. Was not Albert known to posterity – for a short period at any rate – as Albert the Good? No Hanoverian prince would ever have qualified for that title!

Nothing symbolized more perfectly the new standards of conduct now expected of the monarchy than the conclusion of Thackeray's account of the reign of George IV. We have seen how the great novelist, in his highly popular lectures on the 'Four Georges', had lambasted the poor Prince Regent. In his last words to his well-heeled audience, he struck a new note.

The heart of Britain still beats kindly for George III, not because he was wise and just, but because he was pure in life, honest in intent, and because according to his lights he worshipped Heaven. I think we acknowledge in the inheritrix of his sceptre a wiser rule and a life as honourable and pure; and I am sure the future painter of our manners will pay a willing allegiance to that good life, and be loyal to the memory of that unsullied virtue.

The future painter of Victorian manners, as he watches Thackeray busy putting royalty on an impossible pedestal, can only feel the deepest sympathy for the next inheritor of the title of Prince of Wales. He arrived on 8 November 1841. He was the second child of Queen Victoria and was her first son. He was christened Albert Edward. He arrived in the world with that promptness which remained with him all his life. The high officers of state were still required to be present at the birth if not actually in the bedroom, but Prince Albert may have seized the chance offered by the Queen's many false alarms to modify this out-of-date custom. At any rate, he sent the summons to the Palace rather late in the proceedings. Sir Robert Peel, the new Prime Minister, got there just in time. The Archbishop of Canterbury was not so nimble. He had the mortification of hearing his church bells ringing to announce the joyful event while he was still on his way to it. The birth of the Prince also brought consternation in some unlikely places, including the Mayor's parlour at Chester. By ancient custom, the birth of a future Prince of Wales, who would also become Earl of Chester, brought with it the grant of a baronetcy to the Mayor of the city. Unfortunately, Prince Edward arrived on the very day when the mayoralty was changing hands. A furious wrangle arose between the incoming and the outgoing mayor as to who should have the honour. The infant slept peacefully through it all, unaware of all the troubles that lay in store for him. They would arise from one simple fact. By nature, Edward was born a Hanoverian, with all the instincts and gifts to make him another Prince of Pleasure. But he was to grow up in a world where royalty was busy obeying Thackeray's instruction to live a life 'honourable and pure'. The Prince would certainly always strive to be honourable and would succeed admirably. The second part of Thackeray's commandments would prove rather more difficult.

As he started to grow, Victoria and Albert looked anxiously at the heir to the throne. The little boy was affectionate and healthy, but, in contrast to his sister, he seemed backward. By the time he was seven it was clear that his education had to be taken seriously in hand. With the aid of his confidential adviser, Baron Stockmar, the Prince Consort drew up a comprehensive syllabus known in the family as the Plan. The Prince was given a small suite in Buckingham Palace and embarked upon an intensive course of serious study. Once again a royal parent was setting out to produce a model Prince of Wales. When we see the host of subjects in which the unfortunate 'Bertie' was expected to become expert – from French and Latin to constitutional law – we can only cry, about all royal parents, 'Will they never learn?'. The Prince was to be put through the educational mangle with Germanic thoroughness.

Yet what other course was open to the Queen and Prince Albert? They wanted to do their duty, not only to their son but to the state. Surely their successor should be as well educated as possible and have the best instructors available. His parents would set him an example of high-minded devotion to hard work. But what if the Prince proved to be uneducable? Victoria and Albert had early doubts about Edward when they saw him side by side with the bright-eyed Victoria. The Queen must often have sighed, 'If only Vicky had been a boy!' The young prince grew up with an inferiority complex. The diarist Greville, who had excellent opportunities for observing the royal family at close quarters, noted that 'the hereditary and unailing antipathy of our Sovereigns to their Heir Apparent seems thus early to be taking root, and the Q. does not much like the child'. Bertie may not have been academically gifted but, as things turned out, he acquired social graces and a gift for reading men's characters that proved far more useful to him than book learning when he came to the throne.

All this lay in the future. In the meantime the Prince had to plough on through his syllabus under the watchful eye of the Prince Consort. The Plan also effectively isolated the Prince from all contact with the outside, sinful world, with all its subtle and dangerous temptations. His tutor, Mr Gibbs, once suggested that the regime was, perhaps, a little too severe, but the Prince Consort was adamant. He was sure that in the end the Plan would turn Edward into a cultured gentleman fit to follow in his footsteps. Queen Victoria agreed. In her eyes Albert could do no wrong. On 25 August 1857, she wrote to her son and his sisters in these emphatic terms; 'You may thank God for joining us all to your dearest, perfect father.' And she continued, 'None of you can *ever* be proud enough of being the *child* of SUCH a father.'

Prince Edward certainly admired and loved his father, but he was a little in awe of him – as well he might be. He was only too conscious of how far he fell below that impossible ideal. Another royal personage was more to his taste. Napoleon III, Emperor of the French, and his wife Eugénie, came to England on a state visit. The Prince noted in the diary he had been ordered to keep by his father, 'The Emperor is a short person. He has very long moustachios, but short hair. The Empress is very pretty.' In 1856 he accompanied his parents on their return visit to Paris. He was delighted with what he saw. The French were charmed by his good looks, and for the first time in his life the Prince of Wales found himself being praised and admired for his own personality. It was the beginning of his life long devotion to France, to the French and their way of life, and above all to their elegant and witty women. At the end of the visit he begged the Empress to ask his mother to let him stay a few more days in Paris. The Empress suggested that perhaps his parents might not be able to do without their children at home in England. 'Not do without us!' Bertie replied. 'Don't fancy that. They don't want us and there are six more of us at home.'

For the moment, however, it was back to the Plan. The Prince kept on trying his best and still felt his parents were disappointed in his progress. When he reached the age of sixteen the rigours of the Plan began to be relaxed. The Prince was given an annual allowance of £100 and allowed to choose his own clothes for the first time. The Queen was a little worried by this bold step. She wrote to him: 'We do not wish to control your own tastes and fancies, which, on the contrary, we wish you to indulge and develop, but we do *expect* that you will never wear anything *extravagant* or *slang*!' The Prince never did. He grew up deeply conscious of fashion and sartorial elegance. In his maturity he became a fashion-setter himself.

The educational process also began to take on a wider amplitude. The Prince was dispatched on carefully supervised cultural tours to Germany and Italy. He visited Spain, and everywhere he went, those who met him remarked on his charm and his early mastery of the social graces. This was a side of him that his family had not yet seen but the Prince was preparing a role for himself in the future. He would never be an intellectual, but he would be a master of the art of understanding men and the still more difficult art of understanding women.

Prince Albert still cherished the hope that his son would yet take some interest in the arts and sciences. He sent him to Oxford but again took care to insulate him from the dangers of undergraduate life. Oxford, the Prince Consort maintained, was a place for study, a refuge from the world and its distractions. Bertie did his best, but he found Oxford and the high-minded dons who were allowed to meet him distinctly hard going.

In the Long Vacation of 1860 he had a chance at last to prove to himself and his parents that he was not altogether a loss when it was a question of taking up his future royal duties. He was sent on a tour of Canada and the United States. This was the first time that a Prince of Wales had visited the New World, and certainly the first time that one had entered the United States since the War of Independence. In both Canada and the U.S.A. there were still old anxieties and resentments lurking below the surface. There was deep antipathy between the Protestant and Catholic provinces of Canada and republican feeling was still strong in the United States. The Prince navigated these minefields with surprising and unexpected skill. He charmed everyone with his obvious enjoyment of the tour and his tactful disregard of protocol when the occasion required. He left a Canada completely captivated by his easy manner.

He was taken to see Niagara Falls, and from the suspension bridge watched the daring French acrobat, Blondin, cross the abyss on a tightrope, wheeling a man in a wheelbarrow before him. The Prince presented the acrobat with a purse of gold, and Blondin offered to wheel the Prince back on the tightrope to the American side. The Prince accepted the offer with boyish enthusiasm but his entourage hurriedly intervened. Bertie was persuaded to enter the United States in a more orthodox way, by a bridge over to Detroit.

His success in Canada was repeated in the United States. He went as far west as Chicago in a special train provided by the government, and then returned to Washington, where he made a great impression by planting a tree at Mount Vernon, Washington's home. The sight of the great-grandson of George III paying tribute to the man who had led the revolt of the United States from British rule seemed to heal all the old bitterness between the two great English-speaking nations. New York went wild about him, and his only regret was his inability to dance with the numerous pretty girls he saw at the official ball held in his honour. Protocol demanded that he should partner the middle-aged wives of powerful politicians. When, at last, Bertie returned home, his parents were visibly impressed by his success. The Queen noted that her son deserved 'the highest praise'. He himself felt a new confidence. He found it a little hard to settle down again at Oxford, and even more so at Cambridge where he was also sent for a short spell.

The time had come for him to enter the Army, and with his army service came disaster – the first and perhaps the major crisis in his life, a mishap that was to alter his relations with his mother and affect his whole early career. It was a crisis that could only have occurred in the heyday of Victorian respectability.

In 1861 the Prince had gone into camp at The Curragh in Ireland with the 1st Battalion, the Grenadier Guards. The Queen and the Prince Consort had been discussing with him possible plans for his marriage, but the Prince had insisted that if he did marry it would only be for love – the first Prince of Wales in our history who had dared to make such a declaration since the Black Prince. He would still have to marry within the royal caste, of course, and with a Protestant princess; the country would not tolerate any other choice. As he compiled his list of eligible Protestant princesses the Prince Consort confessed himself dismayed by their scarcity. There was one, however, who might just about do. To give her all her resplendent titles, she was Princess Alexandra Caroline Marie Charlotte Louise Julie of Schleswig-Holstein-Sonderburg-Glucksburg, the daughter of Prince Christian who had recently been recognized as the heir of the King of Denmark, King Frederick. King Frederick was hardly a popular monarch. He was a drunken debauchee, who had been divorced and whose people were only too keen to see him in his grave. They eagerly awaited the accession of Prince Christian, who was highly respectable and lived quietly on his modest salary. Princess Alexandra had been brought up to live simply, but she was surrounded by an affectionate family. Luckily for Bertie, she was also beautiful.

Vicky, Bertie's eldest sister had married the Crown Prince of Prussia. She tactfully arranged for him to meet Alix in – of all romantic places – the cathedral at Speyer. She and the Bishop of Speyer took a sudden interest in some obscure frescos, leaving the two young people alone before the altar of St Bernard. The ruse worked. Bertie declared himself pleased with the young lady. When he returned to England, he asked for Alix and her father to be invited to Windsor, where he could see her again before finally making up his mind.

So matters stood when Prince Albert suddenly received a profound shock which, as he said, had caused him the greatest pain he had yet felt in life. Lord Torrington, 'one of the greatest gossips in London', had told him of a scandal that was 'going the rounds of the Clubs', a story that Bertie was having an affair with an actress. A 'searching inquiry' revealed that the story was only too true. When the Prince had been in camp with the Guards in The Curragh, his fellow officers had smuggled a pretty young actress named Nellie Clifton into his quarters and as a result, the heir to the throne had, as the Victorians expressed it, 'lost his purity'. Nellie could not resist boasting about it. Prince Albert and the Queen were deeply shocked. The Prince wrote earnestly to his son, urging him to fight the good fight and admonished him that he 'must not, he dared not be lost'. The consequences, said the Prince, would be too dreadful, not only for the country but for the world. He journeyed down to Madingley Hall, near Cambridge, to see his erring son face to face. Bertie made a disarmingly moving and contrite confession, but refused to reveal the names of the young officers who had led him into temptation. The Prince praised him for this and then forgave him. The important thing now was to look to the future.

But when Prince Albert returned from his interview with the Prince of Wales, the Queen was distressed to find that he looked tired and ill. She thought that he might have become exhausted when Bertie had lost the way during a walk they had taken together in the grounds of Madingley Hall. The Prince complained of catarrh and of pains in his limbs. He had to take to his bed. The doctors diagnosed typhoid and, on 14 December 1861, Prince Albert died. The Prince of Wales was still at Cambridge, but the Queen had refused to call him earlier to the bedside of his dying father. She had formed the totally mistaken idea that Bertie's conduct had been the cause of Albert's death. She admitted that for some time afterwards she could not look on him without a shudder.

Her grief was profound, even extravagant, passing all reasonable bounds. She felt that her own life had also come to an end. Time stopped in the royal palaces. The dead Prince's rooms were to remain exactly as they were on that fatal December day. After the funeral it was better that Bertie should go abroad, anything rather than have him near her to remind her of the cause of her pain. The Prince of Wales was nothing if not dutiful to his mother. His behaviour was impeccable. He went off on a tour of the Middle East and Jerusalem which his father had planned for him before his death. He returned and, equally dutifully, married his Danish princess. The bride enchanted the country when she arrived. Tennyson, the Poet Laureate, burst into song.

Sea King's daughter from over the sea,
                                    Alexandra,
Saxon and Norman and Dane are we
But all of us Danes in our welcome of thee,
                                    Alexandra.

When she eventually came to Windsor, Alexandra touched the Queen's heart by kneeling before her. Victoria led her and Bertie to the vast memorial she had built to the Prince Consort at Frogmore. There beside his effigy she joined their hands together with the words, '*He* gives you his blessing'.

The wedding took place in St George's Chapel at Windsor with the Queen watching the ceremony from a gallery, still dressed in her mourning clothes and her widow's cap. The honeymoon was spent at Osborne where nothing had been changed since the death of the Prince Consort. No wonder the Crown Prince of Prussia had called it 'that gloomy vault'. It is remarkable that the marriage, almost presided over by the spirit of the dead Prince Albert, turned out to be so successful. The bride loved her husband and declared that she would have married him if he had been a cowboy and not a prince. He, as the world knows only too well, was not exactly faithful to her. With his Hanoverian inheritance this could hardly be expected. But he never lost his affection and respect for her. He was a martinet when it came to punctuality, the politeness of kings, but he never reproached her for her habit of being late for nearly everything. She, equally tactfully ignored his penchant for pretty women. They settled into married life at Marlborough House and the Prince and Princess of Wales became the centre of what some of the more straight-laced and censorious of their subjects christened the 'Marlborough House Set'.

The tone of the Prince and his friends may have seemed rakish and Regency-like to outsiders and critics, but they made no allowances for certain difficult factors that were to affect the way the Prince was to live for the next twenty-five years. The first was the strange seclusion into which the Queen withdrew after the death of her husband. It was months before she could bear to meet her Privy Council, and then she sat in the next room and relayed her replies to her Councillors through her confidential clerk. It was almost two years before she drove abroad, and the public became a little restless. In March 1864, a poster appeared outside Buckingham Palace, 'These commanding premises to be let or sold, in consequence of the late occupant's declining business'. The Queen, however, felt that she was doing enough for the country by attending conscientiously to her state papers, performing the onorous task that falls to all sovereigns of 'doing her boxes'. But she had left, as it were, a social vacuum. The Prince and Princess of Wales had to fill the gap. They had to establish a second court. The British expect to see their sovereigns as well as to hear of their devotion to duty.

The Prince had vitality. He enjoyed society. He needed lively and agreeable people around him. He naturally chose them from the world of hunting, shooting, racing and the stage. His income was by no means adequate for this enlarged social round, and he didn't mind including financiers and business men in his circle. They gave him good advice in investing his money. The Prince had had quite enough of high-minded conversation among intellectuals in his youth. Now he felt there was no need for him to pretend an interest he did not feel. The Queen's seclusion meant that he had to shoulder an additional burden of public duties. He had to fulfil that endless schedule of opening docks and buildings, laying foundation stones and presiding at charitable committees that is the unescapable lot of royalty in a democracy. The Prince went through it all with good will, but in his spare time he felt he had a right to relax. If he preferred to take his pleasure at Newmarket, shooting on his estate at Sandringham or *'engarçon'* in France on the Riviera, he did not see why he should be criticized.

There was another aspect of the Queen's retirement that affected the way the Prince conducted himself. Victoria may have sought seclusion but she never let go the real reins of power. Her ministers still reported to her. She still insisted on being kept fully informed about affairs, and resolutely refused to let the Prince have any part in them. She could not bring herself to forget the shock of his escapade on The Curragh, and all that she heard of the 'goings on' at Marlborough House confirmed her in her feeling that, however dutiful and devoted he might be to her personally, he was still not reliable. Even when he grew older and more mature, she still persisted in her refusal to let him see state papers. Disraeli showed them to him surreptitiously and Gladstone again suggested that the Prince should be allowed to sit in on Cabinet deliberations. All in vain. The Prince continued to hope for some significant employment and it was suggested that he might even become Viceroy of Ireland. Nothing came of it.

In all this we can trace something of the old tension, even jealousy, between the monarch and the heir to the throne that we have traced for so long through our history. Victoria, on one occasion, wrote candidly to the Home Secretary that it would be most undesirable to place the Prince of Wales in a position of competing, as it were, for popularity with the Queen. The Prince was left in the air. He felt that he had given proof of his capacity for taking a position of authority. It is hard to blame him if, denied a chance to expend his energies in affairs of state, he spent it in affairs of the heart.

The inevitable scandals followed. His name was publicized in connection with a society divorce, and even more disconcertingly with an incident during a gambling session at the country house of Tranby Croft in Yorkshire, when one of the guests was accused of cheating at baccarat. The very fact that the Prince was gambling was bad enough. Worse still was the game itself, for baccarat was then forbidden by law in England. The Prince survived the scandal, as he had so many of the criticisms levelled at him over the years. The Press had been outspoken in its comments on many occasions, and there had even been some talk of republicanism in certain political circles. The Queen's strange dependence on her Highland servant John Brown was a constant target for gossip and the radical and free-thinking M.P., Charles Bradlaugh, published a savage diatribe entitled *The Impeachment of the House of Brunswick*, in which he raked over every scandal that had affected the Hanoverians and hinted at some in the Prince's own conduct.

The Prince certainly had a succession of lady friends and their names have acquired a certain romance with the passing years. Lillie Langtry, the Countess of Warwick, Mrs Keppel all played their part in creating the legend, but the Prince was no reckless, roistering Regency-type rake. His manners in public were correct and he did not permit undue familiarity. He may have tolerated La Goulue, the dancer at the Moulin Rouge in Paris, calling across to him 'Ullo Wales, you buy me champagne?' but the unfortunate guest who presumed to call him by the nickname of 'Tum-Tum', was banned for ever from the royal presence. He may have enjoyed his food and cigars, his annual trips to France and his visits to Homburg, but behind the cigar-smoke and the gargantuan dinners of the period, he talked to presidents, statesmen and men of affairs. In the long, long period of waiting before he ascended the throne – and over forty years passed between the death of the Prince Consort and that of Queen Victoria – he had accumulated a vast knowledge of European politics and of the men who moulded them. This was of immense importance to him when he came at last to the throne.

There was anxiety in some quarters on his accession. How would the lover of Mrs Langtry and the man who led his horse in after winning the Derby, the bon vivant and the card-player conduct himself when he had to undertake the full responsibilities of kingship. He surprised both his ministers and himself. He was conscientious in his duty, wise in his relations with his ministers and invaluable when it came to foreign affairs. Not for nothing was he known as 'The Uncle of Europe'. It was suggested that the antipathy he felt for William II – he thought the posturings and sword rattling of the German Emperor vulgar – and his partiality for France may have influenced the trend of British policy leading up to the First World War. This is putting the influence of Edward VII on far too high a plane. He was a careful, constitutional monarch and knew exactly where to draw the line between advice and interference. But he sat in the centre of affairs like a wise old uncle whom his nephews were happy to consult. He was delighted. At long last he was able to prove that he was something more than a Victorian version of the Prince of Pleasure.

All for Love

'I'd crowns resign to make her mine.'
From *The Lass of Richmond Hill*

Lord Derby was once the recipient of a remarkable declaration by King George V about his children's education. 'My father was frightened of his mother. I was frightened of my father, and I am damned well going to see to it that my children are frightened of me.' King George was certainly wrong about the relations between his father and Queen Victoria and his father did his best not to frighten him. But he certainly put the fear of the Lord into his own children. Again we come to the age-old clash between the monarch and his heir, between father and son, placed in a modern setting but with all its ancient anguish. This particular clash ended in a national scandal and the abdication of a king.

The abdication of Edward VIII was the biggest shock that the British monarchy received in modern times, and to seek its real cause we must go as far back as the early days of his father, George V. King George was a man firmly rooted in the morals and standards of the nineteenth century, a man of Victorian certainties and above all, a man who had never expected to become king. That role had been reserved for his elder brother Prince Albert Victor, 'The Prince of Wales who Never Was'. Maybe this was just as well, for the Prince – known as Eddy in the royal family – was, in the words of Queen Victoria, 'unsatisfactory'. Even his birth was not exactly 'satisfactory'. His mother, Princess Alexandra, had gone to see her husband play ice-hockey on the frozen Virginia Water. She suddenly felt unwell, and no wonder. She had been whirled at high speed over the ice in a sledge. She was hurried back home in the nick of time. Her second son George arrived on a better prepared occasion in 1865. It is tempting if un-scientific to trace the difference in their characters from the circumstances of their birth. Prince Eddy was unreliable. Prince George was solid and dependable. The two boys, the eldest of a large family, were brought up together. Queen Alexandra, who cherished all her children with an almost cloying affection, admitted that her eldest son was 'a little slow and dawdly'. Prince Eddy, unfortunately, remained slow and 'dawdly' all through his short life. Perhaps his backwardness was not entirely his own fault, for it has been suggested that he may have inherited a touch of his mother's deafness and a slight predisposition to epilepsy – the *'petit mal'* as it used to be called euphemistically. Whatever the cause his lethargy was a constant source of anxiety to his parents.

The Prince of Wales was determined not to repeat the mistakes made by his own father, and tried to treat his children with understanding and affection. Luckily his second son, Prince George, was a bright, attractive boy with a lively interest in everything around him. The Prince arranged that, as far as possible, the two boys should be brought up together in the hope that some of George's liveliness might rub off onto the lethargic Eddy. Their tutor was the Rev. John Dalton, who had come to royal notice as a curate at Whippingham, the parish church of Osborne. He eventually acquired a further claim to fame as the father of Hugh Dalton, the Labour Chancellor of the Exchequer. Dalton was a fine scolar and a man of method. He obviously succeeded with Prince George, who inherited his tutor's sense of order, but Prince Eddy defied all his earnest efforts.

The Dalton curriculum may seem a little tough for two small boys. At Sandringham they got up at seven o'clock and had lessons in English and geography before breakfast. After a merciful break for breakfast for an hour came Bible study and history. Then on to Euclid and algebra, before a dose of Latin or French to give the boys an appetite for lunch at two o'clock. The afternoon was devoted to healthy, open-air pursuits if the weather permitted. After that it was back to English and 'prep' until 'lights out' at eight o'clock.

A formidable routine on the face of it, and suspiciously like the syllabus laid down by Prince Albert, but by all accounts Dalton administered it with flexibility and understanding. Prince George clearly retained his respect and affection for his tutor, and regarded him as a personal friend until Dalton died as Dean of Windsor in 1931 after a long and eventful life.

While Dalton felt he was succeeding with Prince George he became uneasy over the progress of Prince Eddy. As the second son, Prince George was destined for the Navy. At the tender age of twelve he was due to join the *Britannia* at Dartmouth. Dalton urged that Prince Eddy should go with him. The two boys, brought up together in the secluded, enclosed world that inevitably surrounded princes in those days, were emotionally very close to each other. Prince George hero-worshipped his unsatisfactory elder brother. Dalton therefore wrote to their father:

> Prince Albert requires the stimulus of Prince George's company to make him work at all ... Difficult as the education of Prince Albert is now, it would be doubly so if Prince George were to leave him. Prince George's lively presence is his mainstay and chief incentive to exertion.

Even the Navy failed to stir Prince Eddy – not even when the period at Dartmouth was followed by three years cruising around the world in the training ship *Bacchante*. The patient Rev. Dalton went along too. While Prince George was busy with his naval duties Prince Eddy struggled to study with his tutor. Still the good clergyman felt that he was failing to inspire his lethargic pupil. There was now nothing for it but to send the Prince off to Cambridge. Maybe contact with the bright young men of the university might do something.

It is strange how difficult it is for those outside the circle to judge the real character of royal personages. Does the glamour of a title render them blind to any defects? The Governor of Gibraltar, General Napier, actually thought that Prince Eddy's phlegmatic bearing concealed a deeply contemplative nature. He wrote of the two boys: 'The youngest is the most lively and popular, but I think the elder is best suited to his situation – he is shy and not demonstrative, but does the right thing as a young gentleman in a quiet way.' The comments of Lady Geraldine Somerset were even more surprising, and distinctly unfair to Dalton; she described Eddy as '*charming*, as nice a youth as could be, simple, unaffected, unspoilt, affectionate, but his *ignorance*! What on earth stupid Dalton has been about all these years ...'

Cambridge succeeded no better than the Rev. John Dalton. The Prince had rooms in Trinity College and lived the life of the average aristocratic undergraduate. In other words, he completely ignored the academic side of the university. One of his instructors admitted, ruefully, that it seemed scarcely worth while pressing the Prince to attend lectures. 'He hardly knows the meaning of the word *to read*.'

Private tuition, the Navy, and university had all failed to arouse Prince Eddy. Would the Army do any better? It is touching to see how the royal parents clutched at the hope that the next move would surely do the trick and turn the potential heir to the throne into the sort of prince of whom his grandfather, Prince Albert, might have been proud.

The Army proved no more effective than the Navy. The Prince joined the fashionable Tenth Hussars, but his only indication of interest in military affairs was his opinion that his commanding general was a lunatic. When the Duke of Cambridge dropped in to see how his nephew was getting on, and suggested to his Colonel that Prince Eddy might show him his skill in some elementary manoeuvres, the Colonel turned pale at the thought and declared that the Prince would not have the slightest idea how to set about it.

There was one branch of study however at which he was clearly becoming expert. He was obviously an immediate success with the ladies. The Prince of Wales had an uneasy feeling that his own pleasant vices, and those traits in his character on which he now tended to reproach himself, were going to reappear with redoubled force in his eldest son. However lethargic the Prince had appeared in pursuit of his studies, there was no lethargy at all in his pursuit of women. His photograph in his Hussars uniform, with his moustache waxed and turned up at the ends with a military swagger, shows a young man busy turning himself into a young rake.

Scandal soon gathered around his name. Even fashionable ladies threw themselves recklessly at his feet. Sarah Bernhardt claimed that he was the father of her son, Maurice. The gutter press gave him its constant attention, and made him the hero of the most sensational and unlikely stories. One of the most absurd of them credited poor Eddy with being Jack the Ripper. His name was also associated with one of the most sensational scandals that rocked late Victorian society. In 1892 the police raided a male brothel in Clarendon Street and collected a remarkable netful of patrons, nearly all of whom belonged to the higher ranks of society. The most prominent of them was Lord Arthur Somerset, who was actually the Prince of Wales's Superintendent of the Stables. He was known by one of those curious nicknames so characteristic of Victorian and Edwardian society as 'Podge'. The Prince of Wales was deeply shocked and 'poor Podge' smartly slipped away across the Channel to the safety of France. Prince Eddy's name does not appear in any of the official records and, knowing his penchant for the ladies, it is in the highest degree unlikely that the Clarendon Street establishment would have had any attractions for him. But it is symbolic of the sort of reputation that Prince Eddy had already acquired that it was widely rumoured that the Government itself had been involved in a hush-up.

Clearly it was high time the last resort was tried. Prince Eddy must get married. Perhaps it was with this in mind that the Queen made him Duke of Clarence and Avondale, a title that did not go down too well with the gentlemen of the Press who pointed out that the only previous duke of that name who had left any mark on our history was Shakespeare's 'false, fleeting Clarence', who was supposed to have been drowned in a butt of malmsey.

The new Duke showed himself willing when it came to matrimony, but once again his conduct was 'unsatisfactory'. Several eligible princesses were produced, but Prince Eddy caused a shudder to run through the highest royal circles and indeed through the government, by producing a candidate himself.

It is illuminating to follow the ins-and-outs of the affair for they give us a vivid idea of the pressures under which royal personages have to pass their lives, with their most intimate feelings subject to official scrutiny, their most innocent acts liable to public censure and misunderstanding. It may have been thought that Prince Eddy's announcement that he intended to marry would have been received with general approval. At last, the wayward prince was going to settle down. The young man who would one day ascend the British throne had become respectable. He was going to conform to the accepted image of royalty as a model of propriety and the guardian of social standards.

Unfortunately, Prince Eddy's choice of bride caused consternation on two counts – she was French and she was a Roman Catholic. Hélène d'Orleans was the daughter of the Comte de Paris, who was the head of the House of Orleans and therefore a claimant to the throne of France. But in 1890 there was no throne of France. The country was strictly republican. Hélène declared that she was willing to be converted to Protestantism to marry her prince, but her father, the Comte, was a fiercely bigoted Catholic. His consent to Hélène's conversion was deeply in doubt, and this brought into play once again that Act of Settlement of 1701 which had barred the Stuarts from returning to the throne and had caused such anxiety to the Prince Regent and Mrs Fitzherbert. The Prince would lose his right to the throne if he married a Papist. A pretty imbroglio! And everyone close to the unhappy Eddy rushed to express their doubts. The first in the field was naturally the Queen herself and her letter of May 1890, was a magisterial rebuke.

I have heard it rumoured that you have been thinking and talking of Princess Hélène d'Orleans. I can't believe this for you know that I told you (as I did your parents who agreed with me) that such a marriage is *impossible*. None of our family can marry a Catholic without losing all their rights.

Prince Eddy's mother, Princess Alexandra, however, proved more sympathetic. She was always emotional about her children and cherished a romantic view of their marriages. She may have secretly rejoiced that Princess Hélène was French not German, and did not come from that select Teutonic circle of minor royalty which seemed destined to supply royal brides to Britain in perpetuity. Whatever her motive, she set out to foster what the Prime Minister, Lord Salisbury, was starting to describe – with ironic detachment – as 'the Royal Idyll'. She arranged that Eddy's married sister, the Duchess of Fife, should invite the Comte de Paris and Hélène to her Richmond home. Furthermore, the two lovers were then invited by the Fifes to come to Mar Lodge near Braemar, where Princess Alexandra advised them to carry out a daring manoeuvre. They were to face Queen Victoria in person and beg her to change her mind.

This was an act of high courage. Distinguished soldiers and statesmen, even Bismark himself, had confessed to have quailed before the prospect of an interview with the Widow of Windsor. The Queen was at Balmoral, and Princess Alexandra sent off the two trembling young people with a packed lunch in the carriage to keep up their strength and resolution. To everyone's surprise, the Queen relented and Prince Eddy was able to write in triumph to his brother George.

> I naturally expected that grandmother would be furious and say that it was quite impossible, etc. But instead of that she was quite nice about it and promised to help us as much as possible which she is now doing', Then he added, slyly; I believed what pleased her most was my taking Hélène into her saying we had arranged it entirely between ourselves without consulting our parents first. This you know is not quite true but she believed it.

What the Queen would have said if she had known that Princess Alexandra had planned the whole thing can easily be imagined. But the Princess guessed that behind the sometimes forbidding manner of the Queen lay a heart that could still be touched by romance. She had guessed right, but to the dismay of Lord Salisbury and his ministers. Letters, memoranda and dispatches flew in all directions. That most subtle and sinuous of statesmen, Mr Balfour, appeared hurriedly at Balmoral and reported to his uncle, Lord Salisbury, in that curiously detached style of his which reads as if he were examining human beings as curious insects under a microscope.

Will it be believed that neither the Queen, nor the young Prince, nor Princess Hélène, see anything that is not romantic, interesting, touching and praiseworthy in the young lady giving up her religion *to which she still professes devout attachment* in order to marry the man on whom she has set her heart!

And further sentences reveal that slight touch of elegant cynicism which was the Balfour trademark. He gave it as his opinion that

the Comtesse de Paris was more certain that it is good to be Queen of England than she is that it is bad to marry a Protestant. The Comte de Paris, on the other hand, is said to be a strict Roman Catholic – 'But not bigoted', says the Queen. I shall be surprised, however, if he is not bigoted enough to object to his daughter changing her creed for a crown.

Stirred by Mr Balfour, Lord Salisbury himself went into action with a powerful and elaborate memorial to the Queen. In it he indicated in no uncertain manner that Prince Eddy's marriage could not possibly, be regarded as a private matter for the royal family alone. The full Cabinet must be consulted. National feeling throughout our history 'has always been hostile to France. Since the Wars of the Roses we have had no French Queen except Henrietta Maria. Has the feeling of the people so changed that the French origin of their Queen will not change their feeling towards the French?'

Lord Salisbury went on to outline other horrendous possibilities. What if the Princess later on went back on her conversion or, worse still, persuaded the Prince to change his own religion? What was the exact position under the Act of Settlement of 1701. Poor Eddy! It was hard for a man who only wanted to marry the girl of his choice – as any other young man in Britain might wish – to be bombarded with the Wars of the Roses, Queen Henrietta Maria, and the Act of Settlement and all.

In the end, it was the Comte de Paris who solved the whole problem. He performed the unexpected feat of surprising Mr Balfour. He refused to allow his daughter to change her religion and marry a Protestant.

Sir Francis (later Viscount) Knollys, Private Secretary to the Prince of Wales and the most discreet of royal servants, was moved to remark privately that poor Prince Eddy had been made a fool of. 'In the meantime he declares that he will never marry anyone else, which I believe people have said before in similar cases.'

So it transpired. Within months Prince Eddy's engagement was officially announced. His bride was now to be Princess Mary of Teck. Her mother was Princess Mary Adelaide, the Duke of Cambridge's sister and therefore the Queen's first cousin. The Duke of Teck was German, it is true, but Princess Mary, or May as her family called her, had been born in Kensington Palace and had lived most of her life in England. Queen Victoria highly approved of her. She was intelligent, well educated and with an interest in the arts. She was naturally reserved in manner but, as events were to prove, this reserve concealed a character of great courage, resolution and sound judgement.

Poor May had need of all these qualities, when, almost within a month of the day fixed for the wedding, 27 February 1892 Eddy suddenly sickened and was compelled to take to his bed at Sandringham. The doctors diagnosed influenza, for a violent epidemic of the infection had broken out in London at the same time. The patient became delirious with a high fever. His condition worsened, and soon after 14 December – the fateful day on which Prince Albert, the Prince Consort, had died – his grandson, Prince Albert Victor also passed away.

The family grief was almost as overwhelming as Queen Victoria's for her beloved Albert. Alexandra in particular seemed inconsolable. Following the example of the Queen she turned the room in which her son had died into a sort of shrine, with the Union Jack draped over the bed and the dead prince's watch, brush and comb and even his cake of soap kept exactly as he had left them. The nation shared the family grief. A popular ballad expressed it thus:

A nation wrapped in mourning
Sheds bitter tears today,
For the noble Duke of Clarence
And fair young Princess May.

The better informed however were only too well aware that 'noble' was not exactly the description to apply to the dead prince. Prince Eddy himself was aware of his own limitations and admitted to his friends that he knew his father had been disappointed in him, and that he was not up to what the Prince of Wales expected of him. Nor, we might add, to what the nation expected of him as well. Sad though the prince's death had been to those nearest to him, it must be admitted that for the monarchy and for Britain it was a lucky escape. The national luck continued, for in place of the luckless and unsatisfactory Eddie they were now to get the eminently respectable, solidly dutiful, Prince George.

When he came to the throne, George V was fond of describing himself as a typical Englishman. He was no cosmopolitan like his father. 'England', he said, 'is good enough for me. I like my country best, climate or no, and I'm staying in it.' This very insularity was part of his strength as a king. He was transparently honest, a man of his word, conscientious, honourable and utterly reliable. He was almost proud of the fact that he was no intellectual. His subjects saw their own national characteristics reflected in him and respected him for it. He made an admirable constitutional monarch. He was genuinely surprised by the warmth of the acclaim given to him on the occasion of his Jubilee. As he heard the cheering in the East End he said, 'I did not know that they felt like that about me.' 'It's a rum thing,' he told the Archbishop of Canterbury, 'After all I am a very ordinary fellow.' Was he quite as ordinary as he thought? Had he not almost unconsciously disciplined himself to become a complete contrast to his 'unsatisfactory' elder brother Eddy. Was it the awful example of Prince Albert Victor that had turned the bright, inquisitive young naval cadet into the bluff, intimidating figure of the King, who did not understand his children?

His first son, the future Edward VIII, was born in June 1894 at White Lodge in Richmond Park. The little prince thus passed the first few years of his life in the full light of Victorian prosperity and power. Britain was at the height of her international prestige, the centre of an Empire on which the sun never set. This was his father's world that had set the standards by which George V was to live to his dying day. His son was to see that world shattered in the First World War. He would have to adapt the business of being royal to the new world where all the Victorian certainties were gone.

Queen Victoria died in 1901 and the reign of Edward VII began. His son George now became Prince of Wales and his father immediately began to initiate him into the business of government. From the beginning Edward showed his son the state papers and guided him in the way that the monarchy functions. This was a complete contrast to Queen Victoria's regime. King Edward remembered his own distress at the way she had excluded him from the governmental machine. He made no such mistake with his own son. The King gave Prince George confidence and in return the Prince gave his father unswerving loyalty and affection. It is all the more strange and even tragic that the same link was never established between King George V and his own son, when the time came. In the fascinating memoirs, some of the most honest written by royalty, the Duke of Windsor, as he became after his abdication, admitted that in his youth the words that most terrified him were those of the footman announcing, 'Sir, your father wishes to see you in his study.' Yet it seems that the Prince was happy when he was a little boy. He made long visits to Windsor where he was on excellent terms with his grandfather. There are charming anecdotes about their relationship. On one occasion he interrupted King Edward's conversation at table and received a gentle reprimand. He sat silent and then the King gave him permission to speak. 'It's too late, now, grandfather,' said the little Prince. 'There was a caterpillar on your lettuce, but you've eaten it.'

The shades of the prison house began to grow around David, as he was called in the family, when he had to start his education. His first tutor, Henry Hassall, seemed to have been selected by his father more for his sporting prowess than for his intellectual attainments. He had been a master at a public school after coming down from Oxford but seems to have had no intellectual interest at all. He did, however, realize his own shortcomings and suggested that a term at a public school might do the Prince a world of good. The King, then of course still Prince of Wales, had other ideas. There was to be no Cheam or Gordonstoun for David. Instead he was sent to the naval colleges of Osborne and Dartmouth, an experience which he recollected with horror for the rest of his life. His father had been brought up in the Navy and was therefore convinced that the Senior Service would supply the best training for a future king. 'The Navy will teach David all he needs to know', was his brusque comment; above all, that discipline in life which had been so conspicuously absent in the career of Prince Eddy, King George's unfortunate elder brother.

The naval cadets gave the young Prince a rough time. They were determined that he should not pull rank on them. Once, in a bit of horseplay, they held him out of a window and let the sash fall on his neck to remind him of the fate of one of his ancestors who had got a bit above himself. Edward did not emerge from his training with any taste for naval life. As he said afterwards, he would not advise anyone to sail on a ship he commanded.

He underwent another and unexpected ordeal while still at naval college. The Investiture ceremony was revived after a lapse of nearly three hundred years. The idea was the brain-child of the Bishop of St

Asaph, Dr A. G. Edwards, who had been a doughty opponent of Lloyd George in the long battle over the disestablishment of the Church of Wales. King George himself was being crowned in 1910, and the Bishop persuaded Lloyd George, then Chancellor of the Exchequer, that the ceremony would heal old wounds and add to the prestige of the Principality. Lloyd George took up the idea with enthusiasm. Caernarfon Castle, the birthplace of the first Prince of Wales, was chosen as the natural setting for the ceremony, and the ritual last performed under James I was carefully studied and followed. The Prince wore white satin breeches, a surcoat edged with ermine and gold embroidery and a white sash around his waist. He had a coronet on his head and carried a sword and sceptre. The day was hot. 1911 had an exceptionally fine summer and the Prince almost fainted in the heat. He felt embarrassed in his costume – 'a preposterous rig', he called it, and he worried about the ragging he would inevitably receive from the cadets when he returned to college. But the ceremony made a great impression, not only in Wales but throughout the country. Public attention was now focused on the Prince. It was never to leave him.

In all the photographs of his youth, his face has an air of sadness about it. Smiles are rare. Later in life he complained that his parents never demonstrated their affection for him. His father did not mean to be unkind but he was a disciplinarian, and his mother found it hard to display any fondness. She hated her pregnancies and said about her children, 'I have always to remember that their father is also their king.' The Prince of Wales grew up craving for an affection that he never received. He was thus a shy young man, and betrayed his nervousness by characteristic mannerisms, such as suddenly clasping his right wrist with his left hand or tugging at his collar as if it was too tight around his neck. He felt an acute inferiority complex at this time which was not helped by being sent to Magdalen College, Oxford, as an undergraduate. He saw little of his fellow undergraduates but surprised them by playing the bagpipes in his room. The bagpipes became a permanent passion. They were his only means of artistic expression. He had been brought up in a household where literature and the arts were never discussed.

His father showed no curiosity about new developments in the intellectual or scientific world in Britain. Sir Harold Nicholson, when working on the official biography of George V, wrote to his wife that it seemed incredible but, as far as he could discover, all the King had done with his spare time was to shoot birds and stick stamps in an album. Small wonder that the President of Magdalen's verdict on the

Prince of Wales's career at Oxford, was the crisp statement, 'Bookish he will never be'. On the Prince's side, he was glad to get away from Oxford and join the Grenadier Guards. Army life suited him better.

Before he joined his unit, the Prince went on a tour through Germany. It was a strange, uneasy time. The war clouds were already gathering. The Prince stayed with his royal relatives, met Count Zeppelin and took photographs everywhere – he had become as keen on the camera as on the bagpipes. This visit to Germany left him with a feeling of friendship for the country which even the World War did not break.

The tragedy of World War One left a deep mark on the Prince. He had expected to go to France with his regiment but Lord Kitchener refused. When the Prince protested that he had other brothers at home so it would not matter if he was killed, Kitchener agreed, with his usual disconcerting honesty, that it wouldn't matter a bit if he got killed, 'but', he said, 'I cannot take the chance of the enemy taking you prisoner.' But as the war deepened in horror, the King felt that he had no option but to let the Prince go overseas. He was not to go into the front line but was to serve on the staff. But the Prince wanted desperately to share in the experience and anguish of his own generation. Time and again he managed to dodge his watch-dogs and get up into the trenches. The soldiers admired his determination to share their dangers and his coolness under fire. The generals refused to let him take part in any attack and he was sent to the Italian front – where he flew over the enemy lines – and the Middle East. He did his best to face the realities of war. When he visited the hospitals, he made a point of visiting the most serious cases. On one occasion, when the authorities attempted to hide a hideously wounded patient from him, he insisted on going to the bedside. He knelt down and kissed the poor man on the cheek.

He came back a changed man, mature and anxious to play a part in rebuilding that new Britain which he was now sure lay ahead. He also came back with a new prestige. His popularity was immense. This handsome young man, who had been through the ordeal of the War, seemed to become the very symbol of the hopes of the younger generation. His father however seemed to be strangely unaware of all this, and failed to understand the change that had come over his son. The only role he could think of for the Prince was to send him on long tours of the Commonwealth. He set out on the first of these in 1919 on board the battleship *Renown*, and for many years he continued to travel around the world. Few princes, before the age of the aeroplane, could have visited so many places and shaken hands with so many people on so many public occasions. He was a great success as an informal ambassador but still his father continued to feel that he was not yet mature enough or reliable enough. He was going through the same disconcerting experience as his grandfather had endured under Queen Victoria. King George not only refused his son access to the state papers but actively discouraged him from talking to his ministers as well.

The Prince reacted to this in the way that princes have done down the ages. He enjoyed himself in the new Jazz Age. The newspapers reported his activities around the night clubs, dancing the night away. He further horrified his father by taking up flying, and, less successfully, steeplechasing. He suffered a series of well-publicized falls and had to abandon the sport. As he entered his forties he was still without a real role in the state or a purpose in life. He took up golf and developed an interest in gardening at his 'grace and favour' residence at Fort Belvedere, six miles from Windsor Castle. The house had been built by William, Duke of Cumberland, but George IV's favourite architect, Wyatville, had furnished it with towers and battlements. It was a sort of Regency folly. 'What do you want that old place for?' growled the King. 'For those damned weekends, I suppose.' The Prince became very fond of it. 'I came to love it,' he says in his memoirs, 'as I loved no other material thing.' 'My Get-away-from-people house' he called it. Here he could entertain his friends, including the succession of ladies whose names the gossip-writers continually linked with his. He had always felt the need for affection, for a more permanent attachment than the passing fancies of his youth. For some time he was deeply committed to Mrs Dudley Ward then even more deeply to Thelma, Lady Furness. The time was approaching when another attachment – far deeper than any of the foregoing – would come to dominate and then profoundly change his life.

Lady Furness had introduced him to a fellow American, Mrs Wallis Simpson, who came from an old family in Baltimore. She had married a pilot in the American Air Force, but after a divorce, had married again. Her second husband was Mr Ernest Simpson from America who looked very English and had actually served in the Grenadier Guards. Wallis Simpson was not an outstanding beauty but she was witty, understanding and sympathetic. She immediately sensed the Prince's problems, his feelings of frustration. Soon those in the inner circle were aware that there was something special about the relationship of the Prince with the lady from Baltimore. This was no passing infatuation. Wallis Simpson seemed to be fitting into the scene at Fort Belvedere. That acute observer of the London social scene, 'Chips' Channon, noted in his diary that Wallis seemed to have got complete power over the Prince. He summed her up as a 'Jolly, plain, intelligent, quiet, unpretentious and unprepossessing little woman', but admitted that she had greatly improved the Prince and he was 'obviously madly infatuated'. He also noted that Mrs Simpson was discreet. A few days before the wedding of the Duke of Kent she had been presented to the King. This was the only time they ever met, and it is doubtful if he realized the important position she now occupied in the life of his son.

This was the state of affairs when on 20 January 1936, King George V died after a reign of over twenty-five years. He had been there so long and had represented so perfectly the feelings of the country in many ways, that his subjects felt that a whole era of our history had come to an end. The nation nevertheless prepared to give a warm welcome to the new King. He had still retained his popularity. They may no longer have thought of him as their Prince Charming, but they respected him for his work with the ex-service men and the concern he had expressed for the unemployed. They regarded him as a democratic prince, who, when he came to the throne, would throw open the windows of a court which had perhaps got a little too set and formal for the modern world. Politically, the new king might be more inclined to look with favour at the discipline of Mussolini's Italy. He had seen the Italian collapse at Caporetto during the War and had been surprised at the order he thought he saw in the new post-war Italy. But he was not unaware of the dangers of dictatorship. He would have been a thoroughly constitutional king. As such he was welcomed and acclaimed. The country was moved when the new King went on his celebrated tour of the Welsh mining valleys. When faced with the realities of life on the dole, he burst out, 'Something must be done. I will do all I can to assist you.' With those words, he had raised expectations that he would be, as that well-known modern critic of the monarchy, Mr Willie Hamilton says, 'the most radical sovereign in centuries'.

Then came the thunderclap. The nation heard, for the first time that their new, radical and sympathetic sovereign was proposing to marry a twice divorced American. London society, the Press and the top politicians may have known all about Mrs Simpson for a long time. Some of the more sophisticated circles may have well sympathized with the King in his dilemma. The average man and woman in Britain, the very people that the King thought would be solidly behind him, just could not take it. Their children sang in the playground;

Hark, the Herald Angels sing,
Mrs Simpson's pinched our King.

The nation listened to the Abdication broadcast with sadness and sympathy, but it did not alter their feeling that the King had to go. As one of his biographers put it; 'He had stepped out of his fairy tale. Prince Charming might marry a princess; he might marry a Cinderella; but he certainly could not marry a Mrs Simpson.'

Yet marry her he did, in France after leaving his throne. Few men have given up so much for love. For love it was. He and Wallis remained deeply and touchingly devoted to each other until the end. This was their great compensation in the difficult days that followed. They may have married like characters in a fairy tale, but, as the Duke and Duchess of Windsor they hardly lived happily ever after. The Duke was deeply distressed that his wife never received full acknowledgement from the rest of his family. Queen Mary found it difficult to forgive her son who, she felt, had put his own personal love before his love for his country.

Ex-kings find it hard to make a new position for themselves. The Duke became Governor of the Bahamas during the Second World War. He and the Duchess returned to live in France. Slowly the family rift healed. The Duke died in 1972. Time has soothed the bitterness of the Abdication and even touched it with the light of romance. But we can still regret the loss of that bright young Prince, with all his gifts, denied the chance of fulfilling his promise and fading into the dim light of exile. We can only murmur, with another figure who gave all for love, Shakespeare's Othello, 'But yet the pity of it, Iago! O, Iago, the pity of it Iago!'

11

A Prince for the Future

'Among our ancient mountains
And from our lovely vales,
Oh, let the prayer re-echo:
"God bless the Prince of Wales!" '

GEORGE LINLEY

Prince Charles Philip Arthur George was born on the evening of 14 November 1948 at Buckingham Palace. I have reason to remember the time, the place and the hour for I had been waiting with the crowd outside the palace for long hours, waiting to see if it was going to be a boy or a girl. I would then describe the crowd's reactions for the B.B.C. Fifty-five years had passed since the birth of the last boy who had become Prince of Wales. King George VI had come to the throne in the difficult days that followed the unhappy abdication of his brother. His heir was Princess Elizabeth. There had been a suggestion in Parliament that the King should create his daughter Princess of Wales in her own right. The King however turned the suggestion down. He saw practical difficulties in its way. If the Princess married, would her husband – who would not be the monarch's eldest son – bear the title? Could there be a Prince Consort of Wales? King George was clearly right to dismiss the idea. Now, on that November night there was a chance that we would again have a Prince of Wales in the future. I watched the equerry walk slowly across the palace forecourt. He affixed the bulletin to the railings and a great roar went up from the crowd and an exultant shout, 'It's a boy!' The cars sounded their horns as they circled the Victoria Memorial. The crowd chanted, 'We want Philip' and the celebrations outside the Palace went on far into the night. It was all a remarkable contrast to the way royal births were treated in the past. There was no hurried rush of Privy Councillors to the royal bedside to bear witness to the legitimacy of the birth, as occurred with James II and the Old Pretender. Nor was the occasion marked simply by a quiet paragraph in the *Gazette*, as in the arrival of the future Edward VIII. The birth of Prince Charles marked the arrival of the modern publicity machine at the Palace door. Prince Charles would grow up in an age when the spotlight would beat down on the royal family with a cunning and ferocity unknown even in the days before the Second World War.

Princess Elizabeth and Prince Philip had to take the monarchy into the modern world and they sensibly decided that their children were to be brought up to be aware of all the changes going on so rapidly around them. It is fascinating to compare the education and subsequent career of Prince Charles with that of his immediate predecessor, the Duke of Windsor. They seem poles apart. The poor Duke as a child was kept apart from other children. His education was confined to one man, his tutor. When he was flung into the tough world of Osborne and Dartmouth, he got a shock from which it took him years to recover. Charles on the other hand went through the ordinary education of an upper-class English boy. He went to his preparatory school at Cheam on the Berkshire Downs and then on to his father's old school at Gordonstoun. This again was an innovation. It was the first time that the heir to the throne had gone through this educational process, mingling freely with boys of his own age. Gordonstoun is a place for character building and Prince Charles was spared none of its rigours. But there was none of the shock that the Duke of Windsor received at Dartmouth. Charles already knew what to expect, and enjoyed it all. He even did a term at Geelong Grammar School in Australia. The heir to the throne certainly had plenty of variety in his early education. He sat the Oxford and Cambridge Schools Examination Board (Advanced Level) and gained a distinction. He himself chose Cambridge as his university, and insisted on going there on his own merit. He also chose his own college, Trinity, and entered fully into the college life. Here again we think back to the unhappy Duke of Windsor at Magdalen College, Oxford, dogged by his tutor, Mr Hassall, wherever he moved. Prince Charles took part in the college revue, got a half-blue for polo, a sport to which his father introduced him, and buckled down to serious academic study. It cannot be said of Charles, as the President of Magdalen said about his great-uncle, 'Bookish he will never be'. He got a good second in archaeology and then transferred to history. He has always been interested in the history of his own family as well as wider fields. His academic career was a most creditable one, and he went on through the usual periods of training with the services. He naturally went into his father's old service, the Royal Navy and again did well, getting his first command in 1976 in the minehunter, H.M.S. *Bronnington*. How the Duke of Windsor would have envied the

Prince his freedom to enlarge his experience in every walk of life.

In one thing Prince Charles has certainly excelled his predecessors. Of all the Princes of Wales he is the one who has striven hardest to identify himself with the Principality. He spent a term at Aberystwyth university. Here he studied Welsh, and while he would not claim to have mastered the language, he learnt enough, and his pronunciation was good enough, for him to make a public speech at the Urdd Eisteddfod. It surprised and delighted everyone present. He must be the only member of the royal family ever to accomplish this linguistic feat. Lloyd George coached the Duke of Windsor for the Investiture, but then it was a matter of a simple sentence. Prince Charles spoke for a quarter of an hour. He has retained his interest and connection with Wales and makes constant visits to the Principality.

The Queen herself recognized the importance of linking the honour to the realities of Welsh life. She chose the occasion of the Commonwealth Games in Cardiff in 1958 to announce the creation of Charles as Prince of Wales, and his Investiture duly took place at Caernarfon Castle in 1969. Again we contrast Prince Charles's reactions to those of his great-uncle. The Duke of Windsor had felt acutely embarrassed by the whole business, above all by the 'preposterous rig' he had to wear. Prince Charles's dress was far more appropriate and his stay at Aberystwyth had given him a better appreciation of the Welsh background.

Not everyone in Wales approved of the Investiture. Plaid Cymru, the Welsh Nationalist party, boycotted the ceremony. There were other, even violent, demonstrations. But it would be true to say that these were the work of a minority, and Prince Charles accepts the fact that, as the world stands today, not everyone looks with a favourable eye on the institution of monarchy. He knows that royalty must move with the times, but it is not enough for a Prince of Wales to be democratic, to 'go walk-about' and smile and handshake on all possible occasions. He has to show that royalty is relevant to present-day Britain and that it has a worthwhile role to play in the future. If any man can do this, it is surely Prince Charles.

His wedding to Lady Diana Spencer released an astonishing wave of public enthusiasm. Even more astonishing was the public reaction to the announcement that the Princess of Wales was expecting a child. Once again I stood outside Buckingham Palace, the traditional scene of a royal birth. But again the royal family had moved with the times. On the advice of Mr George Pinker, the royal gynaecologist, Princess Diana went to St Mary's Hospital, Paddington, but the crowd maintained tradition and gathered outside the Palace for the vital moment when the official bulletin would be affixed to the railings. I was carried back thirty odd years as again the delighted shouts went up, 'It's a boy'. There was wave after wave of cheering, the motor cars sounded in triumphant and raucous symphony of horns, and champagne bottles specially brought for the occasion were uncorked with gusto on the pavement. The arrival of Prince William Arthur Philip Louis had been celebrated with enthusiasm for the institution of monarchy in Britain, a sort of 'gut-feeling' that goes back into the furthest recesses of our history, throughout the whole length of the story we have been tracing in this account of the Princes of Wales. How long this feeling will continue depends as much on the personalities of our future monarchs as on the decision of the politicians. If there is one lesson to be drawn from our story it is this. A Prince who can adapt to the spirit of his times stays. The Prince who cannot goes. The future of the monarchy may quite literally be eventually in the hands of the child who, if all goes well, will become the twenty-second Prince of Wales.

Further Reading

Suggested here are a few selected works from the vast wealth of historical writing about Britain which have a bearing on the story of the Princes of Wales.

For the native Princes of Wales, consult Sir J. E. Lloyd's *History of Wales from the Earliest Times to the Edwardian Conquest*. This should now be checked against the numerous articles in the *Welsh Historical Review* and supplemented by such authoritative books as *The Welsh Church in the Middle Ages* (Professor Glanmor Williams) and the same author's *Owen Glendower, The King's Works in Wales* (Dr. A. T. Taylor) and *The Welsh in Their History* (Professor Gwyn A. Williams).

For the early English Princes of Wales see *Edward II* (Harold Hutchison): *The Black Prince* (Herbert Cole); *The Knight and Chivalry* (Richard Barber) and the Chronicles of Jean Froissart. The lives of the later medieval princes are covered in *The Age of Plantagenet and Valois* (K. L. Fowler); *The Hollow Crown* (H. F. Hutchinson); *Victor of Agincourt* (J. H. Wylie and W. T. Waugh) and *The History of the Reign of Henry IV* (J. H. Wylie). Other important works include *Richard II* (P. M. Wilson), *The Wars of the Roses* (J. T. Lander); and *The Life and Reign of Edward IV* (C. L. Scofield).

The early Tudors are well covered by Professor Chrimes in his *Henry VII* and by J. D. Machie in *The Early Tudors*. The advent of the Stuarts is detailed in *King James VI and I* by D. Harris Wilson, and there is a classical survey of the reign of Charles I and the subsequent Civil War in C. V. Wedgwood's *The King's Peace* and *The King's War. The Later Stuarts* (Sir George Clark) brings us on to *The Age of Queen Anne* (Sir George Trevelyan).

Sir J. R. Plumb is an inspiring guide through the complexities of the eighteenth century. Sir George Young has given a sympathetic account to 'Poor Fred' and there are the vivid memoirs of such people as Hervey and the *Letters of George III* have now been published. We enter the Regency in the company of Rhys Gronow, Creever and Greville, all of whom wrote vivid memoirs, and Roger Fulford in his *George IV* began the rehabilitation of the Prince of Pleasure. There are excellent biographies of *Queen Victoria* by Lytton Strachey and Elizabeth Longford; of *Edward VII* by Philip Magnus and of *Queen Mary* by J. Pope-Henessey. The tragic story of the Duke of Windsor is traced in the Duke's own autobiography, *A King's Story*, in the Duchess's *The Heart has its Reasons* and in Sir Harold Nicholson's *King George V*.

There has been any amount of popular books about the present Prince of Wales and Lady Diana, but, happily, it will be many a long day before we shall need official biographies of them.

Illustrations and acknowledgements

The author and his publishers make grateful acknowledgement to the owners and photographic agencies listed here for their permission to reproduce pictures.

page
33 Caernarfon Castle. Keystone Press Agency Ltd.
    Edward II. *The First Prince of Wales* by Philip Morris. BBC Hulton Picture Library.
    Edward III and The Black Prince. The Prince paying homage to his father. The British Library.
34 Edward III. Electrotype of Effigy in Westminster Abbey. The National Portrait Gallery.
    Richard II kneeling before St Edmund Martyr, Edward the Confessor and John the Baptist. BBC Hulton Picture Library.
36 Prince Hal being knighted by Richard II in Ireland. The British Library.
    Valle Crucis Abbey in the midst of Owen Glendower country. Photograph Howard Moore, Woodmansterne Ltd.
    Scene from the film *Henry V*. The Rank Organization.
38 Henry VI, artist unknown. The National Portrait Gallery.
    Tewkesbury Abbey. Woodmansterne Ltd.
    Richard III, artist unknown. The National Portrait Gallery.
39 Edward IV, artist unknown. The National Portrait Gallery.
    Edward V and the Duke of York in The Tower by Hippolyte Delaroche. The Trustees, The Wallace Collection, London.
40 Portrait of Henry VII by M. Sittow. The National Portrait Gallery.
    Prince Arthur, eldest son of Henry VII artist unknown. Reproduced by gracious permission of Her Majesty the Queen.
73 Memorial to Llywelyn the Last, Cilmery. Photograph by Derry Brabbs from *Wales* by Wynford Vaughan-Thomas published by Michael Joseph Ltd.
    Effigy of the Black Prince, Canterbury Cathedral. Photograph Nicholas Servian FIIP, Woodmansterne Ltd.
74 George I by Sir Godfrey Kneller 1716. The National Portrait Gallery.
    George II, after Sir Godfrey Kneller, the first Hanoverian king who was also Prince of Wales. The National Portrait Gallery.
75 *Nell Gwynn and the infant Duke of St Albans* by Sir Peter Lely. Denys Eyre Bower Collection, Chiddingstone Castle, Kent.
    The State Barge of Frederick Prince of Wales. The National Maritime Museum, London.
76 *The Lover's Dream*, cartoon by Gillray of the Prince Regent. The British Museum.
    Coronation Banquet of King George IV at Westminister Hall. The National Portrait Gallery.
77 Princess Charlotte and Prince Leopold of Saxe-Coburg by George Dance. The National Portrait Gallery.

INDEX

First names in *italics* refer to the Princes of Wales. Page references in **bold** indicate illustrations.